D0002220

RESEARCH DESIGN

Qualitative, Quantitative, and Mixed Methods Approaches

SECOND EDITION

John W. Creswell

University of Nebraska, Lincoln

SAGE Publications
International Educational and Professional Publisher
Thousand Oaks ▪ London ▪ New Delhi

Copyright © 2003 by Sage Publications, Inc.

All rights reserved. No part of this book may be reproduced or utilized in any form or by any means, electronic or mechanical, including photocopying, recording, or by any information storage and retrieval system, without permission in writing from the publisher.

Cover image copyright © Sheldan Collins/Corbis; used by permission.

For information:

Sage Publications, Inc.
2455 Teller Road
Thousand Oaks, California 91320
E-mail: order@sagepub.com

Sage Publications Ltd.
6 Bonhill Street
London EC2A 4PU
United Kingdom

Sage Publications India Pvt. Ltd.
M-32 Market
Greater Kailash I
New Delhi 110 048 India

Printed in the United States of America

Library of Congress Cataloging-in-Publication Data

Creswell, John W.
  Research design: Qualitative, quantitative, and mixed method
approaches / by John W. Creswell.— 2nd ed.
      p. cm
Includes bibliographical references and indexes.
  ISBN 0-7619-2441-8 (c) — ISBN 0-7619-2442-6 (pbk.)
  1. Social sciences—Research—Methodology.
2. Social sciences—Statistical methods. I. Title.
  H62 .C6963 2002
  300'.7'2—dc21

03 04 05 10 9 8 7 6 5 4 3

Acquiring Editor:	C. Deborah Laughton
Editorial Assistant:	Veronica Novak
Production Editor:	Diana E. Axelsen
Copy Editor:	A. J. Sobczak
Typesetter:	C&M Digitals (P) Ltd., Chennai, India
Cover Designer:	Michelle Lee

Brief Contents

Detailed Contents

Analytic Contents

Introduction to Designing Research

The Purpose Statement

Research Questions and Hypotheses

The Use of Theory

Preface

This book advances a framework, a process, and compositional approaches for designing qualitative, quantitative, and mixed methods research in the human and social sciences. Increased interest in and use of qualitative research, the emergence of mixed methods approaches, and continuing use of the traditional forms of quantitative designs have created a need for this book's unique comparison of the three approaches to inquiry. This comparison begins with preliminary consideration of knowledge claims for all three approaches, a review of the literature, and reflections about the importance of writing and ethics in scholarly inquiry. The book then addresses the key elements of the process of research: writing an introduction; stating a purpose for the study; identifying research questions and hypotheses; using theory; defining, delimiting, and stating the significance of the study; and advancing methods and procedures for data collection and analysis. At each step in this process, the reader is taken through qualitative, quantitative, and mixed methods approaches.

The cover illustration depicts a mandala, a Hindu or Buddhist symbol of the universe. Creation of a mandala, much like creation of a research design, requires looking at the "big picture" as well as tremendous attention to detail—a mandala made of sand can take days to create because of the precise positioning of the pieces, which sometimes are individual grains of sand. The mandala also shows the interrelatedness of the parts of a whole, again reflecting research design, in which each element shapes a complete study.

AUDIENCE

This book was prepared for graduate students and faculty who seek assistance in preparing a plan or proposal for a scholarly journal article, dissertation, or thesis. At a broader level, the book may be useful as both a reference book and a text for graduate courses. To best take advantage of the design features in this book, the reader needs a basic familiarity with qualitative and quantitative research; however, terms will be explained and recommended strategies advanced for those needing introductory assistance in the design process. This book also is intended for a broad audience in the social and human sciences. Readers' comments to the first edition of this book indicate that individual users came from many disciplines and fields. I hope that researchers in fields such as marketing, management, criminal justice, psychology, sociology, K-12 education, higher and postsecondary education, nursing, health sciences, urban studies, family research, and other areas will find this edition useful.

FORMAT

In each chapter, I share examples drawn from varied disciplines. These examples are drawn from books, journal articles, dissertation proposals, and dissertations. Though my primary specialization is in education, the illustrations are intended to be inclusive of the social and human sciences. They reflect issues in social justice and examples of studies with marginalized individuals in our society, as well as the traditional samples and populations studied by social researchers. Inclusiveness also extends to methodological pluralism in research today, and the discussion incorporates alternative philosophical ideas, diverse modes of inquiry, and numerous procedures.

This book is not a detailed method text; instead, I highlight the essential features of research design. The coverage of research strategies of inquiry is limited to frequently used forms: experiments and surveys in quantitative research; phenomenology, ethnography, grounded theory, case studies, and narrative research in qualitative research; and concurrent, sequential, and transformative designs in mixed methods research. Although students preparing a dissertation proposal should find this book helpful, topics related to the politics of presenting and negotiating a study with graduate committees are addressed thoroughly in other texts.

Consistent with accepted conventions of scholarly writing, I have tried to eliminate any words or examples that convey a sexist or ethnic orientation. Examples were selected to provide a full range of gender and cultural orientations. Favoritism also did not play into my use of qualitative and quantitative discussions—the reader will find that I sometimes begin with qualitative examples and sometimes with quantitative examples. Readers should note that in the longer examples cited in this book, many references are made to other writings. Only the reference to the work I am using as an illustration will be cited here, not the entire list of references embedded within any particular example.

As with the first edition, I have maintained features to improve the readability and understandability of the material. These features are bullets to emphasize key points, numbered points to stress steps in a process, longer passages with annotations to provide the reader with key research ideas being incorporated into the passages, and emphasized words to help researchers build their vocabulary of quantitative, qualitative, and mixed methods approaches. At the end of each chapter are both writing exercises, with which to practice the principles learned in the chapter, and annotated lists of additional readings, consisting of references to other texts that will provide a more complete understanding of the material covered.

In this second edition of the book, new features have been added in response to developments in research and reader feedback:

- Mixed methods research has been added to quantitative and qualitative approaches. In each chapter, I discuss the process of designing a mixed methods proposal or plan in addition to presenting the other two approaches.

- The writing chapter, found at the end of the book in the first edition, has been moved to the third chapter at the front of the book. Indeed, before writing a proposal, authors need to consider basic writing features.

- Ethics has also been included in a more substantive way. In the third chapter, I devote an entire section to ethical issues that may arise in quantitative, qualitative, and mixed methods designs. Ethical issues should be anticipated appropriately at the start of a project.

- Many new initiatives have occurred in qualitative research since I authored the first edition of this book. The chapter on qualitative procedures, Chapter 10, reflects much new thinking on this topic, including developments in advocacy, participatory, and emancipatory approaches to research that have now become central to most qualitative inquiry.

- Likewise, mixed methods research has expanded and come into its own as an approach to inquiry since I authored the first edition. The chapter in the first edition titled "Combining Qualitative and Quantitative Research" is appropriately called "Mixed Methods Procedures" in this edition, and I have entirely rewritten this chapter to reflect thinking that has emerged during the last decade.

- In every chapter, I have added updated references within the chapter as well as new references for "additional reading" so that the reader can combine some of the classic reading with new works.

- In discussing research questions and hypotheses, I have provided more examples and clarified instructions for writing different forms. Additional specific illustrations were added for qualitative, quantitative, and mixed methods approaches.

OUTLINE OF CHAPTERS

This book is divided into two parts. Part I consists of steps that researchers need to consider before they develop their proposals or plans for research. Part II discusses the actual steps in composing a proposal and plan. A brief summary of each chapter follows.

Part I: Preliminary Considerations

This part of the book discusses preparing for the process of design. It contains Chapters 1 through 3.

Chapter 1: A Framework for Design

In this chapter, I discuss the importance of having a framework for designing research. This framework involves bringing together claims being made about what constitutes knowledge, a strategy of inquiry, and specific methods. Three approaches result from this interconnection: qualitative, quantitative, and mixed methods. This chapter will help a researcher identify the three approaches and choose which approach to use for a particular study.

Chapter 2: Review of the Literature

Reviewing the literature about a topic is another preliminary step to proposal design. This chapter identifies specific strategies that will be helpful in searching and reviewing the resources available for designing a study.

Chapter 3: Writing Strategies and Ethical Considerations

Also necessary before beginning the process of proposal design are development of a sense of the overall writing structure and anticipation of ethical considerations that may arise during the research. This chapter provides outlines for quantitative, qualitative, and mixed methods research proposals and considers ethical issues that often arise during studies.

Part II: Designing Research

This part of the book describes the steps in the research process. It contains the remaining chapters of the book, Chapters 4 through 11.

Chapter 4: The Introduction

It is important to properly introduce a research study. This requires identifying the research problem or issue, framing this problem within the existing literature, pointing out deficiencies in the literature, and targeting the study for an audience. This chapter provides a systematic method for designing a scholarly introduction to a proposal or study.

Chapter 5: The Purpose Statement

At the beginning of research proposals, authors mention the central purpose or intent of the study. This passage is the most important statement in the entire proposal. In this chapter, the reader will learn how to write this statement for quantitative, qualitative, and mixed methods studies and will learn a "script" useful in the writing process.

Chapter 6: Research Questions and Hypotheses

The questions and hypotheses addressed by the researcher serve to narrow and focus the purpose of the study. As another major signpost in a project, the set of research questions and hypotheses needs to be written carefully. In this chapter, the reader will learn how to write both qualitative research questions and quantitative research questions and hypotheses, as well as how to employ both forms in writing mixed methods questions and hypotheses. Numerous examples serve to illustrate these processes.

Chapter 7: The Use of Theory

Theories serve different purposes in the three forms of inquiry. In quantitative research, they provide a proposed explanation for the relationship among variables being tested by the investigator. In qualitative research, they may often serve as a lens for the inquiry or are generated during the study. In mixed methods studies, researchers employ them in many ways, including those associated with quantitative and qualitative approaches. This chapter provides an overview of how theory might be used in the three approaches to research and cites specific examples to illustrate these uses.

Chapter 8: Delimitations, Limitations, and Significance

All researchers set certain restrictions or boundaries around what their studies will address. These boundaries define terms used in the study, delimit the scope of the inquiry, limit the practices used, and target the significance of the proposed study for different audiences. This chapter helps a reader design each of these sections for a proposal or plan.

Chapter 9: Quantitative Methods

Quantitative methods involve the processes of collecting, analyzing, interpreting, and writing the results of a study. Specific methods exist in both survey and experimental research that relate to identifying a sample and population, specifying the strategy of inquiry, collecting and analyzing data, presenting the results, making an interpretation, and writing the research in a manner consistent with a survey or experimental study. In this chapter, the reader will learn the specific procedures for designing survey or experimental methods.

Chapter 10: Qualitative Procedures

Qualitative approaches to data collection, analysis, and report writing differ from the traditional, quantitative approaches. Use of purposeful sampling, collection of open-ended data, analysis of text or pictures, representation of information in figures and tables, and personal interpretation of the findings all inform qualitative procedures. This chapter advances steps in designing qualitative procedures, and it illustrates these procedures with examples from phenomenology, grounded theory, ethnography, case studies, and narrative research.

Chapter 11: Mixed Methods Procedures

Mixed methods procedures employ aspects of both quantitative methods and qualitative procedures. In designing these procedures, researchers need to convey the intent of mixed methods research and its applications in the social and human sciences. Then the procedures involve identifying the type of mixed methods strategy of inquiry, the data collection and analysis approaches, the researcher's role, and the overall structure guiding the proposed study. This chapter will provide the reader with an overview of mixed methods research as practiced today and indicate the steps taken in designing a mixed methods procedure for a proposed study.

Designing a study is a difficult and time-consuming process. This book will not necessarily make the process easier, but it should provide specific skills useful in the process, knowledge about the steps involved in the process, and a practical guide to composing and writing scholarly research. Before the steps of the process unfold, I recommend that proposal developers think through their approach to research, conduct a literature review on their topic, develop an outline of topics to include in a proposal design, and begin anticipating potential ethical issues that may arise in the research. Part I introduces these topics.

Acknowledgments

This book could not have been written without the encouragement and ideas of the hundreds of students in the doctoral level "Proposal Development" course that I have taught at the University of Nebraska–Lincoln over the years. Specific former students and editors were instrumental in its development: Dr. Sharon Hudson, Dr. Leon Cantrell, the late Nette Nelson, Dr. De Tonack, Dr. Ray Ostrander, and Diane Greenlee. Since the publication of the first edition of the book, I have also become indebted to the students in my introductory research methods courses and to individuals who have participated in my mixed methods seminars. These courses have been my "laboratories" for working out ideas, incorporating new ones, and sharing my experiences as a writer and researcher. In addition, I am grateful for the insightful suggestions provided by the following reviewers: Susan E. Dutch, Westfield State College; Hollis Glaser, University of Nebraska; Steve Guerriero, Antioch New England School; Gladys Hildreth, University of Kentucky; Nancy Leech, Colorado State University; Martha Montero-Sieburth, University of Massachusetts, Boston; David Morgan, Colorado State University; and Kathleen Young, University of New Mexico.

I also could not have produced this book without the support and encouragement of my friends at Sage Publications. Sage is and has been a first-rate publishing house. I especially owe much to my editor and mentor, C. Deborah Laughton. Throughout a decade of work with Sage, C. Deborah has always provided thoughtful guidance, a great eye for design, and encouragement for me as a writer and researcher.

PART I

Preliminary Considerations

■ Chapter 1
A Framework for Design

■ Chapter 2
Review of the Literature

■ Chapter 3
Writing Strategies and
Ethical Considerations

P art I will address several preliminary considerations that are necessary before designing a
proposal or a plan for a study. These considerations per-
tain to selecting an approach or framework for the overall
design (i.e., quantitative, qualitative, or mixed methods),
reviewing the literature to understand how a proposed
study adds or extends prior research, and employing—at
the outset—good writing and ethical practices.

CHAPTER ONE

A Framework for Design

In the past two decades, research approaches have multiplied to a point at which investigators or inquirers have many choices. For those designing a proposal or plan, I recommend that a general framework be adopted to provide guidance about all facets of the study, from assessing the general philosophical ideas behind the inquiry to the detailed data collection and analysis procedures. Using an extant framework also allows researchers to lodge their plans in ideas well grounded in the literature and recognized by audiences (e.g., faculty committees) that read and support proposals for research.

What frameworks exist for designing a proposal? Although different types and terms abound in the literature, I will focus on three: quantitative, qualitative, and mixed methods approaches. The first has been available to the social and human scientist for years, the second has emerged primarily during the last three or four decades, and the last is new and still developing in form and substance.

This chapter introduces the reader to the three approaches to research. I suggest that to understand them, the proposal developer needs to consider three framework elements: philosophical assumptions about what constitutes *knowledge claims*; general procedures of research called *strategies of inquiry*; and detailed procedures of data collection, analysis, and writing, called *methods*. Qualitative, quantitative, and mixed methods approaches frame each of these elements differently, and these differences are identified and discussed in this chapter. Then typical scenarios that combine the three elements are advanced, followed by the reasons why one would choose one approach over another in designing a study. This discussion will not be a philosophical treatise on the nature of knowledge, but it will provide a practical grounding in some of the philosophical ideas behind research.

THREE ELEMENTS OF INQUIRY

In the first edition of this book, I used two approaches—qualitative and quantitative. I described each in terms of different philosophical assumptions about the nature of reality, epistemology, values, the rhetoric of research, and methodology (Creswell, 1994). Several developments in the last decade have caused a reexamination of this stance.

- Mixed methods research has come of age. To include only quantitative and qualitative methods falls short of the major approaches being used today in the social and human sciences.

- Other philosophical assumptions beyond those advanced in 1994 have been widely discussed in the literature. Most notably, critical perspectives, advocacy/participatory perspectives, and pragmatic ideas (e.g., see Lincoln & Guba, 2000; Tashakkori & Teddlie, 1998) are being extensively discussed. Although philosophical ideas remain largely "hidden" in research (Slife & Williams, 1995), they still influence the practice of research and need to be identified.

- The situation today is less quantitative *versus* qualitative and more how research practices lie somewhere on a continuum between the two (e.g., Newman & Benz, 1998). The best that can be said is that studies *tend* to be more quantitative or qualitative in nature. Thus, later in the chapter I introduce *typical* scenarios of quantitative, qualitative, and mixed methods research.

- Finally, the practice of research (such as writing a proposal) involves much more than philosophical assumptions. Philosophical ideas must be combined with broad approaches to research (strategies) and implemented with specific procedures (methods). Thus, a framework is needed that combines the elements of philosophical ideas, strategies, and methods into the three approaches to research.

Crotty's (1998) ideas established the groundwork for this framework. He suggested that in designing a research proposal, we consider four questions:

1. What epistemology—theory of knowledge embedded in the theoretical perspective—informs the research (e.g., objectivism, subjectivism, etc.)?

2. What theoretical perspective—philosophical stance—lies behind the methodology in questions (e.g., positivism and postpositivm, interpretivism, critical theory, etc.)?

Elements of Inquiry

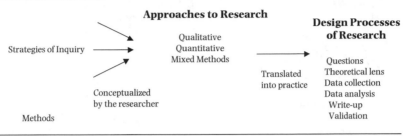

Figure 1.1 Knowledge Claims, Strategies of Inquiry, and Methods Leading to Approaches and the Design Process

3. What methodology—strategy or plan of action that links methods to outcomes—governs our choice and use of methods (e.g., experimental research, survey research, ethnography, etc.)?

4. What methods—techniques and procedures—do we propose to use (e.g., questionnaire, interview, focus group, etc.)?

These four questions show the interrelated *levels* of decisions that go into the process of designing research. Moreover, these are aspects that inform a choice of approach, ranging from the broad assumptions that are brought to a project to the more practical decisions made about how to collect and analyze data.

With these ideas in mind, I conceptualized Crotty's model to address three questions central to the design of research:

1. What knowledge claims are being made by the researcher (including a theoretical perspective)?

2. What strategies of inquiry will inform the procedures?

3. What methods of data collection and analysis will be used?

Next, I drew a picture, as shown in Figure 1.1. This displays how three elements of inquiry (i.e., knowledge claims, strategies, and methods) combine to form different approaches to research. These approaches, in turn, are translated into processes in the design of research. Preliminary steps in designing a research proposal, then, are to assess the knowledge claims brought to the study, to consider the strategy of inquiry that will be used, and to identify specific methods. Using these three elements, a

Table 1.1   Alternative Knowledge Claim Positions

Postpositivism	Constructivism
Determination	Understanding
Reductionism	Multiple participant meanings
Empirical observation and measurement	Social and historical construction
Theory verification	Theory generation
Advocacy/Participatory	**Pragmatism**
Political	Consequences of actions
Empowerment issue-oriented	Problem-centered
Collaborative	Pluralistic
Change-oriented	Real-world practice oriented

researcher can then identify either the quantitative, qualitative, or mixed methods approach to inquiry.

Alternative Knowledge Claims

Stating a *knowledge claim* means that researchers start a project with certain assumptions about how they will learn and what they will learn during their inquiry. These claims might be called paradigms (Lincoln & Guba, 2000; Mertens, 1998); philosophical assumptions, epistemologies, and ontologies (Crotty, 1998); or broadly conceived research methodologies (Neuman, 2000). Philosophically, researchers make claims about what is knowledge (ontology), how we know it (epistemology), what values go into it (axiology), how we write about it (rhetoric), and the processes for studying it (methodology) (Creswell, 1994). Four schools of thought about knowledge claims will be discussed: postpositivism, constructivism, advocacy/participatory, and pragmatism. The major elements of each position are presented in Table 1.1. In discussions to follow, I will attempt to translate the broad philosophical ideas of these positions into practice.

Postpositive Knowledge Claims

Traditionally, the postpositivist assumptions have governed claims about what warrants knowledge. This position is sometimes called the "scientific method" or doing "science" research. It is also called quantitative research, positivist/postpositivist research, empirical science, and postpostivism. The last term, "postpositivism," refers to the thinking after positivism, challenging the traditional notion of the absolute truth of knowledge (Phillips & Burbules, 2000) and recognizing that we cannot be "positive" about our claims of knowledge when studying the behavior and actions of humans. The postpositivist tradition comes from 19th-century writers such as Comte, Mill, Durkheim, Newton, and Locke (Smith, 1983), and it has been most recently articulated by writers such as Phillips and Burbules (2000).

Postpositivism reflects a deterministic philosophy in which causes probably determine effects or outcomes. Thus, the problems studied by postpositivists reflect a need to examine causes that influence outcomes, such as issues examined in experiments. It is also reductionistic in that the intent is to reduce the ideas into a small, discrete set of ideas to test, such as the variables that constitute hypotheses and research questions. The knowledge that develops through a postpositivist lens is based on careful observation and measurement of the objective reality that exists "out there" in the world. Thus, developing numeric measures of observations and studying the behavior of individuals become paramount for a postpositivist. Finally, there are laws or theories that govern the world, and these need to be tested or verified and refined so that we can understand the world. Thus, in the scientific method—the accepted approach to research by postpostivists—an individual begins with a theory, collects data that either supports or refutes the theory, and then makes necessary revisions before additional tests are conducted.

In reading Phillips and Burbules (2000), one can gain a sense of the key assumptions of this position, such as the following:

1. That knowledge is conjectural (and anti-foundational)—absolute truth can never be found. Thus, evidence established in research is always imperfect and fallible. It is for this reason that researchers do not prove hypotheses and instead indicate a failure to reject.

2. Research is the process of making claims and then refining or abandoning some of them for other claims more strongly warranted. Most quantitative research, for example, starts with the test of a theory.

3. Data, evidence, and rational considerations shape knowledge. In practice, the researcher collects information on instruments based on measures completed by the participants or by observations recorded by the researcher.

4. Research seeks to develop relevant true statements, ones that can serve to explain the situation that is of concern or that describes the causal relationships of interest. In quantitative studies, researchers advance the relationship among variables and pose this in terms of questions or hypotheses.

5. Being objective is an essential aspect of competent inquiry, and for this reason researchers must examine methods and conclusions for bias. For example, standards of validity and reliability are important in quantitative research.

Socially Constructed Knowledge Claims

Others claim knowledge through an alternative process and set of assumptions. Social constructivism (often combined with interpretivism; see Mertens, 1998) is such a perspective. The ideas came from Mannheim and from works such as Berger and Luckmann's *The Social Construction of Reality* (1967) and Lincoln and Guba's *Naturalistic Inquiry* (1985). More recent writers who have summarized this position are Lincoln and Guba (2000), Schwandt (2000), Neuman (2000), and Crotty (1998), among others. Assumptions identified in these works hold that individuals seek understanding of the world in which they live and work. They develop subjective meanings of their experiences—meanings directed toward certain objects or things. These meanings are varied and multiple, leading the researcher to look for the complexity of views rather than narrowing meanings into a few categories or ideas. The goal of research, then, is to rely as much as possible on the participants' views of the situation being studied. The questions become broad and general so that the participants can construct the meaning of a situation, a meaning typically forged in discussions or interactions with other persons. The more open-ended the questioning, the better, as the researcher listens carefully to what people say or do in their life setting. Often these subjective meanings are negotiated socially and historically. In other words, they are not simply imprinted on individuals but are formed through interaction with others (hence social constructivism) and through historical and cultural norms that operate in individuals' lives. Thus, constructivist researchers often address the "processes" of interaction among individuals. They also focus on the specific contexts in which people live and work in order to understand the historical and cultural settings of the participants. Researchers recognize that their own background shapes their interpretation, and they "position themselves" in the research to acknowledge how their interpretation flows from their own personal, cultural, and historical experiences. The researcher's intent, then, is to make sense of (or interpret) the meanings others have about the world. Rather than starting with a theory (as in postpostivism), inquirers generate or inductively develop a theory or pattern of meaning.

For example, in discussing constructivism, Crotty (1998) identified several assumptions:

1. Meanings are constructed by human beings as they engage with the world they are interpreting. Qualitative researchers tend to use open-ended questions so that participants can express their views.

2. Humans engage with their world and make sense of it based on their historical and social perspective—we are all born into a world of meaning bestowed upon us by our culture. Thus, qualitative researchers seek to understand the context or setting of the participants through visiting this context and gathering information personally. They also make an interpretation of what they find, an interpretation shaped by the researchers' own experiences and backgrounds.

3. The basic generation of meaning is always social, arising in and out of interaction with a human community. The process of qualitative research is largely inductive, with the inquirer generating meaning from the data collected in the field.

Advocacy/Participatory Knowledge Claims

Another group of researchers claims knowledge through an advocacy/participatory approach. This position arose during the 1980s and 1990s from individuals who felt that the postpostivist assumptions imposed structural laws and theories that did not fit marginalized individuals or groups or did not adequately address issues of social justice. Historically, some of the advocacy/participatory (or emancipatory) writers have drawn on the works of Marx, Adorno, Marcuse, Habermas, and Freire (Neuman, 2000). More recently, works by Fay (1987), Heron and Reason (1997), and Kemmis and Wilkinson (1998) can be read for this perspective. In the main, these inquirers felt that the constructivist stance did not go far enough in advocating for an action agenda to help marginalized peoples. These researchers believe that inquiry needs to be intertwined with politics and a political agenda. Thus, the research should contain an action agenda for reform that may change the lives of the participants, the institutions in which individuals work or live, and the researcher's life. Moreover, specific issues needed to be addressed that speak to important social issues of the day, issues such as empowerment, inequality, oppression, domination, suppression, and alienation. The advocacy researcher often begins with one of these issues as the focal point of research. This research also assumes that the inquirer will proceed collaboratively so as to not further marginalize the participants as a result of the inquiry. In this sense, the participants may help design questions, collect data, analyze information, or receive rewards for participating in the research. The "voice" for the participants becomes a united voice for reform and change. This advocacy may mean providing a voice for these participants, raising their consciousness, or advancing an agenda for change to improve the lives of the participants.

Within these knowledge claims are stances for groups and individuals in society that may be marginalized or disenfranchised. Therefore, theoretical perspectives may be integrated with the philosophical assumptions that construct a picture of the issues being examined, the people to be studied, and the changes that are needed. Some of these theoretical perspectives are listed below.

- *Feminist perspectives* center and make problematic women's diverse situations and the institutions that frame those situations. Research topics may include policy issues related to realizing social justice for women in specific contexts or knowledge about oppressive situations for women (Olesen, 2000).

- *Racialized discourses* raise important questions about the control and production of knowledge, particularly knowledge about people and communities of color (Ladson-Billings, 2000).

- *Critical theory* perspectives are concerned with empowering human beings to transcend the constraints placed on them by race, class, and gender (Fay, 1987).

- *Queer theory* focuses on individuals calling themselves lesbians, gay, bisexuals, or transgendered people. The research can be less objectifying, can be more concerned with cultural and political means, and can convey the voices and experiences of individuals who have been suppressed (Gamson, 2000).

- *Disability inquiry* addresses the meaning of inclusion in schools and encompasses administrators, teachers, and parents who have children with disabilities (Mertens, 1998).

These are diverse groups and topics, and my summaries here are inadequate generalizations. It is helpful to view the summary by Kemmis and Wilkinson (1998) of key features of the advocacy or participatory forms of inquiry:

1. Participatory action is recursive or dialectical and is focused on bringing about change in practices. Thus, at the end of advocacy/participatory studies, researchers advance an action agenda for change.

2. It is focused on helping individuals free themselves from constraints found in the media, in language, in work procedures, and in the relationships of power in educational settings. Advocacy/participatory studies often begin with an important issue or stance about the problems in society, such as the need for empowerment.

3. It is emancipatory in that it helps unshackle people from the constraints of irrational and unjust structures that limit self-development and self-determination. The aim of advocacy/participatory studies is to create a political debate and discussion so that change will occur.

4. It is practical and collaborative because it is inquiry completed "with" others rather than "on" or "to" others. In this spirit, advocacy/participatory authors engage the participants as active collaborators in their inquiries.

Pragmatic Knowledge Claims

Another position about claims on knowledge comes from the pragmatists. Pragmatism derives from the work of Peirce, James, Mead, and Dewey (Cherryholmes, 1992). Recent writers include Rorty (1990), Murphy (1990), Patton (1990), and Cherryholmes (1992). There are many forms of pragmatism. For many of them, knowledge claims arise out of actions, situations, and consequences rather than antecedent conditions (as in postpositivism). There is a concern with applications—"what works"—and solutions to problems (Patton, 1990). Instead of methods being important, the problem is most important, and researchers use all approaches to understand the problem (see Rossman & Wilson, 1985). As a philosophical underpinning for mixed methods studies, Tashakkori and Teddlie (1998) and Patton (1990) convey the importance for focusing attention on the research problem in social science research and then using pluralistic approaches to derive knowledge about the problem. According to Cherryholmes (1992), Murphy (1990), and my own interpretations of these writers, pragmatism provides a basis for the following knowledge claims:

1. Pragmatism is not committed to any one system of philosophy and reality. This applies to mixed methods research in that inquirers draw liberally from both quantitative and qualitative assumptions when they engage in their research.

2. Individual researchers have a freedom of choice. They are "free" to choose the methods, techniques, and procedures of research that best meet their needs and purposes.

3. Pragmatists do not see the world as an absolute unity. In a similar way, mixed methods researchers look to many approaches to collecting and analyzing data rather than subscribing to only one way (e.g., quantitative or qualitative).

4. Truth is what works at the time; it is not based in a strict dualism between the mind and a reality completely independent of the mind. Thus, in mixed methods research, investigators use both quantitative and qualitative data because they work to provide the best understanding of a research problem.

5. Pragmatist researchers look to the "what" and "how" to research based on its intended consequences—where they want to go with it. Mixed methods researchers need to establish a purpose for their "mixing," a rationale for the reasons why quantitative and qualitative data need to be mixed in the first place.

6. Pragmatists agree that research always occurs in social, historical, political, and other contexts. In this way, mixed methods studies may include a postmodern turn, a theoretical lens that is reflexive of social justice and political aims.

7. Pragmatists believe (Cherryholmes, 1992) that we need to stop asking questions about reality and the laws of nature. "They would simply like to change the subject" (Rorty, 1983, p. xiv).

Thus, for the mixed methods researcher, pragmatism opens the door to multiple methods, different worldviews, and different assumptions, as well as to different forms of data collection and analysis in the mixed methods study.

Table 1.2	Alternative Strategies of Inquiry	
Quantitative	*Qualitative*	*Mixed Methods*
Experimental designs Non-experimental designs, such as surveys	Narratives Phenomenologies Ethnographies Grounded theory Case studies	Sequential Concurrent Transformative

Strategies of Inquiry

The researcher brings to the choice of a research design assumptions about knowledge claims. In addition, operating at a more applied level are strategies of inquiry (or traditions of inquiry, Creswell, 1998; or methodologies, Mertens, 1998) that provide specific direction for procedures in a research design. Like knowledge claims, strategies have multiplied over the years as computer technology has pushed forward data analysis and the ability to analyze complex models, and as individuals have articulated new procedures for conducting social science research. These strategies of inquiry contribute to our overall research approach. The major strategies employed in the social sciences are discussed in Chapters 9, 10, and 11 of this book. Rather than cover all or a large number of strategies, these chapters focus on those frequently used in the social sciences. Here I will introduce those that will be discussed later and that are cited in examples of research throughout the book. An overview of these strategies is shown in Table 1.2.

Strategies Associated With the Quantitative Approach

During the late 19th century and throughout the 20th, strategies of inquiry associated with quantitative research were those that invoked the postpositivist perspectives. These include the true experiments and the less rigorous experiments called quasi-experiments and correlational studies (Campbell & Stanley, 1963), and specific single-subject experiments (Cooper, Heron, & Heward, 1987; Neuman & McCormick, 1995). More recently, quantitative strategies involved complex experiments with many variables and treatments (e.g., factorial designs and repeated measure designs). They also included elaborate structural equation models that incorporated causal paths and the identification of the collective strength of multiple variables. In this book, we will focus on two strategies of inquiry: experiments and surveys.

● *Experiments* include true experiments, with the random assignment of subjects to treatment conditions, as well as quasi-experiments that use nonrandomized designs (Keppel, 1991). Included within quasi-experiments are single-subject designs.

● *Surveys* include cross-sectional and longitudinal studies using questionnaires or structured interviews for data collection, with the intent of generalizing from a sample to a population (Babbie, 1990).

Strategies Associated With the Qualitative Approach

In qualitative research, the numbers and types of approaches also became more clearly visible during the 1990s. Books have summarized the various types (such as the 19 strategies identified by Wolcott, 2001), and complete procedures are now available on specific qualitative inquiry approaches. For example, Clandinin and Connelly (2000) have constructed a picture of what "narrative researchers do," Moustakas (1994) discussed the philosophical tenets and the procedures of the phenomenological method, and Strauss and Corbin (1990, 1998) have explicated the procedures of grounded theory. Wolcott (1999) has summarized ethnographic procedures, and Stake (1995) has identified the processes of case study research. In this book, illustrations will be drawn from the following strategies:

● *Ethnographies*, in which the researcher studies an intact cultural group in a natural setting over a prolonged period of time by collecting, primarily, observational data (Creswell, 1998). The research process is flexible and typically evolves contextually in response to the lived realities encountered in the field setting (LeCompte & Schensul, 1999).

● *Grounded theory*, in which the researcher attempts to derive a general, abstract theory of a process, action, or interaction grounded in the views of participants in a study. This process involves using multiple stages of data collection and the refinement and interrelationship of categories of information (Strauss & Corbin, 1990, 1998). Two primary characteristics of this design are the constant comparison of data with emerging categories and theoretical sampling of different groups to maximize the similarities and the differences of information.

- *Case studies*, in which the researcher explores in depth a program, an event, an activity, a process, or one or more individuals. The case(s) are bounded by time and activity, and researchers collect detailed information using a variety of data collection procedures over a sustained period of time (Stake, 1995).

- *Phenomenological research*, in which the researcher identifies the "essence" of human experiences concerning a phenomenon, as described by participants in a study. Understanding the "lived experiences" marks phenomenology as a philosophy as well as a method, and the procedure involves studying a small number of subjects through extensive and prolonged engagement to develop patterns and relationships of meaning (Moustakas, 1994). In this process, the researcher "brackets" his or her own experiences in order to understand those of the participants in the study (Nieswiadomy, 1993).

- *Narrative research*, a form of inquiry in which the researcher studies the lives of individuals and asks one or more individuals to provide stories about their lives. This information is then retold or restoried by the researcher into a narrative chronology. In the end, the narrative combines views from the participant's life with those of the researcher's life in a collaborative narrative (Clandinin & Connelly, 2000).

Strategies Associated With the Mixed Methods Approach

Less well known than either the quantitative or qualitative strategies are those that involve collecting and analyzing both forms of data in a single study. The concept of mixing different methods probably originated in 1959, when Campbell and Fiske used multiple methods to study validity of psychological traits. They encouraged others to employ their "multimethod matrix" to examine multiple approaches to data collection in a study. This prompted others to mix methods, and soon approaches associated with field methods such as observations and interviews (qualitative data) were combined with traditional surveys (quantitative data) (S. D. Sieber, 1973). Recognizing that all methods have limitations, researchers felt that biases inherent in any single method could neutralize or cancel the biases of other methods. Triangulating data sources—a means for seeking convergence across qualitative and quantitative methods—were born (Jick, 1979). From the original concept of triangulation emerged additional reasons for mixing different types of data. For example, the results from one method can help develop or inform the other method (Greene, Caracelli, & Graham, 1989). Alternatively, one method can be nested within another method to provide insight into different levels or units of analysis (Tashakkori & Teddlie, 1998). Or the methods can serve a larger, transformative purpose to change and advocate for marginalized groups, such as women, ethnic/racial minorities, members of gay and lesbian communities, people with disabilities, and those who are poor (Mertens, 2003).

These reasons for mixing methods have led writers from around the world to develop procedures for mixed methods strategies of inquiry and to take the numerous terms found in the literature, such as multi-method, convergence, integrated, and combined (Creswell, 1994) and shape procedures for research (Tashakkori & Teddlie, 2003).

In particular, three general strategies and several variations within them will be illustrated in this book:

- *Sequential* procedures, in which the researcher seeks to elaborate on or expand the findings of one method with another method. This may involve beginning with a qualitative method for exploratory purposes and following up with a quantitative method with a large sample so that the researcher can generalize results to a population. Alternatively, the study may begin with a quantitative method in which theories or concepts are tested, to be followed by a qualitative method involving detailed exploration with a few cases or individuals.

- *Concurrent* procedures, in which the researcher converges quantitative and qualitative data in order to provide a comprehensive analysis of the research problem. In this design, the investigator collects both forms of data at the same time during the study and then integrates the information in the interpretation of the overall results. Also, in this design, the researcher nests one form of data within another, larger data collection procedure in order to analyze different questions or levels of units in an organization.

- *Transformative* procedures, in which the researcher uses a theoretical lens (see Chapter 7) as an overarching perspective within a design that contains both quantitative and qualitative data. This lens provides a framework for topics of interest, methods for collecting data, and outcomes or changes anticipated by the study. Within this lens could be a data collection method that involves a sequential or a concurrent approach.

Table 1.3   Quantitative, Qualitative, and Mixed Methods Procedures

Quantitative Research Methods	Qualitative Research Methods	Mixed Methods Research Methods
Predetermined Instrument based questions Performance data, attitude data, observational data, and census data Statistical analysis	Emerging methods Open-ended questions Interview data, observation data, document data, and audiovisual data Text and image analysis	Both predetermined and emerging methods Both open- and closed-ended questions Multiple forms of data drawing on all possibilities Statistical and text analysis

Research Methods

The third major element that goes into a research approach is the specific methods of data collection and analysis. As shown in Table 1.3, it is useful to consider the full range of possibilities for data collection in any study, and to organize these methods by their degree of predetermined nature, their use of closed-ended versus open-ended questioning, and their focus for numeric versus non-numeric data analysis. These methods will be developed further in Chapters 9 through 11 as quantitative, qualitative, and mixed methods.

Researchers collect data on an instrument or test (e.g., a set of questions about attitudes toward self-esteem) or gather information on a behavioral checklist (e.g., where researchers observe a worker engaged in using a complex skill). On the other end of the continuum, it might involve visiting a research site and observing the behavior of individuals without predetermined questions or conducting an interview in which the individual is allowed to talk openly about a topic largely without the use of specific questions. The choice of methods by a researcher turns on whether the intent is to specify the type of information to be collected in advance of the study or to allow it to emerge from participants in the project. Also, the type of data may be numeric information gathered on scales of instruments or more text information, recording and reporting the voice of the participants. In some forms of data collection, both quantitative and qualitative data are collected. Instrument data may be augmented with open-ended observations, or census data may be followed by in-depth exploratory interviews.

THREE APPROACHES TO RESEARCH

The knowledge claims, the strategies, and the method all contribute to a research approach that *tends* to be more quantitative, qualitative, or mixed. Table 1.4 creates distinctions that may be useful in choosing an approach for a proposal. This table also includes practices of all three approaches that will be emphasized in the remaining chapters of this book.

Definitions can help further clarify the three approaches:

● A *quantitative* approach is one in which the investigator primarily uses postpositivist claims for developing knowledge (i.e., cause and effect thinking, reduction to specific variables and hypotheses and questions, use of measurement and observation, and the test of theories), employs strategies of inquiry such as experiments and surveys, and collects data on predetermined instruments that yield statistical data.

● Alternatively, a *qualitative* approach is one in which the inquirer often makes knowledge claims based primarily on constructivist perspectives (i.e., the multiple meanings of individual experiences, meanings socially and historically constructed, with an intent of developing a theory or pattern) or advocacy/participatory perspectives (i.e., political, issue-oriented, collaborative, or change oriented) or both. It also uses strategies of inquiry such as narratives, phenomenologies, ethnographies, grounded theory studies, or case studies. The researcher collects open-ended, emerging data with the primary intent of developing themes from the data.

● Finally, a *mixed methods* approach is one in which the researcher tends to base knowledge claims on pragmatic grounds (e.g., consequence-oriented, problem-centered, and pluralistic). It employs strategies of inquiry that involve collecting data either simultaneously or sequentially to best understand research problems. The

Table 1.4 Qualitative, Quantitative, and Mixed Methods Approaches

Tend to or Typically	Qualitative Approaches	Quantitative Approaches	Mixed Methods Approaches
Use these philosophical assumptions	Constructivist/Advocacy/ Participatory knowledge claims	Postpositivist knowledge claims	Pragmatic knowledge claims
Employ these strategies of inquiry	Phenomenology, grounded theory, ethnography, case study, and narrative	Surveys and experiments	Sequential, concurrent, and transformative
Employ these methods	Open-ended questions, emerging approaches, text or image data	Closed-ended questions, predetermined approaches, numeric data	Both open- and closed-ended questions, both emerging and predetermined approaches, and both quantitative and qualitative data and analysis
Use these practices of research, as the researcher	Positions himself or herself Collects participant meanings Focuses on a single concept or phenomenon Brings personal values into the study Studies the context or setting of participants Validates the accuracy of findings Makes interpretations of the data Creates an agenda for change or reform Collaborates with the participants	Tests or verifies theories or explanations Identifies variables to study Relates variables in questions or hypotheses Uses standards of validity and reliability Observes and measures information numerically Uses unbiased approaches Employs statistical procedures	Collects both quantitative and qualitative data Develops a rationale for mixing Integrates the data at different stages of inquiry Presents visual pictures of the procedures in the study Employs the practices of both qualitative and quantitative research

Research Approach	Knowledge Claims	Strategy of Inquiry	Methods
Quantitative	Postpositivist assumptions	Experimental design	Measuring attitudes, rating behaviors
Qualitative	Constructivist assumptions	Ethnographic design	Field observations
Qualitative	Emancipatory assumptions	Narrative design	Open-ended interviewing
Mixed methods	Pragmatic assumptions	Mixed methods design	Closed-ended measures, open-ended observations

Figure 1.2 Four Alternative Combinations of Knowledge Claims, Strategies of Inquiry, and Methods

data collection also involves gathering both numeric information (e.g., on instruments) as well as text information (e.g., on interviews) so that the final database represents both quantitative and qualitative information.

To see how these three elements (knowledge claims, strategies, and methods) combine in practice, I have drafted several typical scenarios of research, as shown in Figure 1.2.

● *Quantitative* approach: postpositivist knowledge claims, experimental strategy of inquiry, and pre- and posttest measures of attitudes

In this scenario, the researcher tests a theory by specifying narrow hypotheses and the collection of data to support or refute the hypotheses. An experimental design is used in which attitudes are assessed both before and after an experimental treatment. The data are collected on an instrument that measures attitudes, and the information collected is analyzed using statistical procedures and hypothesis testing.

● *Qualitative* approach: constructivist knowledge claims, ethnographic design, and observation of behavior

In this situation the researcher seeks to establish the meaning of a phenomenon from the views of participants. This means identifying a culture-sharing group and studying how it developed shared patterns of behavior over time (i.e., ethnography). One of the key elements of collecting data is to observe participants' behaviors by participating in their activities.

- *Qualitative* approach: participatory knowledge claims, narrative design, and open-ended interviewing

For this study, the inquirer seeks to examine an issue related to oppression of individuals. To study this, the approach is taken of collecting stories of individual oppression using a narrative approach. Individuals are interviewed at some length to determine how they have personally experienced oppression.

- *Mixed methods* approach: pragmatic knowledge claims, collection of both quantitative and qualitative data sequentially

The researcher bases the inquiry on the assumption that collecting diverse types of data best provides an understanding of a research problem. The study begins with a broad survey in order to generalize results to a population and then focuses, in a second phase, on detailed qualitative, open-ended interviews to collect detailed views from participants.

CRITERIA FOR SELECTING AN APPROACH

Given these three approaches, what factors affect a choice of one approach over another for the design of a proposal? Three considerations play into this decision: the research problem, the personal experiences of the researcher, and the audience(s) for whom the report will be written.

Match Between Problem and Approach

Certain types of social research problems call for specific approaches. A research problem, as discussed in Chapter 4, is an issue or concern that needs to be addressed (e.g., whether one type of intervention works better than another type of intervention). For example, if the problem is identifying factors that influence an outcome, the utility of an intervention, or understanding the best predictors of outcomes, then a quantitative approach is best. It is also the best approach to use to test a theory or explanation. On the other hand, if a concept or phenomenon needs to be understood because little research has been done on it, then it merits a qualitative approach. Qualitative research is exploratory and is useful when the researcher does not know the important variables to examine. This type of approach may be needed because the topic is new, the topic has never been addressed with a certain sample or group of people, or existing theories do not apply with the particular sample or group under study (Morse, 1991).

A mixed methods design is useful to capture the best of both quantitative and qualitative approaches. For example, a researcher may want to both generalize the findings to a population and develop a detailed view of the meaning of a phenomenon or concept for individuals. In this research, the inquirer first explores generally to learn about what variables to study and then studies those variables with a large sample of individuals. Alternatively, researchers may first survey a large number of individuals, then follow up with a few of them to obtain their specific language and voices about the topic. In these situations, the advantages of collecting both closed-ended quantitative data and open-ended qualitative data prove advantageous to best understand a research problem.

Personal Experiences

Into this mix of choice also comes the researcher's own personal training and experiences. An individual trained in technical, scientific writing, statistics, and computer statistical programs who is also familiar with quantitative journals in the library would most likely choose the quantitative design. The qualitative approach incorporates much more of a literary form of writing, computer text analysis programs, and experience in conducting open-ended interviews and observations. The mixed methods researcher needs to be familiar with both quantitative and qualitative research. This person also needs an understanding of the rationales for combining both forms of data so that they can be articulated in a proposal. The mixed methods approach also requires knowledge about the different mixed methods designs that help organize procedures for a study.

Because quantitative studies are the traditional mode of research, carefully worked out procedures and rules exist for the research. This means that researchers may be more comfortable with the highly systematic procedures of quantitative research. Also, for some individuals, it can be uncomfortable to challenge accepted approaches among some faculty by using qualitative and advocacy/participatory approaches to inquiry. On the other hand, qualitative approaches allow room to be innovative and to work more within researcher-designed frameworks. They allow more creative, literary-style writing, a form that individuals may like to use. For advocacy/participatory writers, there is undoubtedly a strong personal stimulus to pursue topics that are of personal interest—issues that relate to marginalized people and an interest in creating a better society for them and everyone.

For the mixed methods researcher, a project will take extra time because of the need to collect and analyze both quantitative and qualitative data. It fits a person who enjoys both the structure of quantitative research and the flexibility of qualitative inquiry.

Audience

Finally, researchers are sensitive to audiences to whom they report their research. These audiences may be journal editors, journal readers, graduate committees, conference attendees, or colleagues in the field. Students should consider the approaches typically supported and used by their advisers. The experiences of these audiences with quantitative, qualitative, or mixed methods studies will shape the decision made about this choice.

SUMMARY

One preliminary consideration before designing a proposal is to identify a framework for the study. Three approaches to research are discussed in this chapter: quantitative, qualitative, and mixed methods research. They contain philosophical assumptions about knowledge claims, strategies of inquiry, and specific research methods. When philosophy, strategies, and methods are combined, they provide different frameworks for conducting research. The choice of which approach to use is based on the research problem, personal experiences, and the audiences for whom one seeks to write.

Writing Exercises

1. Identify a research question in a journal article and discuss what approach would be best to study the question and why.

2. Take a topic that you would like to study, and, using the four combinations of knowledge claims, strategies of inquiry, and methods in Figure 1.2, discuss how the topic might be studied using each of the combinations.

3. Locate a journal article that is either quantitative, qualitative, or mixed methods research. Identify the "markings" as to why it would be one approach and not the others.

ADDITIONAL READINGS

Cherryholmes, C. H. (1992). Notes on pragmatism and scientific realism. *Educational Researcher,14*, August-September, 13-17.

Cleo Cherryholmes contrasts pragmatism with traditional scientific research. The strengths of this article are the numerous citations to writers about pragmatism and a clarification of the alternative versions of pragmatism. Cherryholmes clarifies his own stance by indicating that pragmatism is driven by anticipated consequences, a reluctance to tell a true story, and the idea that there is an external world independent of our minds.

Crotty, M. (1998). *The foundations of social research: Meaning and perspective in the research process*. London: Sage.

Michael Crotty offers a useful framework for tying together the many epistemological issues, theoretical perspectives, methodology, and methods of social research. He interrelates the four components of the research process and shows in Table 1 a representative sampling of topics of each component. He then goes on to discuss nine different theoretical orientations in social research, such as postmodernism, feminism, critical inquiry, interpretivism, constructionism, and positivism.

Kemmis, S., & Wilkinson, M. (1998). Participatory action research and the study of practice. In B. Atweh, S. Kemmis, & P. Weeks (Eds.), _Action research in practice: Partnerships for social justice in education_ (pp. 21-36). New York: Routledge.

Stephen Kemmis and Mervyn Wilkinson provide an excellent overview of participatory research. In particular, they note the six major features of this inquiry approach and then discuss how action research is practiced at the individual, the social, or both levels.

Lincoln, Y. S., & Guba, E. G. (2000). Paradigmatic controversies, contradictions, and emerging confluences. In N. K. Denzin, Y. S. Lincoln, & E. G. Guba (Eds.), _Handbook of qualitative research_ (2nd ed., pp. 163-188). Thousand Oaks, CA: Sage.

Yvonna Lincoln and Egon Guba have provided the basic beliefs of five alternative inquiry paradigms in social science research. These extend the earlier analysis provided in the first edition of the _Handbook_ and include positivism, postpositivism, critical theory, constructivism, and participatory paradigms. Each is presented in terms of ontology (i.e., nature of reality), epistemology (i.e., how we know what we know), and methodology (i.e., the process of research). The participatory paradigm adds another alternative paradigm to those originally advanced in the first edition. After briefly presenting these five approaches, the authors contrast them in terms of seven issues, such as the nature of knowledge and how knowledge accumulates.

Neuman, W. L. (2000). _Social research methods: Qualitative and quantitative aproaches_ (4th ed.). Boston: Allyn and Bacon.

Lawrence Neuman provides a comprehensive research methods text as an introduction to social science research. Especially helpful in understanding the alternative meaning of methodology is Chapter 4, titled "The Meanings of Methodology," in which he contrasts three methodologies—positivist social science, interpretive social science, and critical social science—in terms of eight questions (e.g., What constitutes an explanation or theory of social reality? What does good evidence or factual information look like?)

Phillips, D. C., & Burbules, N. C. (2000). *Postpositivism and educational research*. Lanham, MD: Rowman & Littlefield.

D. C. Phillips and Nicholas Burbules summarize the major ideas of postpositivist thinking. Through two chapters, "What Is Post-positivism?" and "Philosophical Commitments of Postpositivist Researchers," the authors advance major ideas about postpositivism, especially those that differentiate it from positivism. These include knowing that human knowledge is conjectural rather than unchallengeable, and that our warrants for knowledge can be withdrawn in light of further investigations.

CHAPTER TWO

Review of the Literature

I n addition to selecting a quantitative, qualitative, or mixed methods approach, the proposal designer also needs to begin reviewing the scholarly literature. Literature reviews help researchers limit the scope of their inquiry, and they convey the importance of studying a topic to readers.

This chapter continues the discussion about preliminary choices to be made before launching into a proposal. It begins with a discussion about selecting a topic and writing this topic down so that the researcher can continually reflect on it. At this point, researchers also need to consider whether the topic *can* and *should* be researched. Then, the discussion moves into the actual process of reviewing the literature. It begins by addressing the general purpose for using literature in a study, then turns to principles helpful in providing a literature review in qualitative, quantitative, and mixed methods studies.

IDENTIFYING A TOPIC

Before considering what literature to use in a project, first identify a topic to study and reflect on whether it is practical and useful to undertake the study. Describe the topic in a few words or in a short phrase. The topic becomes the central idea to learn about or to explore in a study.

There are several ways in which researchers often gain some insight into their topic when they are beginning their research. My assumption will be that the topic is chosen by the researcher and not by an adviser or committee member. Several strategies can help start the process of identifying a topic.

One way is to draft a brief title for the study. I am surprised at how often researchers fail to draft a title early in their projects. In my opinion, the "working title" becomes a major road sign in research—a tangible idea to keep refocusing on and changing as the project goes on (see Glesne and Peshkin, 1992). I find that in my research, this topic grounds me and provides a sign of what I am studying, as well as a sign often used in conveying to others the central notion of my study. When students first provide their prospectus of a research study to me, I ask them to supply a working title if they do not already have one on the paper.

How would this working title be written? Try completing this sentence: "My study is about. . . ." A response might be "My study is about at-risk children in the junior high" or "My study is about helping college faculty become better researchers." At this stage in the design, frame the answer to the question so that another scholar might easily grasp the meaning of the project. A common shortcoming of beginning researchers is that they frame their study in complex and erudite language. This perspective may result from reading published articles that have undergone numerous revisions before being set in print. Good, sound research projects begin with straightforward, uncomplicated thoughts, easily read and understood.

These easily understood titles should also reflect principles of good titles. Wilkinson (1991) provides useful advice for creating a title: Be brief and avoid wasting words. Eliminate unnecessary words such as "An Approach to" or "A Study of." Use a single title or a double title. An example of a double title is "An Ethnography: Understanding a Child's Perception of War." In addition to Wilkinson's thoughts, consider a title no longer than 12 words, eliminate most articles and prepositions, and make sure that it includes the focus or topic of the study.

Another strategy for topic development is to pose the topic as a brief question. What question needs to be answered in the proposed study? A researcher might ask "What treatment is best for depression?," "What does it mean to be Arabic in American society today?," or "What brings people to tourist sites in the Midwest?" When drafting questions such as these, focus on the key topic in the question as the major signpost for the study. Consider how this question might be expanded later (see Chapters 5 and 6, on the purpose statement and on research questions and hypotheses, respectively) to be more descriptive of your study.

A RESEARCHABLE TOPIC

To actively elevate this topic to a research study calls also for reflecting on whether the topic can and should be researched. A topic *can* be researched if researchers have participants willing to serve in the study. It also can be researched if investigators have resources at key points in the study, such as resources to collect data over a sustained period of time and resources to analyze the information, such as through data analysis or text analysis programs.

The question of *should* is more complex. Several factors might go into this decision. Perhaps the most important is whether the topic adds to the pool of research knowledge available on the topic. A first step in any project is to spend considerable time in the library examining the research on a topic (see later in this chapter for strategies for effectively using the library and library resources). This point cannot be overemphasized. Beginning researchers may advance a great study that is complete in every way, such as in the clarity of research questions, the comprehensiveness of data collection, and the sophistication of statistical analysis. After all that, the researcher may garner little support from faculty committees or conference planners because the study does not add "anything new" to the body of research on a topic. Ask, "how does this project contribute to the literature?" Consider how the study might address a topic that has yet to be examined, extend the discussion by incorporating new elements, or replicate (or repeat) a study in new situations or with new participants.

The issue of whether the topic *should* be studied also relates to whether anyone outside the researcher's own immediate institution or area would be interested in the topic. Given two topics, one that might be of limited, regional interest and one of national interest, I would opt for the latter because its appeal to a general audience will help readers appreciate the worth of the study. Journal editors, committee members, conference planners, and funding agencies all like research that will reach a broad audience. Finally, the *should* issue also relates to the researcher's personal goals. Consider the time it takes to complete a project, revise it, and disseminate the results. Any researcher should consider how the research study and its heavy input of the researcher's time will pay off in enhancing career goals, whether these goals relate to doing more research, obtaining a future position, or advancing toward a degree.

Before proceeding with a proposal or a study, one needs to weigh these factors and ask others for their reaction to a topic. Seek reactions from colleagues, noted authorities in the field, academic advisers and faculty committee members, and colleagues.

PURPOSE OF THE LITERATURE REVIEW

The literature review in a research study accomplishes several purposes. It shares with the reader the results of other studies that are closely related to the study being reported. It relates a study to the larger ongoing dialogue in the literature about a topic, filling in gaps and extending prior studies (Cooper, 1984; Marshall & Rossman, 1999). It provides a framework for establishing the importance of the study as well as a benchmark for comparing the results of a study with other findings. All or some of these reasons may be the foundation for writing the scholarly literature into a study (see Miller, 1991, for a more extensive list of purposes for using literature in a study). Beyond the question of why it is used is the issue of how its use might differ in the three approaches to research.

LITERATURE REVIEWS IN QUALITATIVE, QUANTITATIVE, AND MIXED METHODS RESEARCH

In *qualitative* research, inquirers use the literature in a manner consistent with the assumptions of learning from the participant, and not prescribing the questions that need to be answered from the researcher's standpoint. One of the chief reasons for conducting a qualitative study is that the study is exploratory. This means that not much has been written about the topic or the population being studied, and the researcher seeks to listen to participants and build an understanding based on their ideas.

However, the use of the literature in qualitative research varies considerably. In theoretically oriented qualitative studies such as ethnographies or critical ethnographies, the literature on a cultural concept or a critical theory from the literature is introduced by researchers early in a study as an orienting framework. In grounded theory studies, case studies, and phenomenological studies, literature will serve less to set the stage for the study.

With an approach grounded in learning from participants and variation by type of qualitative research, we see several models for incorporating the literature in a qualitative study. I offer three placement locations. A literature review can be used in any or all of these locations. As shown in Table 2.1, you might include the literature in the introduction to a study. In this placement, the literature provides a useful backdrop for the problem or issue that has led to the need for the study, such as who has been writing about it, who has studied it, and who has indicated the importance of studying the issue. This "framing" of the problem is, of course, contingent on available studies. One can find illustrations of this model in many qualitative studies employing different strategies of inquiry.

TABLE 2.1   Using Literature in a Qualitative Study

Use of the Literature	Criteria	Examples of Suitable Types of Studies
The literature is used to "frame" the problem in the introduction to the study.	There must be some literature available.	Typically used in all qualitative studies, regardless of type.
The literature is presented in a separate section as a "review of the literature."	An approach often acceptable to an audience most familiar with the traditional, positivist, approach to literature reviews.	This approach is used with those studies employing a strong theory and literature background at the beginning of a study, such as ethnographies, critical theory studies.
The literature is presented in the study at the end; it becomes a basis for comparing and contrasting findings of the qualitative study.	This approach is most suitable for the "inductive" process of qualitative research; the literature does not guide and direct the study but becomes an aide once patterns or categories have been identified.	This approach is used in all types of qualitative designs, but it is most popular with grounded theory, where one contrasts and compares his or her theory with other theories found in the literature.

A second form is to review the literature in a separate section, a model typically used in quantitative research. This approach often appears when the audience consists of individuals or readers with a quantitative orientation. Moreover, in theory-oriented qualitative studies, such as ethnographies and critical theory studies or studies with an advocacy or emancipatory aim, the inquirer might locate the theory discussion and literature in a separate section, typically toward the beginning of the study. Third, the researcher may incorporate the related literature in the final section of the study, where it is used to compare and contrast with the results (or themes or categories) that emerged from the study. This model is especially popular in grounded theory studies. I recommend it because it uses the literature inductively.

Quantitative research, on the other hand, includes a substantial amount of literature at the beginning of a study to provide direction for the research questions or hypotheses. In planning a quantitative study, the literature is often used at the beginning of a study to introduce a problem or to describe in detail the existing literature in a section titled "related literature" or "review of literature," or something similar. In addition, the literature is included in the end of a study in which the researcher compares the results of the study with the existing findings in the literature. In this model, the quantitative researcher uses the literature deductively as a framework for the research questions or hypotheses.

A separate section on the "review of the literature" deserves special mention because it is a popular form for writing literature into a study. This literature review might take several different forms, and little consensus exists about a preferable form. Cooper (1984) suggests that literature reviews can be *integrative*, with the researchers summarizing broad themes in the literature. This model is popular in dissertation proposals and dissertations. A second form recommended by Cooper is a *theoretical* review, in which the researcher focuses on extant theory that relates to the problem under study. This form appears in journal articles in which the author integrates the theory into the introduction to the study. A final form suggested by Cooper is a *methodological* review, in which the researcher focuses on methods and definitions. These reviews may provide not only a summary of studies but also an actual critique of the strengths and weaknesses of the method sections. Some authors use this form in dissertations and in "review of related literature" sections in journal articles.

In a *mixed methods* study, the researcher uses either a qualitative or a quantitative approach to the literature depending on the type of mixed methods design being used. In a sequential design, the literature is presented in each phase in a way consistent with the type of design being used in that phase. For example, if the study begins with a quantitative phase, then the investigator is likely to include a substantial literature review that helps to establish a rationale for the research questions or hypotheses. If the study begins with a qualitative phase, then the literature is substantially less, and the researcher may incorporate it more into the end of the study—an inductive approach to literature use. If the researcher advances a concurrent study with an equal weight and emphasis on both qualitative and quantitative data, then the literature may take either qualitative or quantitative forms. Ultimately, the approach to literature use in a mixed methods project will depend on the type of strategy and the relative weight given to the qualitative or quantitative research in the study.

My suggestions, then, for planning to use the literature in a qualitative, quantitative, or mixed methods study are as follows.

- In a *qualitative* study, use the literature sparingly in the beginning of the plan in order to convey an inductive design, unless the qualitative strategy-type requires a substantial literature orientation at the outset.

- Consider the most appropriate place for the literature in a *qualitative* study and base the decision on the audience for the project. Keep in mind placing it at the beginning to "frame" the problem, placing it in a separate section, and using it at the end of a study to compare and contrast with the findings of the current study.

- Use the literature in a *quantitative* study deductively as a basis for advancing research questions or hypotheses.

- Use the literature to introduce the study, describe related literature in a separate section, or compare extant literature with findings in a *quantitative* study plan.

- If a separate "review of the literature" is used, consider whether the review will consist of integrative summaries, theoretical reviews, or methodological reviews. A typical practice in dissertation writing is to advance an integrative review.

- In a *mixed methods* study, use the literature in a way that is consistent with the major type of strategy and the approach—qualitative or quantitative—that is most prevalent in the design.

DESIGN TECHNIQUES

Regardless of whether you write the literature into a qualitative, quantitative, or a mixed methods study, several steps are useful in conducting a literature review.

STEPS IN CONDUCTING A LITERATURE REVIEW

A literature review for a proposal or a research study means locating and summarizing the studies about a topic. Often these summaries are research studies (because you are conducting a research study), but they may also include conceptual articles or thought pieces that provide frameworks for thinking about topics. There is no one way to conduct a literature review, but many scholars proceed in a systematic fashion to capture, evaluate, and summarize the literature.

Step 1   Begin by identifying key words useful in locating materials in an academic library at a college or university. These key words may emerge in identifying a topic, or they may result from preliminary readings in the library.

Step 2   With these key words in mind, next go to the library and begin searching the library catalog for holdings (i.e., journals and books). Most major libraries have computerized databases of their holdings. I suggest focusing initially on journals and books related to the topic. Also, I suggest beginning to search the computerized databases typically reviewed by social science researchers, such as ERIC, PsycINFO, Sociofile, and the Social Science Citation Index (later, these will be reviewed in some detail). These databases are available online using the library's Web site, or they may be available on CD-ROM in a library.

Step 3   I would initially try to locate about 50 reports of research in articles or books related to research on my topic. I would set a priority on the search for journal articles and books because they are easy to locate and obtain. I would determine whether these articles and books are held in my academic library or whether I need to send for them by interlibrary loan or purchase them through a bookstore.

Step 4   Using this initial group of articles, I would then look at the articles and photocopy those that are central to my topic. In the selection process, I would look over the abstract and skim the article or chapter. Throughout this process, I would try simply to obtain a sense of whether the article or chapter will make a useful contribution to my understanding of the literature.

Step 5   As I identify useful literature, I begin designing my literature map, a visual picture of the research literature on my topic. Several possibilities exist for drawing this map (to be discussed later). This picture provides a useful organizing device for positioning my own study within the larger body of the literature on a topic.

Step 6   At the same time that I am organizing the literature into my literature map, I am also beginning to draft summaries of the most relevant articles. These summaries are combined into the final literature review that I write for my proposal or research study. In addition, I am including precise references to the literature using an appropriate style, such as that contained in the American Psychological Association style manual (American Psychological Association, 2001), so that I have a complete reference to use at the end of my proposal or study.

Step 7   After summarizing the literature, I then assemble the literature review, in which I structure the literature thematically or organize it by important concepts addressed in the study. I would end my literature review with a summary of the major themes found in the literature and suggest that we need further research on the topic along the lines of my proposed study.

To build on key points in these seven process steps, we will first consider techniques useful in accessing the literature quickly through databases.

Computerized Databases

Information retrieval has become the next frontier of scientific development for social and human science researchers. Using search engines, researchers can locate online literature for a review. Moreover, library holdings can be scanned quickly using the computerized online catalog system. A survey of academic libraries reported that 98% of 119 academic research libraries had bibliographic records of books and journals "online" for computer accessing (Krol, 1993). Using the Internet, catalog holdings of libraries across the country are also available, an example of which would be the CARL (Colorado Association of Research Libraries) system in Colorado. It provides a wide assortment of online text, indices of model school programs, online book reviews, facts about the metropolitan Denver area, and a database on environmental education (Krol, 1993).

Databases now available in libraries provide an opportunity for researchers to access thousands of journals, conference papers, and materials quickly. Several databases form the toolkit of resources for the social science researcher today.

The ERIC (Educational Resources Information Center) system is available on CD-ROM and online (see www.accesseric.org). This database provides access to nearly 1 million abstracts of documents and journal articles on educational research and practice. ERIC contains two parts: CIJE, the *Current Index to Journals in Education* (Educational Resources Information Center, 1969–) and RIE, *Resources in Education* (Educational Resources Information Center, 1975–). To best utilize ERIC, it is important to identify appropriate "descriptors" for the topic. Researchers can search through a dictionary of terms using the ERIC *Thesaurus* (Educational Resources Information Center, 1975). However, a random search through the *Thesaurus* for descriptors may be time-consuming and futile. Alternatively, you might use the following procedure:

1. Look through the subject index found at the back of each CIJE and RIE or run an ERIC computer search using keywords that seem close to your topic. Look for a research study as similar as possible to your project.

2. When you find a study, examine the descriptors used for that article. Select the major descriptors used to describe that article (see descriptor terms in the abstract).

3. Use these major descriptors in your computer search. In this way, you utilize the descriptors that individuals at the ERIC Clearinghouses have used to catalog articles for the ERIC system. This, in turn, maximizes the possibility of locating articles relevant for the planned study.

The *Social Sciences Citation Index* (Institute for Scientific Information, 1969–   ) is also available on CD-ROM and held in many academic libraries. The SSCI covers about 5,700 journals that represent virtually every discipline in the social sciences. It can be used to locate articles and authors who have conducted research on a topic. It is especially useful in locating studies that have referenced an important study. The SSCI enables you to trace all studies since the publication of the key study that have cited the work. Using this system, you can develop a chronological list of references that document the historical evolution of an idea or study.

Another CD-ROM database *is Dissertation Abstracts International* (University Microfilms, 1938–   ). This database contains abstracts of doctoral dissertations submitted by nearly 500 participating institutions throughout the world. In a full literature review for a dissertation, identify all references, including dissertations, in the search. Look for a few good dissertations from respected institutions that address a topic as close as possible to your topic of study.

To locate research in sociology or on topics that address sociological concepts, search *Sociological Abstracts* (1953–   ), available on a CD-ROM titled Sociofile. *Sociological Abstracts* is available from Cambridge Scientific Abstracts (see its Web site at http://infoshare1.princeton.edu:2003/databases/about/tips/html/sociofile.html). This database contains abstracts to articles in more than 2,500 journals as well as book reviews and abstracts for dissertations and books. For psychological studies, examine PsycINFO (see www.apa.org/psyinfo/about/), the guide to *Psychological Abstracts* (1927–   ). This database indexes more than 850 journals under 16 different categories of information. It is available in academic libraries in CD-ROM form and as a Web site version.

In summary, I recommend the following:

● Use computerized resources available in your academic library, such as CD-ROM or Web site versions to access literature about your topic.

● Access multiple databases to conduct a thorough review of the literature. Search databases such as ERIC, SSCI, PsycINFO, Sociofile, and *Dissertation Abstracts International*.

A Priority for Resources in the Literature

I recommend that researchers establish a priority in a search of the literature. What types of literature might be reviewed, and in what priority? Consider the following:

1. Especially if you are examining a topic for the first time and are unaware of the research on it, start with broad syntheses of the literature, such as overviews found in encyclopedias (e.g., Aikin, 1992; Keeves, 1988). You might also look for summaries of the literature on your topic presented in journal articles or abstract series (e.g., *Annual Review of Psychology*, 1950–).

2. Next, turn to journal articles in respected, national journals, especially those that report research studies. By *research*, I mean that the author or authors pose a question or hypothesis, collect data, and try to answer the question or support the hypothesis. Start with the most recent studies about the topic and then work backward in time. In these journal articles, follow up on references at the end of the articles for more sources to examine.

3. Turn to books related to the topic. Begin with research monographs that summarize the scholarly literature, then consider entire books that are on a single topic or contain chapters written by different authors.

4. Follow this search by looking for recent conference papers on a topic. Often conference papers report the latest research developments. Look for major, national conferences and the papers delivered at them. Most major conferences either require or request that authors submit their papers for inclusion in computerized indexes. Make contact with authors of studies. Seek them out at conferences. Write or phone them asking if they know of studies related to the proposed study and inquire if they have an instrument that might be used or modified for use in your study.

5. If time permits, look at the abstracts of dissertations in *Dissertation Abstracts International* (University Microfilms, 1938–). Dissertations vary immensely in quality, and one needs to be selective in examining these studies. A search of the *Abstracts* might result in one or two relevant dissertations. Once you identify these dissertations, request copies of them through interlibrary loan or through the University of Michigan Microfilm Library.

I placed journal articles first on the list because they are the easiest to locate and duplicate. They also report the "research" about a topic. Dissertations are listed last because they vary considerably in quality and are the most difficult material to locate and reproduce.

Web site articles and research studies also are useful materials. The easy access and ability to capture entire articles makes these sources of material attractive. However, reviewers may not have evaluated and screened these articles for quality, and one needs to be cautious about whether they represent rigorous, thoughtful and systematic research for use in a literature review. Online journals, which are becoming more popular, often include articles that have been examined for standards of quality, and researchers might check to see if the journal has a refereed review board that has published standards of quality used in accepting articles for publication.

A Literature Map of the Research

One of the first tasks for a researcher working with a new topic is to organize the literature about the topic. This enables a researcher to understand how his or her study of the topic adds to, extends, or replicates research already completed.

A useful tool for this task is a literature map of the research about a topic. This map is a visual summary of the research that has been conducted by others, and it is typically represented in a figure. Literature maps are organized in different ways. One is a hierarchical structure, with a top-down presentation of the literature ending at the bottom with a proposed study that will extend the literature. Another might be similar to a flow-chart in which the reader understands the literature unfolding from left to right, with the studies furthest to the right advancing a proposed study that adds to the literature. A third model might be composed of circles, with each circle representing a body of literature and the intersection of the circles indicating the place at which future research is needed. I have seen examples drawn by students of all of these possibilities.

The central idea is that the researcher begins to build a visual picture of existing research about a topic. This literature map presents an overview of existing literature. It will help others—such as a dissertation or master's thesis committee, a group of participants assembled at a conference, or journal reviewers—visualize how the study relates to the larger literature on the topic.

To illustrate a literature map and the process involved in generating one, I will first show a complete map and then discuss some general

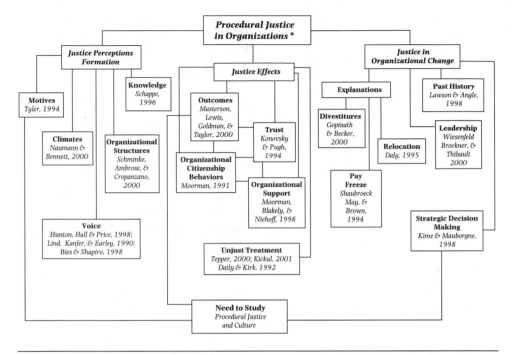

Figure 2.1   A Literature Map

SOURCE: From Janovec (2001). Reprinted by permission of Terese Janovec.
*Employees' concerns about the fairness of and the making of managerial decisions.

guidelines for designing this map. See Figure 2.1, which shows the literature found on the topic of procedural justice in organizations (Janovec, 2001). Janovec's map illustrates a hierarchical design for a map. She used several principles of good map design.

● She placed the topic of the literature review in the box at the top of the hierarchy.

● Next, she took the studies that she found in computer searches, located copies of these studies, and organized them into three broad subtopics (i.e., justice perceptions formation, justice effects, and justice in organizational change). For another map, the researcher may have more or less than four major categories, depending on the extent of publications on the topic.

● Within each box are labels that describe the nature of the studies in the box (i.e., "outcomes").

- Also, within each box are references to major citations illustrating the content of the box. It is useful to use references that are current and illustrative of the topic of the box, and to briefly state the references in an appropriate style manual form for an in-text reference (e.g., Smith, xxxx).

- Consider several levels for the literature map. In other words, major topics lead to subtopics, and then other sub-subtopics.

- Some branches of the chart are more developed than other branches. This depth will depend on the amount of literature available and the depth of the exploration of the literature by the researcher.

- After organizing the literature into a diagram, Janovec considered the branches of the figure that provide a springboard for her proposed study. She placed a "need to study" (or "proposed study") box at the bottom of the map, she briefly identified the nature of this proposed study ("procedural justice and culture"), and she drew lines to past literature that her project would extend. She proposed this study based on ideas suggested by other authors in the "future research" sections of their studies.

Abstracting Studies

When reviewing the content of research studies, researchers record essential information from them for a review of the literature. In this process, researchers need to consider what material to extract from a research study and to summarize in a "review of related literature" section. This is important information when reviewing perhaps dozens if not hundreds of studies. A good literature review summary of a research article reported in a journal might include the following points:

- Mention the problem being addressed.

- State the central purpose or focus of the study.

- Briefly state information about the sample, population, or participants.

- Review key results that relate to the study.

- Depending on whether the review is a methodological review (Cooper, 1984), point out technical and methodological flaws in the study.

When examining an article to develop a summary, there are places in research studies to look for these parts. In well-crafted journal articles, the problem and purpose statements are found and clearly stated in the introduction to the article. Information about the sample, population, or participants is found midway through the article in a method (or procedure) section, and the results are often reported toward the end of the article. In the results sections, look for passages in which the researchers report information to answer or address each research question or hypothesis. For book-length research studies, look for the same points. Consider the following example.

Example 2.1   *Review of a Quantitative Study*

In this example, I will present a paragraph summarizing the major components of a quantitative study (Creswell, Seagren, & Henry, 1979), much like the paragraph might appear in a "review of the literature" section of a dissertation or a journal article. In this passage, I have chosen key components to be abstracted.

> Creswell, Seagren, and Henry (1979) tested the Biglan model, a three-dimensional model clustering thirty-six academic areas into hard or soft, pure or applied, life or non-life areas, as a predictor of chairpersons' professional development needs. Eighty department chairpersons located in four state colleges and one university of a Midwestern state participated in the study. Results showed that chairpersons in different academic areas differed in terms of their professional development needs. Based on the findings, the authors recommended that those who develop in-service programs need to consider differences among disciplines when they plan for programs.

I began with an "in-text" reference in accord with the format in the American Psychological Association style manual, *Publication Manual of the American Psychological Association* (American Psychological Association, 2001). Next, I reviewed the central purpose of the study. I followed the review with information about the data collection. I ended by stating the major results of the study and presenting the practical implications of these results.

How are studies that are not research studies—essays, opinions, typologies, and syntheses of past research—abstracted? When abstracting these non-empirical studies, the researcher should

- Mention the problem being addressed by the article or book

- Identify the central theme of the study

- State the major conclusions related to this theme

- Mention flaws in reasoning, logic, force of argument, and so forth if the review type is methodological

Consider the following example that illustrates the inclusion of these aspects.

Example 2.2   *Review of a Study Advancing a Typology*

Sudduth (1992) completed a quantitative dissertation in political science on the topic of the use of strategic adaptation in rural hospitals. He reviewed the literature in several chapters at the beginning of the study. In an example of summarizing a single study advancing a typology, Sudduth summarized the problem, the theme, and the typology.

> Ginter, Duncan, Richardson, and Swayne (1991) recognize the impact of the external environment on a hospital's ability to adapt to change. They advocate a process that they call environmental analysis which allows the organization to strategically determine the best responses to change occurring in the environment. However, after examining the multiple techniques used for environmental analysis, it appears that no comprehensive conceptual scheme or computer model has been developed to provide a complete analysis of environmental issues (Ginter et al., 1991). The result is an essential part of strategic change that relies heavily on a non-quantifiable and judgmental process of evaluation. To assist the hospital manager to carefully assess the external environment, Ginter et al. (1991) have developed the typology given in Figure 2.1. (p. 44)

Style Manuals

A basic tenet in reviewing the literature is to use an appropriate and consistent reference style. When identifying a useful reference for a literature review, make a complete reference to the source using an appropriate style. For dissertation proposals, graduate students should seek guidance from faculty, dissertation committee members, or department or college officials about the appropriate style manual to use for citing references.

The *Publication Manual of the American Psychological Association* (5th ed.) (American Psychological Association, 2001) is widely used in the fields of education and psychology. The University of Chicago's manual (*A Manual of Style*, 1982), Turabian (Turabian, 1973), and Campbell and Ballou (1977) are also extensively used in the social sciences. Some journals have even developed their own variation of the popular styles. I recommend adopting a style manual early in the planning process and identifying one that is acceptable for your writing audiences.

The most important style manual considerations involve use of in-text citations, end-of-text references, headings, and figures and tables. Some suggestions for scholarly writing using style manuals follow.

- When writing *in-text citations*, keep in mind the appropriate form for types of citations and pay close attention to the format for multiple citations.

- When writing the *end-of-text references*, note whether the style manual calls for them to be alphabetized or numbered. Also, cross-check that each in-text citation is matched by an end-of-text reference.

- The *headings* are ordered in a scholarly paper in terms of levels. First, note how many levels of headings you will have in your research study. Then, refer to the style manual for the appropriate format for each level that you use. Typically, research reports contain between two and four levels of headings.

- If *footnotes* are used, consult the style manual for their proper placement. Footnotes are used less frequently in scholarly papers today than they were a few years ago. If you include them, note whether they go at the bottom of the page or at the end of the paper.

- *Tables* and *figures* have a specific form in each style manual. Note such aspects as bold lines, titles, and spacing in the examples given in the style manual.

In summary, the most important aspect of using a style manual is to be consistent in the approach throughout the manuscript.

A MODEL FOR WRITING THE LITERATURE REVIEW

When composing a review of the literature, it is difficult to determine how much literature to review. To address this problem, I have developed a model that provides parameters for the literature review, especially as it might be designed for a quantitative or mixed methods study that employs a standard literature review section. For a qualitative study, the literature review might explore aspects of the central phenomenon being addressed and divide it into topical areas.

For a quantitative or mixed methods review, write a review of the literature that contains sections about the literature related to major independent variables, major dependent variables, and studies that relate the independent and dependent variables (more material on variables will appear in Chapter 4). This approach seems appropriate for dissertations and for conceptualizing the literature to be introduced in a journal article. Consider a literature review (in a dissertation or proposal) to be composed of five components: an introduction, topic 1 (about the independent variable), topic 2 (about the dependent variable), topic 3 (studies that address both the independent and dependent variables), and a summary. Here is more detail about each section:

1. *Introduce the section* by telling the reader about the sections included in the literature review. This passage is a statement about the organization of the section.

2. Review topic 1, which addresses the scholarly literature about the *independent variable or variables*. With several independent variables, consider subsections or focus on the single most important variable. Remember to address only the literature about the independent variable; keep the literature about the independent and dependent variables separate in this model.

3. Review topic 2, which incorporates the scholarly literature about the *dependent variable or variables*. With multiple dependent variables, write subsections about each variable or focus on a single, important dependent variable.

4. Review topic 3, which includes the scholarly literature that relates the *independent variable(s)* to the *dependent variable(s)*. Here we are at the crux of the proposed study. Thus, this section should be relatively short and contain studies that are extremely close in topic to the proposed study. Perhaps nothing has been written on the topic. Construct a section that is as

close as possible to the topic, or review studies that address the topic at a more general level.

5.   Provide a *summary* of the review that highlights the most important studies, captures major themes in the review, and suggests why we need more research on the topic.

This model focuses the literature review, relates it closely to the variables in the research questions and hypotheses, and sufficiently narrows the study. It becomes a logical point of departure for the method section.

⊞ SUMMARY

Before searching the literature, identify your topic using such strategies as drafting a brief title or stating the central research question to be addressed. Also consider whether this topic can and should be researched by reviewing whether there is access to participants and resources and whether the topic will add to social science knowledge, be of interest to others, and be consistent with personal goals.

Researchers use the scholarly literature in a study to present results of similar studies, to relate the present study to the ongoing dialogue in the literature, and to provide a framework for comparing results of a study with other studies. For qualitative, quantitative, and mixed methods designs, the literature serves different purposes. In qualitative research, the literature helps substantiate the research problem, but it does not constrain the views of participants. A popular approach is to include more literature at the end of a qualitative study than at the beginning. In quantitative research, the literature not only helps to substantiate the problem but also suggests possible questions or hypotheses that need to be addressed. A separate "literature review" section typically is found in quantitative studies. In mixed methods research, the use of literature will depend on the type of strategy of inquiry and the weight given to qualitative or qualitative research in the study.

When conducting a literature review, identify key words for searching the literature, then search the library resources, relying on computerized databases in the library and for fields of study, such as ERIC, PsycINFO, Sociofile, and the Social Science Citation Index. Then, locate articles or books based on a priority of searching first for journal articles and then books. Identify references that will make a contribution to your literature review. Group these studies into a literature map that shows the major categories of studies and positions your proposed study within those categories. Begin writing summaries of the studies, noting complete references according to a style manual (e.g., American Psychological Association, 2001) and extracting information about the research that includes the research problem, the questions, the data collection and analysis, and the final results. Finally, consider the overall structure for organizing these studies. One model is to divide the review into sections according to major variables (a quantitative approach) or major subthemes of the central phenomenon (a qualitative approach) that you are studying.

Writing Exercises

1. Develop a visual map of the literature related to the topic. Include in the map the proposed study, and draw lines from the proposed study to other categories of studies so that a reader can easily see how the study will extend existing literature.

2. Organize a "Review of the Literature" for a quantitative study and follow the model for delimiting the literature to reflect the variables in the study. As an alternative, organize a review of literature for a qualitative study and include it in an introduction as a rationale for the research problem in the study.

3. Identify the number of heading levels in a published journal article. Do this by creating an outline of the levels using appropriate APA (5th ed.) form.

4. Run an ERIC search on a topic by identifying key terms, combining them, and using the Web site www.accesseric.org. As an extention of this exercise, select one of the search results that is close to the type of literature being sought, note the descriptors used, and re-run the ERIC search to obtain literature more central to the literature review.

WRITING EXERCISES

ADDITIONAL READINGS

Locke, L. F., Spirduso, W. W., & Silverman, S. J. (2000). *Proposals that work: A guide for planning dissertations and grant proposals* **(4th ed.). Thousand Oaks, CA: Sage.**

Lawrence Locke, Waneen Spirduso, and Stephen Silverman describe 15 steps in the process of developing a review of literature. These 15 steps involve three stages: developing the concepts that provide the rationale for the study, developing the subtopics for each major concept, and adding the most important references that support each subtopic. These steps involve stages such as identifying the concepts that provide the rationale for the study, selecting the subtopics for each major concept, and adding the most important references that support each subtopic. They also provide a "diagrammatic overview of the related literature" as a model for visualizing the literature.

Merriam, S. B. (1998). *Qualitative research and case study applications in education.* **San Francisco: Jossey-Bass.**

Sharan Merriam provides an extensive discussion about the use of literature in qualitative studies. She identifies steps in reviewing the literature and poses useful criteria for selecting references. These include checking to see if the author is an authority on the topic, how recent the work was published, whether the resource is relevant to the proposed research topic, and the quality of the resource. Merriam further suggests that the literature review is not a linear process of reading the literature, identifying the theoretical framework, and then writing the problem statement. Instead, the process is highly interactive among these steps.

Punch, K. F. (1998). *Introduction to social research: Quantitative and qualitative approaches.* **London: Sage.**

Keith Punch provides a guide to social research that equally addresses quantitative and qualitative approaches. He conceptualizes key differences between the two approaches in several ways. When writing a literature review, Punch notes that the point to concentrate on in the literature varies in different styles of research. Factors that affect when to concentrate on the literature will depend on the style of research, the overall research strategy, and how closely the study will address the directions in the literature.

CHAPTER THREE

Writing Strategies and Ethical Considerations

Before designing a proposal, it is important to consider how to write it. Those considerations should include which topics will convey the best argument for the need and quality of the study. Now is the best time to adopt writing practices that will ensure a consistent and highly readable proposal (and research project). It is also timely to anticipate the ethical issues that will surface during a study and to incorporate good practices into the research proposal. This chapter focuses on arguments and topics to include in a proposal, the adoption of writing strategies for the process of research, and anticipating ethical issues likely to arise in a study.

WRITING THE PROPOSAL

Central Arguments to Make

It is helpful to consider the topics that will go into a proposal. All the topics need to be interrelated so that they provide a cohesive picture of the entire proposed project. An outline of topics will be helpful, but the topics will differ depending on whether the proposal is for a qualitative, quantitative, or mixed methods study. Overall, however, there are central arguments that frame any proposal. They are introduced as nine central arguments by Maxwell (1996). I pose them here as questions to be addressed in a scholarly proposal.

1. What do we need to better understand your topic?

2. What do we know little about in terms of your topic?

3. What do you propose to study?

4. What are the setting and the people that you will study?

5. What methods do you plan to use to provide data?

6. How will you analyze the data?

7. How will you validate your findings?

8. What ethical issues will your study present?

9. What do preliminary results show about the practicability and value of the proposed study?

These nine questions, if adequately addressed in one section for each question, constitute the foundation of good research, and they could provide the overall structure for a proposal. The inclusion of validating findings, ethical considerations (to be addressed shortly), the need for preliminary results, and early evidence of practical significance of the proposed study focus a reader's attention on key elements often overlooked in discussions about proposed projects.

Format for a Qualitative Proposal

Besides these nine questions, it is often helpful to conceptualize in more detail the topics that are included in proposals. Knowledge of these topics is useful at the beginning of proposal development so that you can conceptualize the entire process.

No commonly accepted format exists for a qualitative proposal, although authors such as Berg (2001), Marshall and Rossman (1999), and Maxwell (1996) advance recommendations for topics. A fundamental characteristic should be that the design is consistent with the constructivism/interpretive and advocacy/participatory knowledge claims as mentioned in Chapter 1. With qualitative research now represented by distinct strategies of inquiry, the proposal should also contain the type of inquiry being used as well as detailed procedures of data collection and analysis.

In the light of these points, I propose two alternative models. Example 3.1 is drawn from a constructivist/interpretivist perspective, whereas Example 3.2 is based more on an advocacy/participatory model of qualitative research.

Example 3.1   *A Qualitative Constructivist/Interpretivist Format*

Introduction
    Statement of the problem (including existing literature about the problem)
    Purpose of the study

The research questions
Delimitations and limitations
Procedures
    Characteristics of qualitative research (optional)
    Qualitative research strategy
    Role of the researcher
    Data collection procedures
    Data analysis procedures
    Strategies for validating findings
    Narrative structure
Anticipated ethical issues
Significance of the study
Preliminary pilot findings
Expected outcomes
Appendices: Interview questions, observational forms, timeline,
and proposed budget

In this example, the writer includes only two major sections, the
introduction and the procedures. A review of the literature may be
included, but it is optional, and, as discussed in Chapter 2, the literature
may be included to a greater extent at the end of the study or in the
expected outcomes section. This format does include a special section on
the researcher's role in the study. As described by Marshall and
Rossman (1999), this section would address decisions about gaining
access to the participants and site and negotiating entry to the site
and/or participants. It also includes mentioning the interpersonal skills
the researcher brings to the project and the researcher's sensitivity to
reciprocity or giving back to the people in the study.

Example 3.2   *A Qualitative Advocacy/Participatory Format*

Introduction
    Statement of the problem (including existing literature about
    the problem)
    The advocacy/participatory issue
    Purpose of the study
    The research questions
    Delimitations and limitations
Procedures
    Characteristics of qualitative research (optional)
    Qualitative research strategy
    Role of the researcher

Data collection procedures (including the collaborative
approaches used with participants)
Data recording procedures
Data analysis procedures
Strategies for validating findings
Narrative structure
Anticipated ethical issues
Significance of the study
Preliminary pilot findings
Expected advocacy/participatory changes
Appendices: Interview questions, observational forms, timeline, and
proposed budget

This format is similar to the constructivist/interpretivist format
except that the inquirer is specific about the advocacy/particpatory
issue being explored in the study (e.g., marginalization, empowerment),
advances a collaborative form of data collection, and mentions the
anticipated changes that the research study will likely bring.

Format for a Quantitative Proposal

For a quantitative study, the format conforms to standards easily
identified in journal articles and research studies. The form generally
follows the model of an introduction, a literature review, methods,
results, and discussion. In planning a quantitative study and designing
a dissertation proposal, consider the following format to sketch the
overall plan.

Example 3.3   *A Quantitative Format*

Introduction
    Statement of the problem
    Purpose of the study
    Theoretical perspective
    Research questions or hypotheses
    Definition of terms
    Delimitations and limitations
Review of the literature
Methods
    Type of research design
    Sample, population, and participants

Data collection instruments, variables, and materials
Data analysis procedures
Anticipated ethical issues in the study
Preliminary studies or pilot tests
Significance of the study
Appendixes: Instruments, timeline, and proposed budget

Example 3.3 is a standard format for a social science study, although the order of the sections, especially in the introduction, may vary from study to study (see, for example, Miller, 1991; Rudestam & Newton, 1992). It presents a useful model for designing the sections for a plan for a dissertation or sketching the topics for a scholarly study.

Format for a Mixed Methods Proposal

In a mixed methods design format, the researcher brings together approaches that are included in both the quantitative and qualitative formats (see Creswell, 1999). An example of such a format appears in Example 3.4.

Example 3.4   *A Mixed Methods Format*

Introduction
    Statement of the problem
    Purpose of the study (include both qualitative and quantitative statements and a rationale for mixing methods)
    Research questions (include both qualitative and quantitative)
    Review of the literature (separate section, if quantitative)
Procedures or methods
    Characteristics of mixed methods research
    Type of mixed methods design (including decisions involved in its choice)
    Visual model and procedures of the design
    Data collection procedures
        Types of data
        Sampling strategy
    Data analysis and validity procedures
    Report presentation structure
Role of the researcher
Potential ethical issues

Significance of the study
Preliminary pilot findings
Expected outcomes
Appendixes: Instruments or protocols, outline for chapters, and
    proposed budget

This format shows that the researcher poses both a purpose statement and research questions for quantitative and qualitative components. Further, it is important to specify a rationale for the mixed
methods approach in the study. The researcher also identifies key
elements of this design, such as the type of mixed methods study, a
visual picture of the procedures, and both the quantitative and qualitative data collection procedures and analysis.

WRITING TIPS

Writing as Thinking

Beyond the more general format, proposal developers need to consider the writing process involved in research. One sign of inexperienced
writers is that they prefer to discuss their proposed study rather than
write about it. All experienced writers know that writing is thinking and
conceptualizing a topic. I recommend the following:

- Early in the process of research, write ideas down rather than talk
  about them. Writing specialists see writing as thinking (Bailey,
  1984). Zinsser (1983) discusses the need to get words out of our
  heads and onto paper. Advisers react better when they read the
  printed text on paper than when they hear and discuss a research
  topic with a student or colleague. When a researcher renders ideas
  on paper, a reader can visualize the final product, actually "see"
  how it looks, and begin to clarify ideas. The concept of working ideas
  out on paper has served many experienced writers well.

- Work through several drafts of a paper rather than trying to polish
  the first draft. It is illuminating to see how people think on paper.
  Zinsser (1983) identified two types of writers: the "bricklayer," who
  makes every paragraph just right before going on to the next paragraph, and the "let-it-all-hang-out-on-the-first-draft" writer, who

writes an entire first draft not caring how sloppy it looks or how badly it is written. In between would be someone like Peter Elbow (Elbow, 1973), who recommends that one should go through the iterative process of writing, reviewing, and rewriting. For example, he cites this exercise: With only 1 hour to write a passage, write four drafts (one every 15 minutes) rather than one draft (typically in the last 15 minutes) during the hour. Most experienced researchers write the first draft carefully but do not work for a polished draft; the polish comes relatively late in the writing process. I use Franklin's (1986) three-stage model in my writing:

1. Develop an outline—it could be a sentence or word outline or a visual map of ideas.

2. Write out a draft and then shift and sort ideas, moving around entire paragraphs in the manuscript.

3. Finally, edit and polish each sentence.

The Habit of Writing

Establish the discipline of writing on a continuous and regular basis. Setting the manuscript aside for a long period results in a loss of concentration and effort. The actual writing of words on a page is only part of a more extended process of thinking, collecting information, and reviewing that goes into manuscript production.

Select a time of day to work that is best for you, then use discipline to write at this time each day. Choose a place free of distractions. Boice (1990, pp. 77-78) offers ideas about establishing good writing habits:

●   With the aid of the priority principle, make writing a daily activity, regardless of mood, regardless of readiness to write.

●   If you feel you do not have time for regular writing, begin by charting your daily activities for a week or two in half-hour blocks.

●   Write while you are fresh.

●   Avoid writing in binges.

●   Write in small, regular amounts.

●   Schedule writing tasks so that you plan to work on specific, manageable units of writing in each session.

- Keep daily charts. Graph at least three things: (a) time spent writing, (b) page equivalents finished, and (c) percentage of planned task completed.

- Plan beyond daily goals.

- Share your writing with supportive, constructive friends before you feel ready to go public.

- Try to work on two or three writing projects concurrently.

In addition to these thoughts, one needs to acknowledge that writing moves along slowly and that a writer must ease into writing. Like the runner who stretches before a road race, the writer needs warm-up exercises for both the mind and the fingers. Some leisurely writing activity, such as writing a letter to a friend, brainstorming on the computer, reading some good writing, or studying a favorite poem, can make the actual task of writing easier. I am reminded of John Steinbeck's (1969) "warm-up period" (p. 42) described in detail in *Journal of a Novel: The East of Eden Letters*. Steinbeck began each writing day by writing a letter to his editor and close friend, Pascal Covici, in a large notebook supplied by Covici.

Other exercises may prove useful. Carroll (1990) provides examples of exercises to improve a writer's control over descriptive and emotive passages:

- Describe an object by its parts and dimensions, without first telling the reader its name.

- Write a conversation between two people on any dramatic or intriguing subject.

- Write a set of directions for a complicated task.

- Take a subject and write about it three different ways. (Carroll, 1990, pp. 113-116)

This last exercise seems appropriate for qualitative researchers who analyze their data for multiple codes and themes (see Chapter 10 for qualitative data analysis).

Consider also the implements of writing and the physical location that aids the process of disciplined writing. The implements of writing— a computer, a yellow legal-sized pad, a favorite pen, a pencil, even coffee and Triscuits (Wolcott, 2001)—offer the writer options for ways to be comfortable when writing. The physical setting for writing can also help. Annie Dillard, the Pulitzer prize-winning novelist, avoided appealing workplaces:

> One wants a room with no view, so imagination can meet memory in the dark. When I furnished this study seven years ago, I pushed the long desk against a blank wall, so I could not see from either window. Once, fifteen years ago, I wrote in a cinder-block cell over a parking lot. It overlooked a tar-and-gravel roof. This pine shed under trees is not quite so good as the cinder-block study was, but it will do. (Dillard, 1989, pp. 26-27)

Readability of the Manuscript

Before beginning the process of writing a proposal, consider how you will enhance the readability of it for other people. It is important to use consistent terms, a staging and foreshadowing of ideas, and coherence built into the plan.

- Use *consistent terms* throughout the manuscript. Use the same term each time a variable is mentioned in a quantitative study or a central phenomenon is mentioned in a qualitative study. Refrain from using synonyms for these terms, a problem that causes the reader to work at understanding the meaning of ideas and to monitor subtle shifts in meaning.

- Consider how narrative "thoughts" of different types guide a reader. This concept was advanced by Tarshis (1982), who recommended that writers stage "thoughts" to guide readers. These were of four types:

  1. Umbrella thoughts—the general or core ideas one is trying to get across

  2. Big thoughts—specific ideas or images that fall within the realm of umbrella thoughts and serve to reinforce, clarify, or elaborate upon the umbrella thoughts

  3. Little thoughts—ideas or images whose chief function is to reinforce big thoughts

  4. Attention or interest thoughts—ideas whose purposes are to keep the reader on track, organize ideas, and keep an individual's attention

Beginning researchers, I believe, struggle most with "umbrella" thoughts and "attention" thoughts. A manuscript may include too many "umbrella" ideas, with the content not sufficiently detailed to support large ideas. A clear mark of this problem is a continual shift of ideas from one major idea to another in a manuscript. Often, one will see short paragraphs, like those found written by journalists in newspaper articles. Thinking in terms of a detailed narrative to support "umbrella" ideas may help this problem. Goldberg (1986) not only talks about the power of detail but also illustrates it using the example of the Vietnam memorial in Washington, D.C., where names—even middle names—of 50,000 killed American soldiers are listed.

Lack of "attention" thoughts also derails a good narrative. Readers need "road signs" to guide them from one major idea to the next (Chapters 5 and 6 of this book discuss major road signs in research, such as purpose statements and research questions and hypotheses). Readers need to see the overall organization of the ideas through introductory paragraphs and to be told, in a summary, the most salient points they should remember.

● Use *coherence* to add to the readability of the manuscript. In presenting the topics in this book, I introduce components of the research process to present a systematic whole. For example, the repetition of variables in the title, the purpose statement, the research questions, and the review of the literature headings in a quantitative project illustrates this thinking. This approach builds coherence into the study. Furthermore, emphasizing a consistent order of variables whenever independent and dependent variables are mentioned in quantitative studies also reinforces this idea.

On a more detailed level, coherence builds through connecting sentences and paragraphs in the manuscript. Zinsser (1983) suggests that every sentence should be a logical sequel to the one that preceded it. A useful exercise is the "hook-and-eye" exercise (Wilkinson, 1991) for connecting thoughts from sentence to sentence (or paragraph to paragraph).

The following passage from a draft of a student's paper shows a high level of coherence. It comes from the introductory section to a draft of a qualitative dissertation project about at-risk students. In this passage, I have taken the liberty of drawing "hooks" and "eyes" to connect the ideas from sentence to sentence and from paragraph to paragraph. The objective of the "hook-and-eye" exercise (Wilkinson, 1991) is to connect major thoughts of each sentence and paragraph. If such a connection cannot easily be made, the written passage lacks coherence and the writer needs to add transitional words, phrases, or sentences to establish a clear connection.

Example 3.5   *A Sample Passage Illustrating the Hook-and-Eye Technique*

They sit in the back of the room not because they want to but because it was the place designated to them. Invisible barriers that exist in most classrooms divide the room and separate the students. At the front of the room are the "good" students who wait with their hands poised ready to fly into the air at a moment's notice. Slouched down like giant insects caught in educational traps, the athletes and their following occupy the center of the room. Those less sure of themselves and their position within the room sit in the back and around the edge of the student body.

The students seated in the outer circle make up a population whom for a variety of reasons are not succeeding in the American public education system. They have always been part of the student population. In the past they have been called disadvantaged, low achieving, retards, impoverished, laggards and a variety of other titles (Cuban, 1989; Presseisen, 1988). Today they are called students-at-risk. Their faces are changing and in urban settings their numbers are growing (Hodgkinson, 1985).

In the past eight years there has been an unprecedented amount of research on the need for excellence in education and the at-risk student. In 1983 the government released a document entitled *A Nation At-Risk* that identified problems within the American education system and called for major reform. Much of the early reform focused on more vigorous courses of study and higher standards of student achievement (Barber, 1987). In the midst of attention to excellence, it became apparent the needs of the marginal student were not being met. The question of what it would take to guarantee that all students have a fair chance at a quality education was receiving little attention (Hamilton, 1987; Toch, 1984). As the push for excellence in education increased, the needs of the at-risk student became more apparent.

Much of the early research focused on identifying characteristics of the at-risk student (OERI, 1987; Barber & McClellan, 1987; Hahn, 1987; Rumberger, 1987), while others in educational research called for reform and developed programs for at-risk students (Mann, 1987; Presseisen, 1988; Whelage, 1988; Whelege & Lipman, 1988; Stocklinski, 1991; and Levin, 1991). Studies and research on this topic have included experts within the field of education, business and industry as well as many government agencies.

Although progress has been made in identifying characteristics of the at-risk students and in developing programs to meet their needs, the essence of the at-risk issue continues to plague the American school system. Some educators feel that we do not need further research (DeBlois, 1989; Hahn, 1987). Others call for a stronger network between business and education (DeBlois, 1989; Mann, 1987; Whelege, 1988). Still others call for total restructuring of our education system (OERI, 1987; Gainer, 1987; Levin, 1988; McCune, 1988).

After all the research and studies by the experts, we still have students hanging on to the fringe of education. The uniqueness of this study will shift the focus from causes and curriculum to the student. It is time to question the students and to listen to their responses. This added dimension should bring further understanding to research already available and lead to further areas of reform. Dropouts and potential dropouts will be interviewed in depth to discover if there are common factors within the public school setting that interfere with their learning process. This information should be helpful to both the researcher who will continue to look for new approaches in education and the practitioner who works with these students everyday.

Voice, Tense, and "Fat"

From working with broad thoughts and paragraphs, I move on to the level of writing sentences and words. In Franklin's (1986) terms, one is now working at the "polish" level of writing, a stage addressed late in the writing process. One can find an abundance of writing books about rules and principles to follow concerning good sentence construction and word choice. Wolcott (2001), for example, talks about honing editorial skills to eliminate unnecessary words, delete the passive voice, scale down qualifiers, eliminate overused phrases, and reduce excessive quotations, use of italics, and parenthetical comments. The following additional ideas about active voice, verb tense, and reduced "fat" can strengthen and invigorate scholarly writing.

- Use the active voice as much as possible in scholarly writing. According to Ross-Larson (1982), "if the subject acts, the voice is active. If the subject is acted on, the voice is passive" (p. 29). In addition, a sign of passive construction is some variation of an auxiliary verb, such as "was." Examples include "will be," "have been," and "is being." Writers can use the passive construction when the person acting can logically be left out of the sentence and when what is acted on is the subject of the rest of the paragraph (Ross-Larson, 1982).

- Use strong verbs and verb tenses appropriate for the passage in the study. Lazy verbs are those that lack action ("is" or "was," for example) or those used as adjectives or adverbs.

- A common practice is to use the past tense to review the literature and report results of a study. The future tense would be appropriate at all other times in research proposals and plans. For completed studies, use the present tense to add vigor to a study, especially in the introduction.

- Expect to edit and revise drafts of a manuscript to trim excess words, the "fat," from the prose. Writing multiple drafts of a manuscript is standard practice for most writers. The process typically consists of writing, reviewing, and editing. In the editing process, trim excess words from sentences, such as piled-up modifiers, excessive prepositions, and "the . . . of" constructions (for example, "the study of"), that add unnecessary verbiage to a study (Ross-Larson, 1982). I was reminded of the unnecessary prose that comes into writing by the example mentioned by Bunge (1985):

  > Nowadays you can almost see bright people struggling to reinvent the complex sentence before your eyes. A friend of mine who is a college administrator every now and then has to say a complex sentence, and he will get into one of those morasses that begins, "I would hope that we would be able . . ." He never talked that way when I first met him, but even at his age, at his distance from the crisis in the lives of younger people, he's been to some extent alienated from easy speech. (Bunge, 1985, p. 172)

Begin studying good writing that uses qualitative, quantitative, and mixed methods designs. In good writing, the eye does not pause and the mind does not stumble on a passage. In this present book, I have attempted to draw examples of good prose from human and social science journals such asthe *American Journal of Sociology, The American Cartographer, Journal of Applied Psychology, Administrative Science Quarterly, American Educational Research Journal, Sociology of Education,* and *Image: Journal of Nursing Scholarship.* In the qualitative area, good literature serves to illustrate clear prose and detailed passages. Individuals who teach qualitative research assign classical literature such as *Moby Dick, The Scarlet Letter,* and *The Bonfire of the Vanities* as reading assignments in qualitative courses (Webb & Glesne, 1992). Journals such as *Qualitative Inquiry, Qualitative Research, Symbolic Interaction, Qualitative Family Research,* and *Journal of Contemporary Ethnography* represent good, scholarly journals to examine. In mixed methods research, examine journals that report studies with combined qualitative and quantitative data, including many social science journals, such as *Field Methods.* Examine the numerous journal articles cited in the *Handbook of Mixed Methods in the Social and Behavioral Sciences* (Tashakkori & Teddlie, 2002).

ETHICAL ISSUES TO ANTICIPATE

In addition to conceptualizing the writing process for a proposal, researchers need to anticipate the ethical issues that may arise during their studies. As mentioned earlier, writing about these issues is required in making an argument for a study as well as being an important topic in the format for proposals.

In the literature, ethical issues arise in discussions about codes of professional conduct for researchers and in commentaries about ethical dilemmas and their potential solutions (Punch, 1998). Many national associations have published standards or codes of ethics on their Web sites for professionals in their fields. For example, see

- The American Psychological Association's *Ethical Principles of Psychologists and Code of Conduct,* written in 1992, available at www.apa.org/ethics/code.html

- The American Sociological Association Code of Ethics, adopted in 1997 and available at www.asanet.org/members/ecoderev.html

- The American Anthropological Association's Code of Ethics, approved in June 1998, available at www.aaanet.org/committees/ethics/ethcode.htm

- The American Educational Research Association Ethical Standards, updated in November 2001, available at www.aera.net/about/policy/_vti_cnf/ethics.htm

- The American Nurses Association Code of Ethics for Nurses–Provisions, approved in June 2001, and available at www.ana.org/ethic/chcode.htm

In addition to these codes of ethical practice, writers detail ethical dilemmas for investigators and inquirers (e.g., see Berg, 2001; Punch, 1998; and Sieber, 1998). These issues apply to qualitative, quantitative, and mixed methods research. Moreover, proposal writers need to anticipate them and specify them in their research plans. In the chapters to follow, in Part II, I refer to ethical issues in many stages of the process of research. By foreshadowing them at this point, I hope to encourage the proposal writer to actively design them into sections of a proposal. Although this discussion will not comprehensively cover all ethical issues, it addresses major ones. These issues arise primarily in specifying the research problem (Chapter 4), identifying a purpose statement and research questions (Chapters 5 and 6), and collecting, analyzing, and writing up the results of data (Chapters 9, 10, and 11).

Ethical Issues in the Research Problem Statement

In writing an introduction to a study, the researcher identifies a significant problem or issue to study and presents a rationale for its importance. During the identification of the research problem, it is important to identify a problem that will benefit individuals being studied. A core idea of action/participatory research is that the inquirer will not further marginalize or disempower the study participants. To guard against this, proposal developers can conduct a pilot project to establish trust and respect with the participants so that inquirers can detect any marginalization before the proposal is developed and the study begun.

Ethical Issues in the Purpose Statement and Research Questions

In developing the purpose statement or the central intent and questions for a study, proposal developers need to convey the purpose of the study that will be described to the participants. Deception occurs when participants understand one purpose for a study but the researcher has a different purpose in mind. It is also important for researchers to specify the sponsorship of their study. For example, in designing cover letters for survey research, sponsorship will be an important element in establishing trust and credibility for a mailed survey instrument.

Ethical Issues in Data Collection

As researchers anticipate data collection, they need to respect the participants and the sites for research. Many ethical issues arise during this stage of the research.

● Do not put participants at risk, and respect vulnerable populations. Researchers need to have their research plans reviewed by the Institutional Review Board (IRB) on their college and university campuses. IRB committees exist on campuses because of federal regulations that provide protection against human rights violations. For a researcher, the IRB process requires assessing the potential for risk, such as physical, psychological, social, economic, or legal harm (Sieber, 1998) to participants in a study. Also, the researcher needs to consider the special needs of vulnerable populations, such as minors under the age of 19, mentally incompetent participants, victims, persons with neurological impairments, pregnant women or fetuses, prisoners, and individuals with AIDS. Investigators file research proposals containing the procedures and information about the participants with the IRB campus committee so that the boards can review the extent to which the research being proposed subjects individuals to risk. In addition to this proposal, the researcher develops an *informed consent form* for participants to sign before they engage in the research. This form acknowledges that participants' rights have been protected during data collection. Elements of this consent form include the following (Creswell, 2002):

  – The right to participate voluntarily and the right to withdraw at any time, so that the individual is not being coerced into participation

  – The purpose of the study, so that individuals understand the nature of the research and its likely impact on them

  – The procedures of the study, so that individuals can reasonably expect what to anticipate in the research

- The right to ask questions, obtain a copy of the results, and have their privacy respected

- The benefits of the study that will accrue to the individual

- Signatures of both the participant and the researcher agreeing to these provisions

● Other procedures during data collection involve gaining the permission of individuals in authority (e.g., gatekeepers) to provide access to study participants at research sites. This often involves writing a letter that identifies the extent of time, the potential impact, and the outcomes for the research.

● Researchers need to respect research sites so that the sites are left undisturbed after a research study. This requires that inquirers, especially in qualitative studies involving prolonged observation or interviewing at a site, be cognizant of their impact and minimize their disruption of the physical setting. For example, they might time visits so that they intrude little on the flow of activities of participants.

● In experimental studies, investigators need to collect data so that all participants, and not only an experimental group, benefit from the treatments. This issue may require providing *some* treatment to all groups or staging the treatment so that ultimately all groups receive the beneficial treatment.

● Means need to be considered for reciprocating between the researcher and the participants. In some research situations, power can easily be abused and participants can be coerced into a project. Involving individuals collaboratively in the design and research questions prior to data collection, as well as actively seeking their support during all phases of the research, can help reduce these issues.

● Researchers also need to anticipate the possibility of harmful information being disclosed during the data collection process. For example, a student may discuss parental abuse or prisoners may talk about an escape. In these situations, the ethical code for researchers is to protect the privacy of the participants and to convey this protection to all individuals involved in a study.

Ethical Issues in the Data
Analysis and Interpretation

When the researcher analyzes and interprets both quantitative and qualitative data, issues emerge that call for good ethical decisions. In anticipating a research study, consider the following:

- How the study will protect the anonymity of individuals, roles, and incidents in the project. For example, in survey research, investigators disassociate names from responses during the coding and recording process. In qualitative research, inquirers use aliases or pseudonyms for individuals and places to protect identities.

- Data, once analyzed, need to be kept for a reasonable period of time (e.g., Sieber, 1998, recommends 5-10 years). Investigators should then discard data so that it does not fall into the hands of other researchers who might appropriate it for other purposes.

- Who owns the data once it is collected and analyzed also can be an issue that splits research teams and divides individuals against each other. A proposal might mention this issue of ownership and discuss how it will be resolved, such as through the development of a clear understanding between the researcher, the participants, and possibly the faculty advisors. Berg (2001) recommends the use of "personal agreements" to designate ownership of research data. An extension of this idea is to guard against sharing the data with individuals not involved in the project.

- In the interpretation of data, researchers need to provide an accurate account of the information. This accuracy may require "debriefing" between the researcher and participants in quantitative research (Berg, 2001). It may include, in qualitative research, using one or more of the strategies (see validation strategies in Chapter 10) to check the accuracy of the data with participants or across different data sources.

Ethics in Writing and
Disseminating the Research

The ethical issues do not stop with data collection and analysis; they also extend into the actual writing and dissemination of the final research report. For example:

- Discuss how the research will not use language or words that are biased against persons because of gender, sexual orientation, racial or ethnic group, disability, or age. The *Publication Manual of the American Psychological Association* (5th ed.) (American Psychological Association, 2001) suggests three guidelines. First, present unbiased language at an appropriate level of specificity (e.g., rather than say, "the client's behavior was typically male," state, "the client's behavior was _____ [specify]"). Second, use language that is sensitive to labels (e.g., rather than "400 Hispanics," indicate "400 Mexicans, Spaniards, and Puerto Ricans"). Third, acknowledge participants in a study (e.g., rather than "subject," use the word "participant," and rather than "woman doctor" use "doctor" or "physician").

- Other ethical issues in writing the research will involve the potential of suppressing, falsifying, or inventing findings to meet a researcher's or an audience's needs. These fraudulent practices are not accepted in professional research communities, and they constitute scientific misconduct (Neuman, 2000). A proposal might contain a proactive stance by the researcher to not engage in these practices.

- In planning a study, it is important to anticipate the repercussions of conducting the research on certain audiences and not to misuse the results to the advantage of one group or another.

- Finally, it is important to release the details of the research with the study design so that readers can determine for themselves the credibility of the study (Neuman, 2000). The emphasis on detailed procedures for quantitative, qualitative, and mixed methods research will be emphasized in the chapters to follow.

▓ SUMMARY

It is helpful to consider how to write a research proposal before actually engaging in the process. Consider the nine arguments advanced by Maxwell (1996) as the key elements to include and then use one of the four topical outlines provided to craft a thorough qualitative, quantitative, or mixed methods proposal.

During the writing process, begin putting words down on paper to think through ideas, establish the habit of writing on a regular basis, and use strategies such as applying consistent terms, different levels of narrative thoughts, and coherence to strengthen writing. Writing in the active voice, using strong verbs, and revising and editing will help as well.

Before writing the proposal, it is useful to consider the ethical issues that can be anticipated and described in the proposal. These issues relate to all phases of the research process. With consideration for participants, research sites, and potential readers, studies can be designed that contain ethical practices.

Writing Exercises

1. Develop a topical outline for a quantitative, qualitative, or mixed methods proposal. Include the major topics in the examples included in this chapter.

2. Locate a journal article that reports qualitative, quantitative, or mixed methods research. Examine the introduction to the article, and, using the "hook-and-eye" method illustrated in this chapter, identify the deficiencies in the flow of ideas from sentence to sentence and from paragraph to paragraph.

3. Consider one of the following ethical dilemmas that may face a researcher. Describe ways you might anticipate the problem and actively address it in your research proposal.

   a. A prisoner you are interviewing tells you about a potential breakout at the prison that night. What do you do?

   b. A researcher on your team copies sentences from another study and incorporates them into the final written report for your project. What do you do?

   c. A student collects data for her project from several individuals she has interviewed in families in your city. After the fourth interview, she tells you that she has not received approval for the project from the Institutional Review Board. What do you do?

ADDITIONAL READINGS

Maxwell, J. (1996). *Qualitative research design: An interactive approach.* **Thousand Oaks, CA: Sage.**

Joe Maxwell provides a good overview of the proposal development process for qualitative research that, in many ways, is applicable to quantitative and mixed methods research as well. He states that a proposal is an argument to conduct a study and presents an example that describes nine necessary steps. Moreover, he includes a complete qualitative proposal and analyzes it as an illustration of a good model to follow.

Sieber, J. E. (1998). Planning ethically responsible research. In L. Bickman & D. J. Rog (Eds.), *Handbook of applied social research methods* **(pp. 127-156). Thousand Oaks, CA: Sage.**

Joan Sieber discusses the importance of ethical planning as integral to the process of research design. In this chapter, she provides a comprehensive review of many topics related to ethical issues, such as Institutional Review Boards, informed consent, privacy, confidentiality, and anonymity, as well as elements of research risk and vulnerable populations. Her coverage is extensive, and her recommendations for strategies are numerous.

Wolcott, H. F. (2001). *Writing up qualitative research* **(2nd ed.). Thousand Oaks, CA: Sage.**

Harry Wolcott, an educational ethnographer, has compiled an excellent resource guide addressing numerous aspects of the writing process in qualitative research. It surveys techniques useful in getting started in writing; developing details; linking with the literature, theory, and method; tightening up with revising and editing; and finishing the process by attending to such aspects as the title and appendices. For all aspiring writers, this is an essential book, regardless of whether a study is qualitative, quantitative, or mixed methods.

PART II

Designing Research

This section relates the three approaches—quantitative, qualitative, and mixed methods—to the steps in the process of research. Each chapter addresses a separate step in this process.

CHAPTER FOUR

The Introduction

After having completed a framework and a preliminary literature review, and having given consideration to writing and ethics, a proposal developer turns to the actual design of a study. A process begins of organizing ideas, starting with designing an introduction to a proposal. This chapter discusses the composition and writing of a scholarly introduction to a qualitative, quantitative, or mixed methods proposal. It examines the differences in writing an introduction to these three different types of proposals. Then, to provide a working model of a good introduction, a complete introduction from a published research study is presented. After this, the model is analyzed, section by section, using a framework for writing a good introduction. This framework is based on five key components found in all introductions, regardless of approach to research. This framework consists of establishing the problem leading to the study, reviewing the literature about the problem, identifying deficiencies in the literature about the problem, targeting an audience and noting the significance of the problem for this audience, and identifying the purpose of the proposed study. Because this approach relies on stating the deficiencies of past literature, it will be called a social sciences *deficiencies* model for an introduction.

THE IMPORTANCE OF INTRODUCTIONS

An introduction is the first passage in a journal article, dissertation, or scholarly research study. It sets the stage for the entire study. As Wilkinson (1991) mentions:

> The introduction is the part of the paper that provides readers with the background information for the research reported in the paper. Its purpose is to establish a framework for the research, so that readers can understand how it is related to other research. (p. 96)

Setting the stage for a study, the introduction establishes the issue or concern leading to the research by conveying information about a research problem. Because it is the initial passage in a study or proposal, special care must be given to writing it. Unfortunately, too many authors of research studies do not clearly identify the research problem, leaving the reader to decide for himself or herself the importance of the issue that motivates a study. Further, the research problem is often confused with the research questions—those questions that the investigator would like answered in order to understand or explain the problem.

A research problem can originate from many potential sources. It might spring from an experience researchers have had in their personal lives or workplaces. It may come from an extensive debate that has appeared in the literature for several years. It might develop from policy debates in government or among top executives. The sources of research problems are often multiple.

To this complexity is added the need for introductions to carry the weight of encouraging the reader to read further and to begin to see significance in the study. This facet alone makes introductions difficult to write. The introduction needs to create reader interest in the topic, establish the problem that leads to the study, place the study within the larger context of the scholarly literature, and reach out to a specific audience. All of this is achieved in a concise section of a few pages. Because of the messages they must convey and the limited space allowed, introductions are challenging to write and understand.

Fortunately, there is a template or structure for writing a good, scholarly social science introduction. Before introducing this model, it is necessary to distinguish subtle differences between introductions for qualitative, quantitative, and mixed methods studies.

QUALITATIVE, QUANTITATIVE, AND MIXED METHODS INTRODUCTIONS

A general review of all introductions shows that they follow a similar pattern: The authors announce a problem, and they justify why it needs to be studied. Because problems differ for qualitative, quantitative, and mixed methods studies (as discussed in Chapter 1), the type of problem presented in an introduction will vary depending on the approach. In a *qualitative* project, the author will describe a research problem that can best be understood by exploring a concept or phenomenon. I suggested that qualitative research is exploratory and researchers use it to explore a topic when the variables and theory base are unknown. For example, Morse (1991) says this:

> Characteristics of a qualitative research problem are: (a) the concept is "immature" due to a conspicuous lack of theory and previous research; (b) a notion that the available theory may be inaccurate, inappropriate, incorrect, or biased; (c) a need exists to explore and describe the phenomena and to develop theory; or (d) the nature of the phenomenon may not be suited to quantitative measures. (p. 120)

For example, the problem of urban sprawl (a problem) needs to be explored because it has not been examined in certain areas of a state. Alternatively, kids in elementary classrooms have anxiety that interferes with learning (a problem), and the best way to explore this problem is to go to schools and visit directly with teachers and students. Some qualitative researchers have a theoretical lens through which the problem will be examined (e.g., the inequality of pay among women and men or the racial attitudes involved in profiling drivers on the highways). Thomas (1993) suggests that "critical researchers begin from the premise that all cultural life is in constant tension between control and resistance" (p. 9). This theoretical orientation shapes the structure of an introduction. In the introduction to a study, Beisel (1990), for example, proposed to examine how the theory of class politics explained the lack of success of an anti-vice campaign in one of three American cities. Thus, within some qualitative studies, the approach in the introduction may be less inductive while still relying on the perspective of participants like most qualitative studies. In addition, qualitative introductions may begin with a personal statement of experiences from the author, such as those found in phenomenological studies (Moustakas, 1994). They also may be written from a personal, first-person subjective point of view in which the researcher positions herself or himself in the narrative.

Less variation is seen in *quantitative* introductions. In a quantitative project, the problem is best addressed by understanding what factors or variables influence an outcome. For example, in response to worker cutbacks (a problem for all employees), an investigator may seek to discover what factors influence businesses to downsize. Another researcher may need to understand the high divorce rate among married couples (a problem) and examine whether financial issues contribute to divorce. In both of these situations, the research problem is one in which understanding the factors that explain or relate to an outcome helps the investigator best understand and explain the problem. In addition, in quantitative introductions, researchers sometimes advance a theory to test, and they will incorporate substantial reviews of the literature to identify research questions that need to be answered. The writing of a quantitative introduction may be from the impersonal point of view and the past tense to provide "objectivity" to the language of research.

A mixed methods study can employ either the qualitative or the quantitative approach (or some combination) to writing an introduction. For example, a mixed methods research problem may be one in which a need exists to both understand the relationship among variables in a situation and explore the topic in further depth. A mixed methods project may initially seek to explain the relationship between smoking behavior and depression among adolescents, then explore the detailed views of adolescents and display different patterns of smoking and depression. With the first phase of this project as quantitative, the introduction may include a discussion about a theory that predicts this relationship.

A MODEL FOR AN INTRODUCTION

These differences among the various approaches are small, and they relate largely to the different types of problems associated with qualitative, quantitative, and mixed methods studies. It should be helpful to illustrate an approach to designing and writing an introduction to a research study.

The *deficiencies model* is a general template for writing a solid introduction to a proposal or research study. It is a popular approach used in the social sciences, and once its structure is elucidated, the reader will find it apparent in many scholarly studies. It consists of five parts:

1. The research problem,

2. Studies that have addressed the problem,

3. Deficiencies in the studies,

4. The importance of the study for an audience, and

5. The purpose statement.

An Illustration

Before a review of each component, an illustration will be presented. The example used here is from a quantitative study published by Terenzini, Cabrera, Colbeck, Bjorklund, and Parente (2001) in *The Journal of Higher Education* and titled "Racial and Ethnic Diversity in the Classroom" (reprinted with permission). Following each major section in the structure of the introduction, I will briefly highlight the component of the introduction being addressed by the authors.

Since passage of the Civil Rights Act of 1964 and the Higher Education Act of 1965, America's colleges and universities have struggled to increase the racial and ethnic diversity of their students and faculty members, and "affirmative action" has become the policy-of-choice to achieve that heterogeneity. **[Authors state the narrative hook.]** These policies, however, are now at the center of an intense national debate. The current legal foundation for affirmative action policies rests on the 1978 *Regents of the University of California v. Bakke* case, in which Justice William Powell argued that race could be considered among the factors on which admissions decisions were based. More recently, however, the U.S. Court of Appeals for the Fifth Circuit, in the 1996 *Hopwood v. State of Texas* case, found Powell's argument wanting. Court decisions turning affirmative action policies aside have been accompanied by state referenda, legislation, and related actions banning or sharply reducing race-sensitive admissions or hiring in California, Florida, Louisiana, Maine, Massachusetts, Michigan, Mississippi, New Hampshire, Rhode Island, and Puerto Rico (Healy, 1998a, 1998b, 1999).

In response, educators and others have advanced educational arguments supporting affirmative action, claiming that a diverse study body is more educationally effective than a more homogeneous one. Harvard University President Neil Rudenstine claims that the "fundamental rationale for student diversity in higher education [is] its educational value" (Rudenstine, 1999, p. 1). Lee Bollinger, Rudenstine's counterpart at the University of Michigan, has asserted, "A classroom that does not have a significant representation from members of different races produces an impoverished discussion" (Schmidt, 1998, p. A32). These two presidents are not alone in their beliefs. A statement published by the Association of American Universities and endorsed by the presidents of 62 research universities stated: "We speak first and foremost as educators. We believe that our students benefit significantly from education that takes place within a diverse setting" ("On the Importance of Diversity in University Admissions," *The New York Times,* April 24, 1997, p. A27). **[Authors identify the research problem.]**

Studies of the impact of diversity on student educational outcomes tend to approach the ways students encounter "diversity" in any of three ways. A small group of studies treat students' contacts with "diversity" largely as a function of the numerical or proportional racial/ethnic or gender mix of students on a campus (e.g., Chang, 1996, 1999a; Kanter, 1977; Sax, 1996). . . . A second considerably larger set of studies take some modicum of structural diversity as a given and operationalize students' encounters with diversity using the frequency or nature of their reported interactions with peers who are racially/ethnically different from themselves. . . . A third set of studies examines institutionally structured and purposeful programmatic efforts to help students engage racial/ethnic and/or gender "diversity" in the form of both ideas and people.

These various approaches have been used to examine the effects of diversity on a broad array of student educational outcomes. The evidence is almost uniformly consistent in indicating that students in a racial/ethnically or gender-diverse community, or engaged in a diversity-related activity, reap a wide array of positive educational benefits. . . . **[Authors mention studies that have addressed the problem.]**

Only a relative handful of studies (e.g., Chang, 1996, 1999a; Sax, 1996) have specifically examined whether *the racial/ethnic or gender composition* of the students on a campus, in an academic major, or in a classroom (i.e., structural diversity) has the educational benefits claimed. . . . Whether the degree of racial diversity of a campus or classroom has a *direct* effect on learning outcomes, however, remains an open question. **[Deficiencies in the studies are noted.]**

The scarcity of information on the educational benefits of the structural diversity on a campus or in its classrooms is regrettable because it is the sort of evidence the courts appear to be requiring if they are to support race-sensitive admissions policies. **[Importance of the study for an audience mentioned.]**

This study attempted to contribute to the knowledge base by exploring the influence of structural diversity in the classroom on students' development of academic and intellectual skills. . . . This study examines both the direct effect of classroom diversity on academic/intellectual outcomes and whether any effects of classroom diversity may be moderated by the extent to which active and collaborative instructional approaches are used in the course. **[Purpose of the study identified.]** (pp. 510-512, reprinted by permission of *The Journal of Higher Education*)

The Research Problem in the Study

When researchers begin their studies, they start with one or more paragraphs that convey the specific research problems or issues. They also present, in the first sentence, information to create reader interest. In the sentences that follow the first sentence, authors identify a distinct research problem that needs to be addressed.

In the Terenzini et al. (2001) article, the first sentence accomplishes both objectives: piquing interest in the study and conveying a distinct research problem or issue. What effect did this sentence have? Would it entice a reader to read on? Was it pitched at a level so that a wide audience could understand it? These questions are important for opening sentences called *narrative hooks*, a term drawn from English composition, to draw or "hook" the reader into the study. To learn how to write good narrative hooks, study opening sentences in leading journals in different fields of study. Often, journalists provide good examples in their lead sentences of newspaper and magazine articles. Here are a few examples of lead sentences from social science journals.

- "The transsexual and ethnomethodological celebrity Agnes changed her identity nearly three years before undergoing sex reassignment surgery." (Cahill, 1989, p. 281)

- "Who controls the process of chief executive succession?" (Boeker, 1992, p. 400)

- "There is a large body of literature that studies the cartographic line (a recent summary article is Buttenfield 1985), and generalization of cartographic lines (McMaster 1987)." (Carstensen, 1989, p. 181)

All three of these examples present information easily understood by many readers. The first two—introductions in qualitative studies—demonstrate how reader interest can be created by use of reference to the single participant and by posing a question. The third example, a quantitative-experimental study, shows how one can begin with a literature perspective. All three examples demonstrate well how the lead sentence can be written so that the reader is not taken into a detailed morass of thought, but lowered gently into the topic.

I use the metaphor of the writer lowering a barrel into a well. The *beginning* writer plunges the barrel (the reader) into the depths of the well (the article). The reader sees only unfamiliar material. The *experienced* writer lowers the barrel (the reader, again) slowly, allowing the reader to acclimate to the study. This lowering of the barrel begins with *a narrative hook* of sufficient generality that the reader understands (and can relate to) the topic.

Beyond this first sentence, it is important to clearly identify for the reader the issue or problem that leads to a need for the study. Terenzini et al. (2001) discuss a distinct problem: the struggle to increase the racial and ethnic diversity on American college and university campuses. They note that policies to increase diversity are at "the center of an intense national debate" (p. 509).

In applied social science research, problems arise from issues, difficulties, and current practices. For example, schools may not have implemented multicultural guidelines. the needs of faculty in colleges are such that they need to engage in professional development activities in their departments. minority students need better access to universities. or a community needs to better understand the contributions of its early female pioneers. These are all significant research problems that merit further study and establish a practical issue or concern that needs to be addressed. A *research problem* is the issue that exists in the literature, in theory, or in practice that leads to a need for the study. The research problem in a study begins to become clear when the researcher asks "What is the need for this study?" or "What problem influenced the need to undertake this study?"

When designing the opening paragraphs of a proposal, keep in mind these guidelines:

- Write an opening sentence that will stimulate reader interest as well as convey an issue to which a broad audience can relate.

- As a general rule, refrain from using quotations, especially long ones, in the lead sentence. Quotations raise many possibilities for interpretation and thus create unclear beginnings. However, as is evident in some qualitative studies, quotations can create reader interest.

- Stay away from idiomatic expressions or trite phrases (e.g., "The lecture method remains a 'sacred cow' among most college and university instructors.").

- Consider numeric information for impact (e.g., "Every year an estimated 5 million Americans experience the death of an immediate family member.").

- Clearly identify the research problem (i.e., dilemma, issue) leading to the study. Researchers might ask themselves, "Is there a specific sentence (or sentences) in which I convey the research problem?"

- Indicate why the problem is important by citing references that justify the need to study the problem.

- Make sure that the research problem is framed in a manner consistent with the approach to research in the study (e.g., exploratory in qualitative, examining relationships or predictors in quantitative, and either approach in mixed methods inquiry).

Review Studies Addressing the Problem

After establishing the research problem in the opening paragraphs, Terenzini et al. (2001) next justify the importance of the research problem by *reviewing studies* that have examined the problem. They discussed three "sets of studies" (p. 510) almost as if they had a literature map (as discussed in Chapter 2) in front of them and were simply presenting the major categories of studies about the impact of student diversity on educational outcomes. It is useful to note in their example that they did not review single, isolated studies; instead, they introduced larger groups of studies so that at this point in the article they could present the broader picture of the literature. It is in the "literature review" section, which typically follows an introduction in a quantitative study (sometimes in a qualitative study and in a mixed methods study), that one finds detailed reviews of studies.

The purpose of reviewing studies that have addressed the problem is to justify the importance of the study and to create distinctions between past studies and a proposed study. This component might be called "setting the research problem within the ongoing dialogue in the literature." Researchers do not want to conduct a study that replicates exactly what someone else has studied. New studies need to add to the literature or to extend or retest what others have examined. Marshall and Rossman (1999) talk about setting a study "within a tradition of inquiry and a context of related studies" (p. 43). The ability to frame the study in this way separates novices from more experienced researchers. The veteran understands what has been written about a topic or certain problem in the field. This knowledge comes from years of experience following the development of problems and their accompanying literature.

The question often develops as to what type of literature to review. My best advice would be to review "research" studies in which authors advance research questions and report data to answer them. These studies might be quantitative, qualitative, or mixed methods studies. The important point is that the literature provides studies about the research problem being addressed in the proposal. Another question is "What do I do now? No research has been conducted on my topic." Of course, in some narrowly construed studies or in new, exploratory projects no literature exists to document the research problem. To counter this statement, I often suggest that an investigator think about the literature as an inverted triangle. At the apex of the inverted triangle lies the scholarly study being proposed. This study is narrow and focused (and studies may not exist on it). If one broadens the review of the literature out to the base of the triangle, literature can be found, although it may be only indirectly related to the study at hand. This broad-based literature is reviewed to cast the problem within the literature.

To review the literature related to the research problem for an introduction to a proposal, consider these ideas:

- Refer to the literature by summarizing groups of studies (unlike the focus on single studies in the integrated review in Chapter 2), not individual studies. The intent should be to establish broad areas of research at this juncture in the study.

- To de-emphasize single studies, place the in-text references at the end of a paragraph or at the end of a summary point about several studies.

- Review research studies that used a quantitative, qualitative, or mixed methods approach.

- Find recent literature to summarize (such as that published in the last 10 years) unless an older study exists that has been widely cited by others.

Deficiencies in Past Literature

After advancing the problem and reviewing the literature about the problem, the researcher then identifies *deficiencies* found in this literature. Hence, I use a *deficiencies model* for this template for writing an introduction to a study. The nature of these deficiencies varies from study to study. The literature may be deficient because the authors have not studied specific variables. They may not have explored the topic with a particular group, sample, or population. The literature may need to be replicated or repeated to see if the same findings hold given new samples of people or new sites for study. In any given study, authors may mention one or more of these deficiencies. If other authors have also mentioned these deficiencies—typically in the "suggestions for future research" sections at the end of research studies—then this section can include references to these studies as further justification for the proposed study.

Beyond mentioning the deficiencies, proposal writers need to tell how their planned study will remedy or address these deficiencies. For example, because past studies have overlooked an important variable, a study will include it and analyze its effect. Because past studies have overlooked the examination of Native Americans as a cultural group, a study will include them as the participants in the project.

In the two examples below, the authors point out the gaps or short-comings of the literature. Notice their use of key phrases to indicate the shortcoming: "what remains to be explored," "little empirical research," and "very few studies."

Example 4.1   *Deficiencies in the Literature—Needed Explorations*

For this reason, the meaning of war and peace has been explored extensively by social scientists (Cooper, 1965; Alvik, 1968; Rosell, 1968; Svancarova & Svancarova, 1967-68; Haavedsrud, 1970). What remains to be explored, however, is how veterans of past wars react to vivid scenes of a new war. (Ziller, 1990, pp. 85-86)

Example 4.2   *Deficiencies in the Literature—Few Studies*

Despite an increased interest in micropolitics, it is surprising that so little empirical research has actually been conducted on the topic, especially from the perspectives of subordinates. Political research in educational settings is especially scarce: Very few studies have focused on how teachers use power to interact strategically with school principals and what this means descriptively and conceptually (Ball, 1987; Hoyle, 1986; Pratt, 1984). (Blase, 1989, p. 381)

In summary, when identifying deficiencies in the past literature, proposal developers might do the following:

- Cite several deficiencies to make the case even stronger for a study.

- Identify specifically the deficiencies of other studies (e.g., methodological flaws, variables overlooked).

- Write about areas overlooked by past studies, including topics, special statistical treatments, significant implications, and so forth.

- Discuss how a proposed study will remedy these deficiencies and provide a unique contribution to the scholarly literature.

These deficiencies might be written using a series of short paragraphs that identify three or four shortcomings of the past research or focus on one major shortcoming, as illustrated in the Terenzini et al. (2001) introduction.

Importance of a Study for an Audience

All good writers have the audience in mind. Terenzini et al. (2001) end their introduction by mentioning how courts could use the information of the study to require colleges and universities to support "race-sensitive admissions policies" (p. 512). In addition, the authors might have mentioned the importance of this study for admissions offices and for students seeking admissions as well as the committees that review applications for admission.

The point is that authors need to identify the audiences that will likely profit from a study of the research problem. The more audiences that can be mentioned, the greater the importance of the study and the more it will be seen by readers to have wide application. These audiences will differ from one project to another, and they might include diverse audiences of policy makers, organizations, other researchers, and individuals in work organizations. Reaching out to an audience in an introduction might be accomplished by briefly mentioning the audience (such as the courts in the Terenzini et al. [2001] study) or detailing information for several audiences.

Finally, good introductions to research studies end with a statement of the purpose or intent of the study. Terenzini et al. (2001) ended their introduction this way, and they conveyed that they planned to examine the influence of structural diversity on student skills in the classroom. The purpose statement, a major guiding element of any research study, is the focus of attention in the next chapter.

▓ SUMMARY

This chapter provides advice about composing and writing an introduction to a scholarly study. The first element is to consider how the introduction incorporates the research problems associated with quantitative, qualitative, or mixed methods research. Then, a five-part introduction is suggested as a model or template to use. This model, called the deficiencies model, is based on first identifying the research problem (and including a narrative hook). Then it includes reviewing the literature that has addressed the problem, indicating one or more deficiencies in the past literature and suggesting how a study will remedy these deficiencies. It typically ends by identifying one or more audiences that will profit from proposed study and by advancing the purpose or major intent of the project. Guidelines are provided for writing each component in this introduction to a study.

Writing Exercises

1. Draft several examples of narrative hooks for the introduction to a study and share these with colleagues to determine if the hooks present an issue to which readers can relate.

2. Write the introduction to a proposed study. Include paragraphs setting forth the problem in the study, the related literature about this problem, the deficiencies in the literature, and the audience who would find the study of interest.

3. Locate several research studies published in scholarly journals in a field of study. Review the introductions to the studies and locate the sentence or sentences in which the authors state the research problem or issue in their studies.

WRITING EXERCISES

ADDITIONAL READINGS

Bem, D. J. (1987). Writing the empirical journal article. In M. P. Zanna & J. M. Darley (Eds.), *The compleat academic: A practical guide for the beginning social scientist* (pp. 171-201). New York: Random House.

Daryl Bem emphasizes the importance of the opening statement in published research. He provides a list of rules of thumb for opening statements, stressing the need for clear, readable prose and for a structure that leads the reader step by step to the problem statement. Examples are provided of both satisfactory and unsatisfactory opening statements. Bem calls for opening statements that are accessible to the nonspecialist, yet not boring to the technically sophisticated reader.

Maxwell, J. A. (1996). *Qualitative research design: An interactive approach.* Thousand Oaks, CA: Sage.

Joe Maxwell reflects on the purpose of a proposal for a qualitative dissertation. One of the fundamental aspects of a proposal is to justify the project—to help readers understand not only what you plan to do but also why. He mentions the importance of identifying the issues you plan to address and indicating why they are important issues to study. In an example of a dissertation proposal, he shares the major issues addressed by the author to create an effective argument for the study.

Wilkinson, A. M. (1991). *The scientist's handbook for writing papers and dissertations.* Englewood Cliffs, NJ: Prentice Hall.

Antoinette Wilkinson identifies the three parts of an introduction: the derivation and statement of the problem and a discussion of its nature, the discussion of the background of the problem, and the statement of the research question. Her book offers numerous examples of these three parts together with a discussion of how to write and structure the introduction. Emphasis is placed on ensuring that the introduction leads logically and inevitably to a statement of the research question.

The Purpose Statement

Whereas introductions focus on the problem leading to the study, the purpose statement establishes the direction for the research. In fact, the purpose statement is the most important statement in an entire research study. It orients the reader to the central intent of the study, and from it, all other aspects of the research follow. In journal articles, researchers write the purpose statement into introductions; in dissertations and dissertation proposals, it often stands as a separate section. The purpose statement needs to be written as clearly and concisely as possible.

This entire chapter focuses on the purpose statement because of its significance in a study. I address the reasons for developing purpose statements, advance key principles to use in designing them, and provide examples that illustrate good models.

SIGNIFICANCE AND MEANING OF A PURPOSE STATEMENT

According to Locke, Spirduso, and Silverman (2000), the purpose statement indicates "why you want to do the study and what you intend to accomplish" (p. 9). Unfortunately, method- and proposal-writing texts give little attention to the purpose statement, and writers on method often incorporate the purpose statement into discussions about other topics, such as specifying research questions or hypotheses. Wilkinson (1991), for example, refers to it within the context of the research question and objective. Other authors frame it as an aspect of the research problem (Castetter & Heisler, 1977). Closely examining their discussions indicates that they both are referring to the purpose statement as the central, controlling idea in a study.

For this discussion, I will call this passage the "purpose statement" because it conveys the overall intent of a proposed study. In proposals, researchers need to distinguish clearly between the purpose, the problem in the study, and the research questions. The purpose sets forth the intent of the study and not the problem or issue leading to a need for the study (see Chapter 4). The purpose is also not the research questions— those questions that the data collection will attempt to answer—to be discussed in Chapter 6. Instead, the purpose sets the objectives, the intent, and the major idea of a proposal or a study. This idea builds on a need (the problem) and is refined into specific questions (the research questions).

Given the importance of the purpose statement, it is helpful to set it apart from other aspects of the proposal or study and to frame it as a single sentence or paragraph that readers can identify easily. Although qualitative, quantitative, and mixed methods purpose statements share similar topics, each will be identified below and illustrated with "scripts" for constructing a thorough but manageable purpose statement for a proposal or study.

A QUALITATIVE PURPOSE STATEMENT

A good qualitative purpose statement contains important elements of qualitative research, uses research words drawn from the language of that inquiry (Schwandt, 2001), and employs the procedures of an emerging design based on experiences of individuals in a natural setting. Thus, one might consider several basic design features for writing this statement:

● Use words such as "purpose," "intent," or "objective" to signal attention to this statement as the central controlling idea in a study. Set the statement off as a separate sentence or paragraph and use the language of research by employing words such as "The purpose (or intent or objective) of this study is (was) (will be). . . ." Researchers often use the present or past verb tense in journal articles and dissertations, and the future tense in proposals because researchers are presenting a plan for a study.

● Focus on a single phenomenon (or concept or idea). Narrow the study to one idea to be explored or understood. This focus means that a purpose does not convey "relating" two or more variables or "comparing" two or more groups, as is typically found in quantitative research. Instead, advance a single phenomenon to study, recognizing that the study may evolve into an exploration of relationships or comparisons among ideas. None of these related explorations can be anticipated at the beginning of a qualitative study. For example, a project might begin by exploring "chairperson roles" in enhancing faculty development (Creswell & Brown, 1992). Other qualitative studies might start by exploring "teacher identity" and the marginalization of this identity for a teacher in her school (Huber & Whelan, 1999) or the meaning of "baseball culture" in a study of the work and talk of stadium employees (Trujillo, 1992). These examples all illustrate the focus on a single idea.

● Use action verbs to convey how learning will take place. Action verbs and phrases, such as "describe, "understand," "develop," "examine the meaning of," or "discover," keep the inquiry open and convey an emerging design.

● An emerging design is also enhanced by nondirectional language rather than predetermined outcomes. Use neutral words and phrases, such as exploring the "experiences of individuals" rather than the "successful experiences of individuals." Other words and phrases that may be problematic include "useful," "positive," and "informing"—all words that suggest an outcome that may or may not occur. McCracken (1988) refers to the need in qualitative interviews to let the respondent describe his or her experience. Interviewers (or purpose statement writers) violate the "law of nondirection" in qualitative research (McCracken, 1988, p. 21) by using words that suggest a directional orientation.

● Provide a general working definition of the central phenomenon or idea. Consistent with the rhetoric of qualitative research, this definition is not rigid and set, but tentative and evolving throughout a study based on information from participants. Hence, a writer might use the words, "A tentative definition at this time for _____ (central phenomenon) is. . . ." It should also be noted that this definition is not to be confused with the detailed "definition of terms" section found later in some qualitative proposals. The intent here is to convey to readers at an early stage in a proposal or research study a general sense of the central phenomenon so that they can better understand information that will unfold in the study.

- Include words denoting the strategy of inquiry to be used in data collection, analysis, and the process of research, such as whether the study will use an ethnographic, grounded theory, case study, phenomenological, or narrative approach.

- Mention the participants in the study, such as whether the participants might be one or more individuals, a group of people, or an entire organization.

- Identify the site for the research, such as homes, classrooms, organizations, programs, or events. Describe this site in enough detail so that the reader will know exactly where a study will take place.

Although considerable variation exists in the inclusion of these points in purpose statements, a good dissertation or thesis proposal should mention all of them.

To assist in designing a purpose statement, I include here a "script" that should be helpful in drafting a complete statement. A "script," as used in this book, contains the major words and ideas of a statement and provides space for the researcher to insert information that relates to a project. The "script" for a qualitative purpose statement is this:

The purpose of this _____ (strategy of inquiry, such as ethnography, case study, or other type) study is (was? will be?) to _____ (understand? describe? develop? discover?) the _____ (central phenomenon being studied) for _____ (the participants, such as the individual, groups, organization) at _____ (research site). At this stage in the research, the _____ (central phenomenon being studied) will be generally defined as _____ (provide a general definition).

The following examples may not illustrate perfectly all elements of this "script," but they represent adequate models to study and emulate.

_____

Example 5.1   *A Purpose Statement in a Qualitative Phenomenology Study*

Lauterbach (1993) studied five women who had lost a baby in late pregnancy and their memories and experiences of this loss. Her purpose statement was as follows.

The phenomenological inquiry, as part of uncovering meaning, articulated "essences" of meaning in mothers' lived experiences when their wished-for babies died. Using the lens of the feminist perspective, the focus was on mothers' memories and their "living through" experience. This perspective facilitated breaking through the silence surrounding mothers' experiences; it assisted in articulating and amplifying mothers' memories and their stories of loss. Methods of inquiry included phenomenological reflection on data elicited by existential investigation of mothers' experiences, and investigation of the phenomenon in the creative arts. (Lauterbach, 1993, p. 134)

I found Lauterbach's purpose statement in the opening section of the journal article under the heading "Aim of Study." Thus, the heading calls attention to this statement. "Mothers' lived experiences" would be the central phenomenon, and the author uses the action word "portray" to discuss the "meaning" (a neutral word) of these experiences. The author further defines what experiences will be examined when she identifies "memories" and "lived through" experiences. Throughout this passage, it is clear that Lauterbach will use the strategy of phenomenology. Also, the passage conveys that the participants will be mothers, but later in the article the reader learns that the author interviewed a convenience sample of five mothers, each of whom had experienced a perinatal death of a child in her home.

Example 5.2   *A Purpose Statement in a Case Study*

Kos (1991) conducted a multiple case study of perceptions of reading-disabled middle-school students concerning factors that prevented these students from progressing in their reading development. Her purpose statement read as follows.

The purpose of this study was to explore affective, social, and educational factors that may have contributed to the development of reading disabilities in four adolescents. The study also sought explanation as to why students' reading disabilities persisted despite years of instruction. This was not an intervention study and, although some students may have improved their reading, reading improvement was not the focus of the study. (Kos, 1991, pp. 876-877)

Notice Kos's disclaimer that this study was not a quantitative study measuring of the magnitude of reading changes in the students. Instead, Kos clearly placed this study within the qualitative approach by using words such as "explore." She focused attention on the central phenomenon of "factors" and provided a tentative definition of this phenomenon by mentioning examples, such as "affective, social, and educational." She included this statement under a heading called "Purpose of the Study" to call attention to the statement, and she mentioned the participants who participated in the study. In the abstract and the methodology section, a reader finds out that the study used the inquiry strategy of case study research and that the study took place in a classroom.

Example 5.3   *A Purpose Statement in an*
Ethnographic Study

Rhoads (1997) conducted a 2-year ethnographic study exploring how the campus climate can be improved for gay and bisexual males at a large university. His purpose statement, included in the opening section, was as follows.

> The article contributes to the literature addressing the needs of gay and bisexual students by identifying several areas where progress can be made in improving the campus climate for them. This paper derives from a two-year ethnographic study of a student subculture composed of gay and bisexual males at a large research university; the focus on men reflects the fact that lesbian and bisexual women constitute a separate student subculture at the university under study. (Rhoads, 1997, p. 276)

With intent to improve the campus, this qualitative study falls into the genre of advocacy research as mentioned in Chapter 1. Also, these sentences occur at the beginning of the article to signal the reader about the purpose of the study. The "needs" of these students become the central phenomenon under study, and the author seeks to "identify" areas that can improve the climate for gays and bisexual males. The author also mentioned that the strategy of inquiry will be ethnographic and that the study will involve males (participants) at a large university (site). At this point, the author does not provide additional information about the exact nature of these "needs" or a working definition to begin the article. However, he does refer to "identity" and probes a tentative meaning for that term in the next section of the study.

Example 5.4   *A Purpose Statement in a Grounded Theory Study*

Richie et al. (1997) conducted a qualitative study to develop a theory of the career development of 18 prominent, highly achieving African American Black and White women in the United States working in different occupational fields. In the second paragraph of this study, they stated the purpose statement:

> The present article describes a qualitative study of the career development of 18 prominent, highly achieving African-American Black and White women in the United States across eight occupational fields. Our overall aim in the study was to explore critical influences on the career development of these women, particularly those related to their attainment of professional success. (Richie et al., 1997, p. 133)

In this statement, the central phenomenon is "career development," and the reader learns that the phenomenon will be defined as "critical influences" in the "professional success" of the women. In this study, "success," a directional word, serves to define the sample of individuals to be studied more than to limit the inquiry about the central phenomenon. The authors plan to "explore" this phenomenon, and the reader learns that the participants are all women, in different occupational groups. Grounded theory as a strategy of inquiry is mentioned in the abstract and later in the procedure discussion.

A QUANTITATIVE PURPOSE STATEMENT

Quantitative purpose statements differ considerably from the qualitative models in terms of the language and a focus on relating or comparing variables or constructs. A variable refers to a characteristic or attribute of an individual or an organization that can be measured or observed and that varies among the people or organization being studied (Creswell, 2002). A variable typically will "vary" in two or more categories or on a continuum of scores. Psychologists prefer to use the term *construct* (rather than *variable*), which carries the connotation of more of an abstract idea than a specifically defined term. However, social scientists typically use the term *variable*, and it will be employed in this discussion. Variables often measured in studies include gender, age, socioeconomic status (SES), and attitudes or behaviors such as racism, social control, political power, or leadership. Several texts provide detailed discussions about the types of variables one can use and their scale of measurement (e.g., Isaac & Michael, 1981; Keppel, 1991; Kerlinger, 1979; Thorndike, 1997). Variables are distinguished by two characteristics: temporal order and their measurement (or observation).

Temporal order means that one variable precedes another in time. Because of this time ordering, it is said that one variable affects or "causes" another variable, though a more accurate statement would indicate "probable causation." When dealing with studies in the natural setting and with humans, researchers cannot absolutely "prove" cause and effect (Rosenthal & Rosnow, 1991). This time ordering causes researchers in quantitative approaches to think "left to right" (Punch, 1998) and order the variables in purpose statements, research questions, and visual models into left-to-right, cause and effect, presentations. Thus,

- *Independent variables* are variables that (probably) cause, influence, or affect outcomes. They are also called treatment, manipulated, antecedent, or predictor variables.

- *Dependent variables* are variables that depend on the independent variables; they are the outcomes or results of the influence of the independent variables. Other names for dependent variables are criterion, outcome, and effect variables.

- *Intervening or mediating variables* "stand between" the independent and dependent variables, and they mediate the effects of the independent variable on the dependent variable. For example, if students do well on a research methods test (dependent variable), that result may be due to (a) their study preparation (independent variable) and/or (b) their organization of study ideas into a framework (intervening variable) that influenced their grade on the test. The mediating variable, "organization of study," stands between the independent and dependent variables.

- Two other types of variables are control variables and confounding variables. *Control variables* play an active role in quantitative studies. These variables are a special type of independent variable that are measured in a study because they potentially influence the dependent variable. Researchers use statistical procedures (e.g., analysis of covariance) to control for these variables. They may be demographic or personal variables that need to be "controlled" so that the true influence of the independent variable on the dependent can be determined. Another type of variable, a *confounding* (or *spurious) variable*, is not actually measured or observed in a study. It exists, but its influence cannot be directly detected in a study. Researchers comment on the influence of confounding variables, after the study has been completed, because these variables may have operated to explain the relationship between the independent variable and dependent variable, but they were not or could not be easily assessed.

The design of a quantitative purpose statement, therefore, begins with identifying the proposed variables for a study (independent, intervening, dependent, control), drawing a visual model to clearly identify this sequence, and locating and specifying how the variables will be measured or observed. Finally, the intent of using the variables quantitatively will be either to relate variables (as one typically finds in a survey) or to compare samples or groups in terms of an outcome (as commonly found in experiments).

This knowledge helps in the design of the quantitative purpose statement. The major components of a good quantitative purpose statement include a brief paragraph that contains the following:

- Words to signal the major intent of the study, such as "purpose," "intent," or "objective." Start with "The purpose (or objective or intent) of this study is (was) (will be). . . ."

- Identification of the theory, model, or conceptual framework to test in the proposal or study. At this point one does not need to describe it in detail; in Chapter 7 I suggest a separate "Theoretical Perspective" section for this purpose. Mentioning it in the purpose statement provides emphasis on the importance of the theory and foreshadows its use in the study.

- Identification of the independent and dependent variables, as well as any mediating or control variables used in the study.

- Words that connect the independent and dependent variables to indicate that they are being related. Use "the relationship between" two or more variables or a "comparison of" two or more groups.

Most quantitative studies fall into one of these two options for connecting variables in the purpose statement. A combination of comparing and relating might also exist, for example, a two-factor experiment in which the researcher has two or more treatment groups as well as a continuous variable as an independent variable in the study. Although one typically finds studies about comparing two or more groups in experiments, it is also possible to compare groups in a survey study.

- A position or ordering of the variables from left to right in the purpose statement, beginning with the independent variable, followed by the dependent variable. Place intervening variables between the independent and dependent variables. Researchers also place the control variables between the independent and dependent variables. Alternatively, control variables might be placed immediately following the dependent variable, in a phrase such as "controlling for. . . ." In experiments, the independent variable will always be the "manipulated" variable.

- Mention the specific type of strategy of inquiry used in the study. By incorporating this information, the researcher will anticipate the methods discussion and enable a reader to associate the relationship of variables to the inquiry approach.

- Reference to the participants (or the unit of analysis) in the study and mention of the research site for the study.

- A general definition for each key variable in the study, preferably using established definitions. In quantitative research, investigators use set and accepted definitions for variables. The definitions included here are intended to provide a general definition of variables to help the reader best understand the purpose statement. They do not replace specific, operational definitions (details about how variables will be measured) found later in a "Definition of Terms" section in proposals (see Chapter 8).

Based on these points, a quantitative purpose statement "script" can include these ideas:

> The purpose of this _____ (experiment? survey?) study is (was? will be?) to test the theory of _____ that _____ (compares? relates?) the _____ (independent variable) to _____ (dependent variable),

controlling for _____ (control variables) for _____ (participants) at _____ (the research site). The independent variable(s) _____ will be generally defined as _____ (provide a general definition). The dependent variable(s) will be generally defined as _____ (provide a general definition), and the control and intervening variable(s), _____, (identify the control and intervening variables) will be statistically controlled in the study.

The examples to follow illustrate many of the elements in the "script." The first two studies are surveys; the last one is an experiment.

Example 5.5   *A Purpose Statement in a Published Survey Study*

Kalof (2000) conducted a 2-year longitudinal study of 54 college women about their attitudes and experiences with sexual coercion. These women responded to two identical mail surveys administered 2 years apart. The author combined the purpose statement, introduced in the opening section, with the research questions.

> This study is an attempt to elaborate on and clarify the link between women's sex role attitudes and experiences with sexual victimization. I used two years of data from 54 college women to answer these questions: (1) Do women's attitudes influence vulnerability to sexual coercion over a two-year period? (2) Are attitudes changed after experiences with sexual victimization? (3) Does prior victimization reduce or increase the risk of later victimization? (Kalof, 2000, p. 48)

Although Kalof does not mention a theory that she seeks to test, she identifies both her independent variable (sex role attitudes) and the dependent variable (sexual victimization). She positioned these variables from independent to dependent. She also discussed "linking" rather than "relating" the variables to establish a connection between them. This passage also identifies the participants (women) and the research site (a college setting). Later, in the method section, she mentioned that the study was a mailed survey. Although she does not define the major variables, she provides specific measures of the variables in the research questions.

Example 5.6   *A Purpose Statement in a Dissertation*
Survey Study

DeGraw (1984) completed a doctoral dissertation in the field of education on the topic of educators working in adult correctional institutions. Under a section titled "Statement of the Problem," he advanced the purpose of the study.

> The purpose of this study was to examine the relationship between personal characteristics and the job motivation of certified educators who taught in selected state adult correctional institutions in the United States. Personal characteristics were divided into background information about the respondent (i.e., institutional information, education level, prior training, etc.) and information about the respondents' thoughts of changing jobs. The examination of background information was important to this study because it was hoped it would be possible to identify characteristics and factors contributing to significant differences in mobility and motivation. The second part of the study asked the respondents to identify those motivational factors of concern to them. Job motivation was defined by six general factors identified in the educational work components study (EWCS) questionnaire (Miskel & Heller, 1973). These six factors are: potential for personal challenge and development; competitiveness; desirability and reward of success; tolerance for work pressures; conservative security; and willingness to seek reward in spite of uncertainty vs. avoidance. (DeGraw, 1984, pp. 4, 5)

This statement included several components of a good purpose statement. It was presented in a separate section, it used the word "relationship," terms were defined, and the population was mentioned. Further, from the order of the variables in the statement, one can clearly identify the independent variable and the dependent variable.

Example 5.7   *A Purpose Statement in an*
Experimental Study

Booth-Kewley, Edwards, and Rosenfeld (1992) undertook a study comparing the social desirability of responding to a computer version of an attitude and personality questionnaire to the desirability of completing a pencil-and-paper version. They replicated a study completed on college students that used an inventory, called "Balanced Inventory of Desirable Responding" (BIDR), composed of two scales, impression management (IM) and self-deception (SD). In the final paragraph of the introduction, they advance the purpose of the study.

> (W)e designed the present study to compare the responses of Navy recruits on the IM and SD scales, collected under three conditions— with paper-and-pencil, on a computer with backtracking allowed, and on a computer with no backtracking allowed. Approximately half of the recruits answered the questionnaire anonymously and the other half identified themselves. (Booth-Kewley et al., 1992, p. 563)

This statement also reflected many properties of a good purpose statement. The statement was separated from other ideas in the introduction as a separate paragraph, it mentioned that a comparison would be made, and it identified the participants in the experiment (i.e., the unit of analysis). In terms of the order of the variables, the authors advanced them with the dependent variable first, contrary to my suggestion (still, the groups are clearly identified). Although the theory-base is not mentioned, the paragraphs preceding the purpose statement reviewed the findings of prior theory. The authors also do not tell us about the strategy of inquiry, but other passages, especially those related to procedures, discuss the study as an experiment.

A MIXED METHODS PURPOSE STATEMENT

A mixed methods proposal or study needs to convey both quantitative and qualitative purpose statements. These statements need to be identified early in the study in an introduction, and they provide a major signpost for the reader to understand the quantitative and qualitative parts of a study. Several guidelines might direct the organization and presentation of the mixed methods purpose statement:

● Begin with signaling words, such as "The purpose of" or "The intent of."

● Indicate the type of mixed methods design, such as sequential, concurrent, or transformational.

- Discuss a rationale for combining both quantitative and qualitative data in the proposed study. This rationale could be

  – to better understand a research problem by converging (or tri-angulating) both broad numeric trends from quantitative research and the detail of qualitative research;

  – to explore participant views with the intent of using these views to develop and test an instrument with a sample from a population;

  – to obtain statistical, quantitative results from a sample and then follow up with a few individuals to probe or explore those results in more depth;

  – to best convey the needs of a marginalized group or individuals.

- Include the characteristics of a good qualitative purpose statement, such as focusing on a single phenomenon, using action words and nondirectional language, mentioning the strategy of inquiry, and identifying the participants and the research site

- Include the characteristics of a good quantitative purpose state-ment, such as identifying a theory and the variables, relating vari-ables or comparing groups in terms of variables, placing these variables in order from independent to dependent, mentioning the strategy of inquiry, and specifying the participants and research site for the research

- Consider adding information about the specific types of both quali-tative and quantitative data collection

Based on these elements, three mixed methods purpose statement "scripts" are as follows. The first two are sequential studies, and the third is a concurrent study.

> The purpose of this two-phase, sequential mixed methods study will be to explore participant views with the intent of using this information to develop and test an instrument with a sample from a population. The first phase will be a qualitative exploration of a _____ (central phenomenon) by collecting _____ (data) from _____ (participants) at _____ (research site). Themes from this qualitative data will then be developed into an instrument so that _____ (theory, research questions, or hypotheses) can be tested that _____ (relate, compare)

_____ (independent variable) with _____ (dependent variable) for _____ (sample of population) at _____ (research site).

The purpose of this two-phase, sequential mixed methods study will be to obtain statistical, quantitative results from a sample and then follow up with a few individuals to probe or explore those results in more depth. In the first phase, quantitative research questions or hypotheses will address the _____ relationship or comparison of _____ (independent) and _____ (dependent) variables with _____ (participants) at _____ (the research site). In the second phase, qualitative interviews or observations will be used to probe significant _____ (quantitative results) by exploring aspects of the _____ (central phenomenon) with _____ (a few participants) at _____ (research site).

The purpose of this concurrent mixed methods study is to better understand a research problem by converging both quantitative (broad numeric trends) and qualitative (detailed views) data. In the study, _____ (quantitative instruments) will be used to measure the relationship between _____ (independent variable) and _____ (dependent variable). At the same time, the _____ (central phenomenon) will be explored using _____ (qualitative interviews or observations) with _____ (participants) at _____ (the research site).

Example 5.8   *A Mixed Methods Purpose Statement, Convergent Strategy of Inquiry*

Hossler and Vesper (1993) studied student and parent attitudes toward parental savings for the postsecondary education of their children. In this 3-year study, they identified the factors most strongly associated with parental savings and collected both quantitative and qualitative data. Their purpose statement was as follows.

In an effort to shed light on parental saving, this article examines parental saving behaviors. Using student and parent data from a longitudinal study employing multiple surveys over a three-year period, logistic regression was used to identify the factors most strongly associated with parental savings for postsecondary

> education. In addition, insights gained from the interviews of a
> small subsample of students and parents who were interviewed
> five times during the three-year period are used to further examine
> parental savings. (Hossler & Vesper, 1993, p. 141)

This section was contained under the heading "Purpose," and it indicated that both quantitative data (i.e., surveys) and qualitative data (i.e., interviews) were included in the study. Both forms of data were collected during the 3-year period, and the authors might have identified their study as a triangulation or convergence design. Although the rationale for the study is not included in this passage, it is articulated later, in the methods discussion about "Surveys and Interviews." Here we find that "the interviews were also used to explore variables under investigation in greater detail and triangulate findings using quantitative and qualitative data" (Hossler & Vesper, 1993, p. 146).

Example 5.9   *A Mixed Methods Purpose Statement,*
Sequential Strategy of Inquiry

Ansorge, Creswell, Swidler, and Gutmann (2001) studied the use of wireless iBook laptop computers in three teacher education methods courses. These laptop computers enabled students to work at their desks and use a laptop to log directly onto Web sites recommended by the instructors. The purpose statement was as follows.

> The purpose of this sequential, mixed methods study was to first
> explore and generate themes about student use of iBook laptops
> in three teacher education classes using field observations and
> face-to-face interviews. Then, based on these themes, the second
> phase was to develop an instrument and to survey students about
> the laptop use on several dimensions. The rationale for using both
> qualitative and quantitative data was that a useful survey of
> student experience could best be developed only after a preliminary exploration of student use.

In this example, the statement begins with the signal words "the purpose of." It then mentions the type of mixed methods design and contains the basic elements of both an initial qualitative phase and a follow-up quantitative phase. It includes information about both the qualitative data and the quantitative data collection and ends with a rationale for the incorporation of the two forms of data in a sequential design.

▓ SUMMARY

This chapter emphasizes the importance of a purpose statement in a scholarly study. This statement advances the central idea in a study, and as such it is the most important statement in a research proposal or study. In writing a qualitative purpose statement, a researcher needs to identify a single central phenomenon and to pose a tentative definition for it. Also, the researcher employs action words such as "discover," "develop," or "understand." In the process, nondirectional language is used, and the inquirer mentions the strategy of inquiry, the participants, and the research site for the study. In a quantitative purpose statement, the researcher mentions the theory being tested as well as the variables and their relationship or comparison. It is important to position the independent variable first and the dependent variable second. The researcher mentions the strategy of inquiry as well as the participants and the research site for the investigation. In some purpose statements, the researcher also defines the key variables used in the study. In a mixed methods study, the type of strategy is mentioned as well as a rationale for the type of strategy, such as whether the data are collected concurrently or sequentially. Further, many elements of both good qualitative and quantitative purpose statements are included in the statement.

Writing Exercises

1. Using the "script" for a qualitative purpose statement, write the statement by completing the blanks. Make this statement short; write no more than approximately three-quarters of a typed page.

2. Using the "script" for a quantitative purpose statement, write the statement. Also make this statement short, no longer than three-quarters of a typed page.

3. Using the "script" for a mixed methods purpose statement, write a purpose statement. Be sure to include the rationale for mixing quantitative and qualitative data, and incorporate the elements of both a good qualitative and a good quantitative purpose statement.

WRITING EXERCISES

ADDITIONAL READINGS

Creswell, J. W. (2002). *Educational research: Planning, conduct-ing, and evaluating quantitative and qualitative research.* **Upper Saddle River, NJ: Merrill/Pearson.**

In this methods text, I devote a section of one chapter to the topic of writing a purpose statement. The text includes a "script" for both quantitative and qualitative purpose statements. For identify-ing types of quantitative variables, the discussion provides a conceptual framework called the "family" of variables. The book provides several examples of both quantitative and qualitative purpose statements from the literature of education.

Marshall, C., & Rossman, G. B. (1999). *Designing qualitative research* **(3rd ed.). Thousand Oaks, CA: Sage.**

Catherine Marshall and Gretchen Rossman call attention to the major intent of the study, the "purpose of the study." This section is generally embedded in the discussion of the topic, and it is mentioned in a sentence or two. It tells the reader what the results of the research are likely to accomplish. The authors characterize purposes as exploratory, explanatory, descriptive, and emancipa-tory. They also mention that the purpose statement includes the unit of analysis (e.g., individuals, dyads, or groups).

Wilkinson, A. M. (1991). *The scientist's handbook for writing papers and dissertations.* **Englewood Cliffs, NJ: Prentice Hall.**

Antoinette Wilkinson calls the purpose statement the "immediate objective" of the research study. She states that the purpose of the "objective" is to answer the research question. Further, the "objec-tive" of the study needs to be presented in the introduction to a study, although it may be implicitly stated as the subject of the research, the paper, or the method. If stated explicitly, the "objec-tive" is found at the end of the argument in the introduction; it might also be found near the beginning or in the middle, depend-ing on the structure of the introduction.

CHAPTER SIX

Research Questions and Hypotheses

Investigators place signposts in their research to carry the reader through a plan for a study. The first signpost is the purpose statement, which establishes the central direction for the study. From the broad, general purpose statement, the researcher narrows the focus to specific questions to be answered or predictions (i.e., hypotheses) to bo tostod. This chapter addresses the second signpost—the research questions, or hypotheses—in a proposal. The discussion begins by advancing several principles involved in designing qualitative research questions; quantitative research questions, objectives, and hypotheses; and finally, mixed methods research questions.

QUALITATIVE RESEARCH QUESTIONS

In a qualitative study, inquirers state research questions, not objectives (i.e., specific goals for the research) or hypotheses (i.e., predictions that involve variables and statistical tests). These research questions assume two forms: a central question and associated subquestions.

The central question is a statement of the question being examined in the study in its most general form. The inquirer poses this question, consistent with the emerging methodology of qualitative research, as a general issue so as to not limit the inquiry. One might ask "What is the broadest question that can be asked in the study?" Beginning researchers trained in *quantitative* research might struggle with this approach because they are accustomed to the reverse logic: identifying specific questions or hypotheses. The following are guidelines for writing broad, qualitative research questions:

● I recommend that a researcher ask one or two central questions followed by no more than five to seven subquestions. Several subquestions follow each general central question, and the subquestions narrow the focus of the study but leave open the questioning. This approach is well within the limits set by Miles and Huberman (1994), who recommend that researchers write no more than a dozen research questions in all. These questions, in turn, become topics specifically explored in interviews, observations, and documents and archival material. For example, they might be used as key questions the researcher will ask himself or herself in the observational procedure or during an open-ended interview.

● Relate the central question to the specific qualitative strategy of inquiry. For example, the specificity of the questions in ethnography at this stage of the design differs from that in other qualitative strategies. In ethnographic research, Spradley (1980) advanced a taxonomy of ethnographic questions that included mini-tour, experience, native-language, contrast, and verification questions. Similarly, in critical ethnography, the research questions may build on a body of existing literature. These questions become "working guidelines" rather than "truths" to be proven (Thomas, 1993, p. 35). Alternatively, in phenomenology, the questions might be broadly stated without specific reference to the existing literature or a typology of questions. An example is "What is it like for a mother to live with a teenage child who is dying of cancer?" (Nieswiadomy, 1993, p. 151). In grounded theory, the questions may be related to procedures in the data analysis such as open coding ("What are the categories to emerge from interactions between caregivers and patients?") or axial coding ("How does caregiving relate to actions by nurses?").

● Begin the research questions with the words "what" or "how" to convey an open and emerging design. "Why" suggests cause and effect, an approach consistent with *quantitative* research.

● Focus on a single phenomenon or concept.

● Use exploratory verbs that convey the language of emerging design of research. These verbs tell the reader that the study will

   – Discover (e.g., grounded theory)
   – Seek to understand (e.g., ethnography)
   – Explore a process (e.g., case study)

- – Describe the experiences (e.g., phenomenology)
- – Report the stories (e.g., narrative research)

● Use nondirectional language. Delete words that suggest or infer a *quantitative* study, words with a directional orientation such as "affect," "influence," "impact," "determine," "cause," and "relate."

● Expect the research questions to evolve and to change during the study in a manner consistent with the assumptions of an emerging design. Often in *qualitative* studies, the questions are under continual review and reformulation (as in a grounded theory study). This approach may be problematic for individuals accustomed to *quantitative* designs, in which the research questions remain fixed throughout the study.

● Use open-ended questions without reference to the literature or theory unless otherwise indicated by a qualitative strategy of inquiry.

● If the information is not redundant with the purpose statement, specify the participants and the research site for the study.

The following are examples of qualitative research questions drawing on several types of strategies.

Example 6.1   *A Qualitative Central Question*
                   From an Ethnography

Finders (1996) used ethnographic procedures to document the reading of teen magazines by middle-class Euro-American seventh-grade girls. By examining the reading of teen zines (magazines), the researcher could explore how the girls perceive and construct their social roles and relationships as they enter junior high school. She asked one guiding central question in her study:

> How do early adolescent females read literature that falls outside the realm of fiction? (Finders, 1996, p. 72)

This central question begins with "how"; it uses an open-ended verb, "read"; it focuses on a single concept, the "literature" or teen magazines; and it mentions the participants, adolescent females, in the study. Notice how the author crafted a concise, single question that needed to be answered in the study.

Example 6.2   *Central Questions From a Case Study*

Padula and Miller (1999) conducted a multiple case study that described the experiences of women who went back to school, after a time away, in a psychology doctoral program at a major Midwestern research university. The intent was to document the women's experiences, with those experiences intended as aids for feminists and feminist researchers. The authors asked three central questions that guided the inquiry.

(a) How do women in a psychology doctoral program describe their decision to return to school? (b) How do women in a psychology doctoral program describe their reentry experiences? And (c) How does returning to graduate school change these women's lives? (Padula & Miller, 1999, p. 328)

These three central questions all begin with the words "how," they include open-ended verbs such as "describe," and they focus on three areas of the doctoral experience—returning to school, reentering, and changing. They also mention the participants as women in a single doctoral program at a Midwestern research university.

QUANTITATIVE RESEARCH QUESTIONS AND HYPOTHESES

In quantitative studies, investigators use research questions and hypotheses to shape and specifically focus the purpose of the study. Research questions are interrogative statements or questions that the investigator seeks to answer. They are used frequently in social science research and especially in survey studies. Hypotheses, on the other hand, are predictions the researcher holds about the relationship among variables. They are numeric estimates of population values based on data collected from samples. Testing of hypotheses employs statistical procedures in which the investigator draws inferences about the population from a study sample. Hypotheses typically are used in experiments in which investigators compare groups. Advisers often recommend their use in a formal research project, such as a dissertation or thesis, as a means of stating the direction a study will take. Objectives, on the other hand, indicate the goals or objectives for a study. They are used infrequently in social science research. As such, the focus here will be on research questions and hypotheses.

Guidelines for writing good quantitative research questions and hypotheses include the following.

● The use of variables in research questions or hypotheses is typically limited to three basic approaches. The researcher may *compare* groups on an independent variable to see its impact on a dependent variable. Alternatively, the investigator may *relate* one or more independent variables to a dependent variable. Third, the researcher may *describe* responses to the independent, mediating, or dependent variables.

● The most rigorous form of quantitative research follows from a test of a theory (see Chapter 7) and the specification of research questions or hypotheses that are included in the theory.

● The independent and dependent variables must be measured separately. This procedure reinforces the cause and effect logic of quantitative research.

● To eliminate redundancy, write only research questions or hypotheses, not both, unless the hypotheses build on the research questions (as discussed below). Choose the form based on tradition, recommendations from an adviser or faculty committee, or whether past research indicates a prediction about outcomes.

● If hypotheses are used, there are two forms: null and alternative. A *null hypothesis* represents the traditional approach to writing hypotheses. It makes a prediction that in the general population, no relationship or no difference exists between groups on a variable. The wording is "There is no difference (or relationship)" between the groups. The following example illustrates a null hypothesis.

Example 6.3   *A Null Hypothesis*

An investigator might examine three types of reinforcement for children with autism: verbal cues, a reward, and no reinforcement. Then the investigator collects behavioral measures assessing social interaction of the children with their siblings. A null hypothesis might read:

There is no significant difference between the effects of verbal cues, rewards, and no reinforcement in terms of social interaction for children with autism and their siblings.

● The second form of hypothesis, popular in journal articles, is the *alternative hypothesis*. The investigator makes a prediction about the expected outcome for the population of the study. This prediction often comes from prior literature and studies on the topic that suggest a potential outcome that the researcher may expect. For example, the researcher may predict that "Scores will be higher for Group A than for Group B" on the dependent variable or that "Group A will change more than Group B" on the outcome. These examples illustrate a *directional hypothesis*, because an expected prediction (e.g., higher, change more) is made. Another type of alternative hypothesis is *nondirectional*—a prediction is made, but the exact form of differences (e.g., higher, lower, more, or less) is not specified because the researcher does not know what can be predicted from past literature. Thus, the investigator might write, "There is a difference" between the two groups. The following illustrates a directional hypothesis.

Example 6.4   *Directional Hypotheses*

Mascarenhas (1989) studied the differences between type of ownership (state-owned, publicly traded, and private) of firms in the offshore drilling industry. Specifically, the study explored such differences as domestic market dominance, international presence, and customer orientation. The study was a "controlled field study" using quasi-experimental procedures.

Hypothesis 1: Publicly traded firms will have higher growth rates than privately held firms.

Hypothesis 2: Publicly traded enterprises will have a larger international scope than state-owned and privately held firms.

Hypothesis 3: State-owned firms will have a greater share of the domestic market than publicly traded or privately held firms.

Hypothesis 4: Publicly traded firms will have broader product lines than state-owned and privately held firms.

Hypothesis 5: State-owned firms are more likely to have state-owned enterprises as customers overseas.

Hypothesis 6: State-owned firms will have a higher customer-base stability than privately held firms.

Hypothesis 7: In less visible contexts, publicly traded firms will employ more advanced technology than state-owned and privately held firms. (Mascarenhas, 1989, pp. 585-588)

Example 6.5   *Nondirectional and Directional Hypotheses*

Sometimes directional hypotheses are created to examine the relationship among variables rather than to compare groups. For example, Moore (2000) studied the meaning of gender identity for religious and secular Jewish and Arab women in Israeli society. In a national probability sample of Jewish and Arab women, the author identified three hypotheses for study. The first hypothesis is nondirectional and the last two are directional.

H_1: Gender identity of religious and secular Arab and Jewish women are related to different sociopolitical social orders that reflect the different value systems they embrace.

H_2: Religious women with salient gender identity are less sociopolitically active than secular women with salient gender identities.

H_3: The relationships among gender identity, religiosity, and social actions are weaker among Arab women than among Jewish women.

● Unless the study intentionally employs demographic variables as predictors, use nondemographic variables (i.e., measuring attitudes or behaviors) rather than personal demographics as independent variables. Because quantitative studies attempt to verify a theory, demographic variables (e.g., age, income level, educational level, and so forth) typically enter these models as intervening or control variables instead of major independent variables.

● Use the same pattern of word order in the questions or hypotheses to enable a reader to easily identify the major variables. This calls for repeating key phrases and positioning the variables beginning with the independent and concluding with the dependent variables (as also discussed in Chapter 5 on good purpose statements). An example of word order with independent variables stated first in the phrase follows.

Example 6.6   *Standard Use of Language in Hypotheses*

1. *There is no relationship between* utilization of ancillary support services and academic persistence for non-traditional women college students.

2. *There is no relationship* between family support systems and academic persistence for non–traditional aged college women.

3. *There is no relationship between* ancillary support services and family support systems for non-traditional college women.

A Model for Descriptive Questions and Hypotheses

Consider a model for writing questions or hypotheses based on writing descriptive questions that are followed by inferential questions or hypotheses. These questions or hypotheses include both independent and dependent variables. In this model, the writer specifies descriptive questions for *each* independent and dependent variable (and important control or intervening variables) in the study. Inferential questions (or hypotheses) that relate variables or compare groups follow these descriptive questions. A final set of questions, then, may add inferential questions or hypotheses in which variables are controlled.

Example 6.7   *Descriptive and Inferential Questions*

To illustrate this approach, assume that a researcher wants to examine the relationship of critical thinking skills (an independent variable measured on an instrument) to student achievement (a dependent variable measured by grades) in science classes for eighth-grade students in a large metropolitan school district. Further, this researcher controls for the intervening effects of prior grades in science classes and parents' educational attainment. Following the model proposed above, the research questions might be written as follows:

Descriptive Questions

1. How do the students rate on critical thinking skills? (A descriptive question focused on the independent variable)
2. What are the student's achievement levels (or grades) in science classes? (A descriptive question focused on the dependent variable)
3. What are the student's prior grades in science classes? (A descriptive question focused on the control variable of prior grades)
4. What is the educational attainment of the parents of the eighth-graders? (A descriptive question focused on another control variable, educational attainment of parents)

Inferential Questions

5. Does critical thinking ability relate to student achievement? (An inferential question relating the independent and the dependent variables)
6. Does critical thinking ability relate to student achievement, controlling for the effects of prior grades in science and the educational attainment of the eighth-graders' parents? (An inferential question relating the independent and the dependent variables, controlling for the effects of the two controlled variables)

This example illustrates how to organize all the research questions into descriptive and inferential questions. In another example, a researcher may want to compare groups, and the language may change to reflect this comparison in the inferential questions. In other studies, many more independent and dependent variables may be present in the model being tested, and a longer list of descriptive and inferential questions would result. I would recommend this descriptive-inferential model.

This example also illustrates the use of variables to describe as well as relate. It specifies the independent variables in the first position in the questions, the dependent in the second, and the control variables in the third position. It employs demographics as controls rather than central variables in the questions, and a reader needs to assume that the questions flow from a theoretical model.

MIXED METHODS RESEARCH
QUESTIONS AND HYPOTHESES

Mixed methods research presents challenges in writing research questions (or hypotheses) because so little of the literature has addressed this
design step (Creswell, 1999). Authors prefer to make purpose statements rather than specify their research questions. Thus, there is a distinct lack of models on which to base guidelines for writing research
questions into mixed methods studies. By examining a number of these
studies, however, it is possible to identify some characteristics that might
guide the design of the questions.

● Mixed methods studies need to have both qualitative and quantitative research questions (or hypotheses) included in the studies to
narrow and focus the purpose statements.

● These questions and hypotheses need to incorporate the elements of
good questions and hypotheses already addressed in the quantitative and qualitative approaches.

● In a two-phase, sequential project in which the second phase elaborates on the first phase, it is difficult to specify the second-phase
questions in a proposal or plan. After the study is completed, the
researcher can state the questions of both phases in the final report.
In a single-phase project, it is possible to identify the qualitative and
quantitative research questions in the proposal because one set of
questions is not contingent on the other set of questions.

● Some attention should be given to the order of the research questions and hypotheses. In a two-phase project, the order would
consist of the first-phase questions followed by the second-phase
questions so that readers see them in the order in which they will be
addressed in the proposed study. In a single-phase strategy of
inquiry, the questions might be ordered according to the method
that is given the most weight in the design.

● A variation often seen in sequential mixed methods studies is
to introduce the questions at the beginning of each phase. For
example, assume that the study begins with a quantitative phase.
The investigator might introduce hypotheses. Later in the study,

when the qualitative phase is addressed, the qualitative research questions appear.

Example 6.8   *Hypotheses and Research Questions in a Mixed Methods Study*

Houtz (1995) provides an example of a two-phase study with the research hypotheses and questions stated in sections introducing each phase. Her study investigated the differences between middle-school (nontraditional) and junior high (traditional) instructional strategies for seventh- and eighth-grade students and their attitudes toward science and their science achievement. In this two-phase study, the first phase involved assessing pre- and posttest attitudes and achievement using scales and examination scores. Houtz then followed the quantitative results with qualitative interviews with science teachers, the school principal, and consultants. This second phase helped to explain differences and similarities in the two instructional approaches obtained in the first phase.

With a first-phase quantitative study, Houtz mentioned the hypotheses guiding her research:

> It was hypothesized that there would be no significant difference between students in the middle school and those in the junior high in attitude toward science as a school subject. It was also hypothesized that there would be no significant difference between students in the middle school and those in the junior high in achievement in science. (Houtz, 1995, p. 630)

These hypotheses appeared at the beginning of the study as an introduction to the quantitative phase of the study. Prior to the qualitative phase, Houtz raised questions to explore the quantitative results. Focusing in on the achievement test results, Houtz interviewed science teachers, the principal, and the university consultants and asked three questions:

> What differences currently exist between the middle school instructional strategy and the junior high instructional strategy at this school in transition? How has this transition period impacted science attitude and achievement of your students? How do teachers feel about this change process? (Houtz, 1995, p. 649)

Examining this mixed methods study shows that the author included both quantitative and qualitative questions, specified them at the beginning of each phase of her study, and used good elements for writing both quantitative hypotheses and qualitative research questions.

▦ SUMMARY

Research questions and hypotheses narrow the purpose statement and become major signposts for readers of research. Qualitative researchers ask at least one central question and several subquestions. They begin the questions with words such as "how" or "what" and use exploratory verbs, such as "explore" or "describe." They pose broad, general questions to allow the participants to explain their ideas. They also focus initially on one central phenomenon of interest. The questions may mention the participants and the site for the research.

Quantitative researchers write either research questions or hypotheses. These questions or hypotheses include variables that are described, related, categorized into groups for comparison, and measured separately for the independent and dependent variables. In many quantitative proposals, writers use research questions; however, a more formal statement of research employs hypotheses. These hypotheses are predictions about the outcomes of the results, and they may be written as alternative hypotheses specifying the exact results to be expected (more or less, higher or lower of something). They also may be stated in the null form, indicating no difference or no relationship between groups on a dependent variable. Typically in questions and hypotheses, the researcher writes the independent variable(s) first, followed by the dependent variable(s). One model for ordering all the questions in a quantitative proposal is to begin with descriptive questions, followed by the inferential questions that relate variables or compare groups.

Mixed methods research questions should address both the qualitative and the quantitative components in a study. In a proposal, it is difficult to be specific about the second-phase questions when these questions will build or elaborate on the first-phase questions. Typically, if both qualitative and quantitative questions are introduced in a study, their order of sequence in the study suggests their priority in the study. Also, the weight given to the qualitative and quantitative phases will dictate the order of the questions. Finally, one model found in mixed methods studies involves writing the research questions as an introduction to each phase in the study rather than presenting them all at the beginning of the study.

Writing Exercises

1. For a qualitative study, write one or two central questions followed by five to seven subquestions.

2. For a quantitative study, write two sets of questions. The first set should be descriptive questions about the independent and dependent variables in the study. The second set should pose questions that relate (or compare) the independent variable(s) with the dependent variable(s). This follows the model presented in this chapter for combining descriptive and inferential questions.

3. Write research questions for a two-phase, sequential mixed methods project. Include the elements of good questions in both the qualitative and quantitative questions.

4. Return to the working draft of your title. Retitle your study to reflect a qualitative or quantitative approach to the study. To write a qualitative title, consider the suggestions in Chapter 2 and be sure to include the central phenomenon. Use a literary style such as a question. To write a quantitative title, include the major independent and dependent variables and separate them with the conjunction "and." Order the variables from independent to dependent so that they are consistent with the purpose statement and research questions/hypotheses.

ADDITIONAL READINGS

Creswell, J. W. (1999). Mixed-method research: Introduction and application. In G. J. Cizek (Ed.), *Handbook of educational policy* **(pp. 455-472). San Diego: Academic Press.**

In this chapter, I discuss the nine steps in conducting a mixed methods study. These are as follows:

1. determine if a mixed methods study is needed to study the problem;

2. consider whether a mixed methods study is feasible;

3. write both qualitative and quantitative research questions;

4. review and decide on the types of data collection;

5. assess the relative weight and implementation strategy for each method;

6. present a visual model;

7. determine how the data will be analyzed;

8. assess the criteria for evaluating the study; and

9. develop a plan for the study.

In writing the research questions, I recommend developing both qualitative and quantitative questions, and stating within the questions the type of qualitative strategy of inquiry being used.

Morse, J. M. (1994). Designing funded qualitative research. In N. K. Denzin & Y. S. Lincoln (Eds.), *Handbook of qualitative research* **(pp. 220-235). Thousand Oaks, CA: Sage.**

> Janice Morse, a nursing researcher, identifies and describes the major design issues involved in the planning of a qualitative project. She compares several strategies of inquiry and maps the type of research questions used in each strategy. For phenomenology and ethnography, the research calls for meaning and descriptive questions. For grounded theory, the questions need to address "process" questions, whereas in ethnomethodology and discourse analysis, the questions relate to verbal interaction and dialogue. She indicates that the wording of the research question determines the focus and scope of the study.

Tuckman, B. W. (1999). *Conducting educational research* **(5th ed.). Fort Worth, TX: Harcourt Brace College Publishers.**

> Bruce Tuckman provides an entire chapter on constructing hypotheses. He identifies the origin of hypotheses in deductive theoretical positions and in inductive observations. He further defines and illustrates both alternative and null hypotheses and takes the reader through the hypothesis testing procedure.

CHAPTER SEVEN

The Use of Theory

I n *quantitative research*, the hypotheses and research questions are often based on theories that the researcher seeks to test. In *qualitative research*, the use of theory is much more varied. Thus, this book introduces the use of theory at this time in the design process because theory provides an explanation for the variables in questions and hypotheses in quantitative research. In contrast, in a quantitative dissertation, an entire section of a research proposal might be devoted to explicating the theory for the study. Alternatively, in a qualitative study, the inquirer may generate a theory during a study and place it at the end of a project, such as in grounded theory. In other qualitative studies, it comes at the beginning and provides a lens that shapes what is looked at and the questions asked, such as in ethnographies or in advocacy research. In *mixed methods research*, researchers may both test theories and generate them. Moreover, mixed methods research may contain a theoretical lens, such as a focus on feminist, racial, or class issues, that guides the entire study.

The chapter begins by focusing on theory-use in a quantitative study. It reviews a definition of a theory, the placement of it in a quantitative study, and the alternative forms it might assume in a written plan. Procedures in identifying a theory are next presented followed by a "script" of a "theoretical perspective" section of a quantitative research proposal. Then the discussion moves to use of theory in a qualitative study. Qualitative inquirers use different terms, such as theories, patterns, and naturalistic generalizations, to describe the understandings developed in their studies. Sometimes these understandings occur at the beginning of a study; at other times, they appear at the end. Examples illustrate the alternatives available to qualitative researchers. Finally, the chapter turns to the use of theories in mixed methods research and the use of theory in a type of strategy of inquiry—the transformative strategy—that emerged recently in the literature.

QUANTITATIVE THEORY-USE

Definition of a Theory

In *quantitative* research, some historical precedent exists for viewing a theory as a scientific prediction or explanation (see G. Thomas, 1997, for different ways of conceptualizing theories and how they might constrain thought). For example, the definition of a theory, such as the one by Kerlinger (1979), is still valid today. A theory is "a set of interrelated constructs (variables), definitions, and propositions that presents a systematic view of phenomena by specifying relations among variables, with the purpose of explaining natural phenomena" (p. 64).

In this definition, a theory is an interrelated set of constructs (or variables) formed into propositions, or hypotheses, that specify the relationship among variables (typically in terms of magnitude or direction). The systematic view might be an argument, a discussion, or a rationale, and it helps to explain (or predict) phenomena that occur in the world. Labovitz and Hagedorn (1971) add to this definition the idea of a *theoretical rationale*, which they define as "specifying how and why the variables and relational statements are interrelated" (p. 17). Why would an independent variable, X, influence or affect a dependent variable, Y? The theory would provide the explanation for this expectation or prediction. A discussion about this theory, then, would appear in a section of a proposal titled a *theory-base*, a *theoretical rationale*, or a *theoretical perspective*. I prefer the term *theoretical perspective* because it has been popularly used as a required section for a proposal for research when one submits an application to present a research paper at the American Educational Research Association conference.

The metaphor of a rainbow can help to visualize how a theory operates. Assume that the rainbow *bridges* the independent and dependent variables (or constructs) in a study. This rainbow, then, ties together the variables and provides an overarching explanation for *how* and *why* one would expect the independent variable to explain or predict the dependent variable.

Theories develop when researchers test a prediction many times. Recall that investigators combine independent, mediating, and dependent variables based on different forms of measures into hypotheses or research questions. These hypotheses or questions provide information about the type of relationship (positive, negative, or unknown) and its magnitude (e.g., high or low). The hypothesis might be written, "The greater the centralization of power in leaders, the greater the disenfranchisement of the followers." When researchers test hypotheses such as this over and over in different settings and with different populations (e.g., the Boy Scouts, a Presbyterian church, the Rotary Club, and a group of high school students), a theory emerges and someone gives it a name (e.g., a theory of attribution). Thus, theory develops as explanation to advance knowledge in particular fields (G. Thomas, 1997).

Another aspect of theories is that they vary in their breadth of coverage. Neuman (2000) reviews theories at three levels: micro-level, meso-level, and macro-level. Micro-level theories provide explanations limited to small slices of time, space, or numbers of people, such as Goffman's theory of "face work" that explains how people engage in rituals during face-to-face interactions. Meso-level theories link the micro and macro levels. These are theories of organizations, social movement, or communities, such as Collins's theory of control in organizations. Macro-level theories explain larger aggregates, such as social institutions, cultural systems, and whole societies. Lenski's macro-level theory of social stratification, for example, explains how the amount of surplus a society produces increases with the development of the society.

Theories are found in the social science disciplines of psychology, sociology, anthropology, education, and economics, as well as within many subfields. To locate and read about these theories requires searching literature databases (e.g., *Psychological Abstracts*, *Sociological Abstracts*) or reviewing guides to the literature about theories (e.g., see Webb, Beals, & White, 1986).

Form of Theories

Researchers state their theories in several ways, such as a series of hypotheses, "if . . . then" logic statements, or visual models. First, some researchers state theories in the form of interconnected hypotheses. For example, Hopkins (1964) conveyed his theory of influence processes as a series of 15 hypotheses (slightly altered to remove all the male-specific pronouns). For any member of a small group, some hypotheses are:

1. The higher her rank, the greater her centrality.

2. The greater his centrality, the greater his observability.

3. The higher her rank, the greater her observability.

4. The greater his centrality, the greater his conformity.

5. The higher her rank, the greater her conformity.

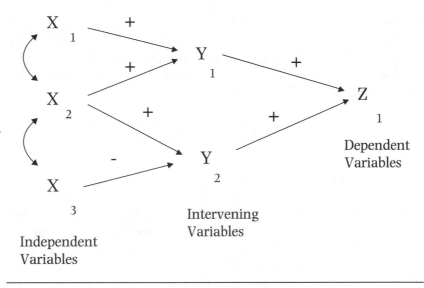

Figure 7.1 Three Independent Variables Influencing a Single
Dependent Variable Mediated by Two Intervening
Variables

6. The greater his observability, the greater his conformity.

7. The greater her conformity, the greater her observability. (p. 51)

A second form is to state a theory as a series of "if . . . then" statements that explain why one would expect the independent variables to
influence or cause the dependent variables. For example, Homans
(1950) explains a theory of interaction:

> If the frequency of interaction between two or more persons
> increases, the degree of their liking for one another will increase,
> and vice versa . . . persons who feel sentiments of liking for one
> another will express those sentiments in activities over and above
> the activities of the external system, and these activities may
> further strengthen the sentiments of liking. The more frequently
> persons interact with one another, the more alike in some respects
> both their activities and their sentiments tend to become. (pp. 112,
> 118, 120)

Third, an author may present a theory as a visual model. It is useful
to translate variables into a visual picture. Blalock (1969, 1985, 1991)
advocates causal modeling and recasts verbal theories into causal
models so that a reader can visualize the interconnections of variables.

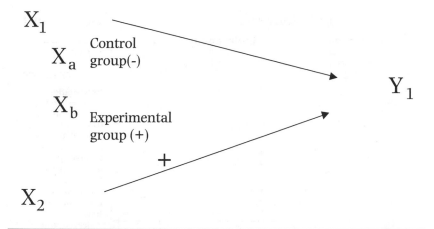

X_1

X_a Control
        group(-)

X_b Experimental
        group (+)

$+$

X_2

Y_1

Figure 7.2 Two Groups Given Different Treatments on X_1 Are
Compared in Terms of Y_1 Controlling for X_2

Two simplified examples are presented here. As shown in Figure 7.1,
three independent variables influence a single dependent variable
mediated by the influence of two intervening variables. Setting up a
diagram such as this one shows the possible causal sequence among
variables, leading to path analytic modeling and more advanced
analyses using multiple measures of variables as found in structural
equation modeling (see Kline, 1998). At an introductory level, Duncan
(1985) provides useful suggestions about the notation for constructing
these visual, causal diagrams:

● Position the dependent variables on the right in the diagram and the
  independent variables on the left.

● Use one-way arrows leading from each determining variable to each
  variable dependent on it.

● Indicate the "strength" of the relationship among variables by
  inserting valence signs on the paths. Use positive or negative
  valences that postulate or infer relationships.

● Use two-headed arrows connected to show unanalyzed relationships between variables not dependent upon other relationships in
  the model.

Though more complicated causal diagrams can be constructed with
additional notation, the model presented here portrays a basic model of
limited variables, such as typically found in a survey research study.

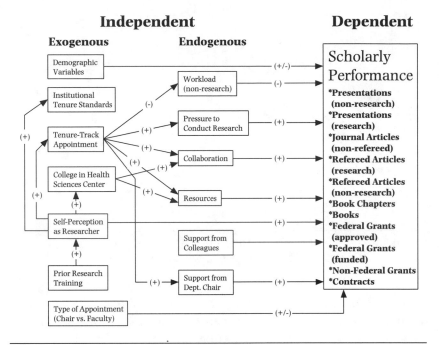

Figure 7.3   A Visual Model of Faculty Scholarly Performance

SOURCE: From P. W. Jungnickel (1990), *Workplace Correlates* and *Scholarly Performance of Pharmacy Clinical Faculty Members*, unpublished proposal, University of Nebraska–Lincoln. Used with permission.

A variation on this theme is to have two independent variables in which one variable compares a control and experimental group and a second variable simply measures an attribute or characteristic. As shown in Figure 7.2, two groups on variable X_1 (X_a and X_b) are compared, along with variable X_2 (a control variable) as they influence Y_1, the dependent variable. This design is a between-groups experimental design. The same rules of notation discussed above apply.

These two visual models are meant only to introduce possibilities for connecting independent and dependent variables to build theories. More complicated designs employ multiple independent and dependent variables in elaborate models of causation (Blalock, 1969, 1985). For example, Jungnickel (1990), in a doctoral dissertation proposal about research productivity among faculty in pharmacy schools, presented a complex visual model as shown in Figure 7.3. Jungnickel asked what factors influence a faculty member's scholarly research performance.

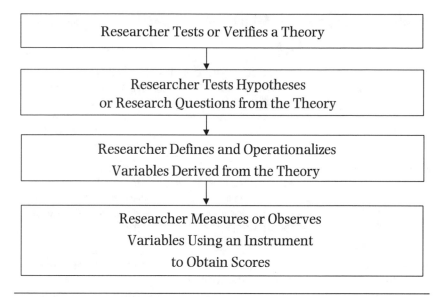

Figure 7.4   The Deductive Approach Typically Used in Quantitative Research

After identifying these factors in the literature, he adapted a theoretical framework found in nursing research (Megel, Langston, & Creswell, 1988). He developed a visual model portraying the relationship among these factors. The model follows the rules for constructing a visual model introduced earlier. He listed the independent variables on the far left, the intervening variables in the middle, and the dependent variables on the right. The direction of influence flowed from the left to the right, and he used "+" and "−" valences to indicate the hypothesized direction.

Placement of Quantitative Theories

In *quantitative* studies, one uses theory deductively and places it toward the beginning of the plan for a study. With the objective of testing or verifying a theory rather than developing it, the researcher advances a theory, collects data to test it, and reflects on the confirmation or disconfirmation of the theory by the results. The theory becomes a framework for the entire study, an organizing model for the research questions or hypotheses and for the data collection procedure. The deductive model of thinking used in a quantitative study is shown in Figure 7.4. The researcher tests or verifies a theory by examining

Table 7.1	Options for Placing Theory in a Quantitative Study	
Placement	Advantages	Disadvantages
In the introduction	An approach often found in journal articles, it will be familiar to readers. It conveys a deductive approach	It is difficult for a reader to isolate and separate theory base from other components of the research process
In the literature review	Theories are found in the literature, and their inclusion in a literature review is a logical extension or part of the literature	It is difficult for a reader to see the theory in isolation from the scholarly review of the literature
After hypotheses or research questions	The theory discussion is a logical extension of hypotheses or research questions because it explains how and why variables are related	A writer may include a theoretical rationale after hypotheses and question, and leave out an extended discussion about the origin and use of the theory
In a separate section	This approach clearly separates the theory from other components of the research process, and it enables a reader to better identify and to understand the theory-base for the study	The theory discussion stands in isolation from other components of the research process and, as such, a reader may not easily connect it with other components of the research process

hypotheses or questions derived from the theory. These hypotheses or questions contain variables (or constructs) that the researcher needs to define. Alternatively, an acceptable definition might be found in the literature. From here, the investigator locates an instrument to use in measuring or observing attitudes or behaviors of participants in a study. Then the investigator collects scores on these instruments to confirm or disconfirm the theory.

This deductive approach to research in the quantitative approach has implications for the *placement of a theory* in a quantitative research study (see Table 7.1). A general guide is to introduce the theory early in a plan or study. This means that the researcher presents it in the introduction, in the literature review section, immediately after hypotheses or research questions (as a rationale for the connections among the variables), or in a separate section of the study. Each placement has its advantages and disadvantages.

I prefer to write the theory into a separate section so that readers can clearly identify the theory from other components of the research process. Such a separate passage provides a complete explication of the theory section, its use, and how it relates to the study I am proposing.

A Model for Writing a Quantitative Theoretical Perspective

Using these ideas, the following presents a model for writing a quantitative theoretical perspective section into a research plan. Assume that the task is to identify a theory that explains the relationship between independent and dependent variables. The following procedure might be used:

1. Look in the discipline-based literature for a theory. If the unit of analysis for variables is individuals, look in the psychology literature; to study groups or organizations, look in the sociological literature. If the project examines individuals and groups, consider the social psychology literature. Of course, theories from other discipline theories may be useful, too (e.g., to study an economic issue, the theory may be found in economics).

2. Look also at prior studies that address the topic or a closely related topic. What theories were used by other authors? Limit the number of theories and try to identify *one overarching theory* that explains the central hypothesis or research question in the study.

3. As mentioned earlier, ask the *rainbow* question that bridges the independent and dependent variables: Why would the independent variable(s) influence the dependent variables?

4. Script out the theory section. Follow these lead sentences: "The theory that I will use will be _____ (name the theory). It was developed by _____ (identify the origin or source for the theory), and it was used to study _____ (identify the topics where one finds the theory being applied). This theory indicates that _____ (identify the propositions or hypotheses in the theory). As

applied to my study, this theory holds that I would expect my independent variable(s) _____ (state independent variables) to influence or explain the dependent variable(s) _____ (state dependent variables) because _____ (provide a rationale based on the logic of the theory)."

Thus, the topics to include in a quantitative theory discussion are the theory to be used, the central hypotheses or propositions of the theory, information about past use of the theory and its application, and statements that reflect how the theory relates to a proposed study. This model is illustrated in the example by Crutchfield (1986) below.

Example 7.1　*A Quantitative Theory Section*

Crutchfield (1986) wrote a doctoral dissertation titled *Locus of Control, Interpersonal Trust, and Scholarly Productivity*. Surveying nursing educators, her intent was to determine if locus of control and interpersonal trust affected the levels of publications of the faculty. Her dissertation included a separate section in the introductory chapter titled "Theoretical Perspective." What follows is this section, including the following points:

● The theory she planned to use

● The central hypotheses of the theory

● Information about who has used the theory and its applicability

● An adaptation of the theory to variables in her study using the "if . . . then" logic

Here is a section of her study, reproduced in its entirety. I added annotations (in bold type) to mark key passages.

Theoretical Perspective

In formulation of a theoretical perspective for studying the scholarly productivity of faculty, social learning theory provides a useful prototype. This conception of behavior attempts to achieve a balanced synthesis of cognitive psychology with the principles of behavior modification (Bower & Hilgard, 1981). Basically, this unified theoretical framework "approaches the explanation of human behavior in terms of a continuous (reciprocal) interaction between cognitive, behavioral, and environmental determinants" (Bandura, 1977, p. vii). **(Author identifies the theory for the study.)**

While social learning theory accepts the application of reinforcements such as shaping principles, it tends to see the role of rewards as both conveying information about the optimal response and providing incentive motivation for a given act because of the anticipated reward. In addition, the learning principles of this theory place special emphasis on the important roles played by vicarious, symbolic, and self-regulating processes (Bandura, 1971).

Social learning theory not only deals with learning, but seeks to describe how a group of social and personal competencies (so-called personality) could evolve out of social conditions within which the learning occurs. It also addresses techniques of personality assessment (Mischel, 1968), and behavior modification in clinical and educational settings (Bandura, 1977; Bower & Hilgard, 1981; Rotter, 1954).**(Author describes social learning theory.)**

Further, the principles of social learning theory have been applied to a wide range of social behavior such as competitiveness, aggressiveness, sex roles, deviance, and pathological behavior (Bandura & Walters, 1963; Bandura, 1977; Mischel, 1968; Miller & Dollard, 1941; Rotter, 1954; Staats, 1975). **(Author describes the use of the theory.)**

Explaining social learning theory, Rotter (1954) indicated that four classes of variables must be considered: behavior, expectancies, reinforcement, and psychological situations. A general formula for behavior was proposed which states: "the potential for a behavior to occur in any specific psychological situation is the function of the expectancy that the behavior will lead to a particular reinforcement in that situation and the value of that reinforcement" (Rotter, 1975, p. 57).

Expectancy within the formula refers to the perceived degree of certainty (or probability) that a causal relationship generally exists between behavior and rewards. This construct of generalized expectancy has been defined as *internal* locus of control when an individual believes that reinforcements are a function of specific behavior, or as *external* locus of control when the effects are attributed to luck, fate, or powerful others. The perceptions of causal relationships need not be absolute positions, but rather tend to vary in degree along a continuum depending upon previous experiences and situational complexities (Rotter, 1966). **(Author explains variables in the theory.)**

In the application of social learning theory to this study of scholarly productivity, the four classes of variables identified by Rotter (1954) will be defined in the following manner.

1. Scholarly productivity is the desired behavior or activity.

2. Locus of control is the generalized expectancy that rewards are or are not dependent upon specific behaviors.

3. Reinforcements are the rewards from scholarly work and the value attached to these rewards.

4. The educational institution is the psychological situation which furnishes many of the rewards for scholarly productivity.

With these specific variables, the formula for behavior which was developed by Rotter (1975) would be adapted to read: The potential for scholarly behavior to occur within an educational institution is a function of the expectancy that this activity will lead to specific rewards and of the value that the faculty member places on these rewards. In addition, the interaction of interpersonal trust with locus of control must be considered in relation to the expectancy of attaining rewards through behaviors as recommended in subsequent statements by Rotter (1967). Finally, certain characteristics, such as educational preparation, chronological age, post-doctoral fellowships, tenure, or full-time versus part-time employment may be associated with the scholarly productivity of nurse faculty in a manner similar to that seen within other disciplines. **(Author applied the concepts to her study.)**

The following statement represents the underlying logic for designing and conducting this study. If faculty believe that: (a) their efforts and actions in producing scholarly works will lead to rewards (locus of control), (b) others can be relied upon to follow through on their promises (interpersonal trust), (c) the rewards for scholarly activity are worthwhile (reward values), and (d) the rewards are available within their discipline or institution (institutional setting), then they will attain high levels of scholarly productivity (pp. 12-16). **(Author concluded with the "if . . . then" logic to relate the independent variables to the dependent variables.)**

QUALITATIVE THEORY-USE

Variation in Theory-Use in Qualitative Research

Qualitative inquirers use theory in their studies in several ways. They employ theory as a broad explanation, much like in *quantitative* research. This theory provides an *explanation* for behavior and attitudes, and it may be complete with variables, constructs, and hypotheses. For example, ethnographers employ cultural themes or "aspects of culture" (Wolcott, 1999, p. 113) to study in their qualitative projects. These might be themes such as social control, language, stability and change, or social organization such as kinship or families (see Wolcott's 1999 discussion about texts that address cultural topics in anthropology). Themes in this context provide a ready-made series of hypotheses to be tested from the literature. Although researchers might not refer to them as theories, they provide broad explanations that anthropologists use to study the culture-sharing behavior and attitudes of people.

Alternatively, qualitative researchers increasingly use a *theoretical lens or perspective* to guide their study and raise the questions of gender, class, and race (or some combination) they would like to address. The case could easily be made that qualitative research of the 1980s underwent a transformation to broaden its scope of inquiry to include these theoretical lenses. These are the theories mentioned earlier in this book, contained in Chapter 1. They provide a lens (even a theory) to guide the researchers as to what issues are important to examine (e.g., marginalization, empowerment) and the people that need to be studied (e.g., women, homeless, minority groups). They also indicate how the researcher positions himself or herself in the qualitative study (e.g., up front or biased from personal, cultural, and historical contexts) and how the final written accounts need to be written (e.g., without further marginalizing individuals, by collaborating with participants). In critical ethnography studies, researchers begin with a theory that informs their studies. This causal theory might be a theory of emancipation or repression (J. Thomas, 1993). Rossman and Rallis (1998) capture, in a few words, the sense of theory as critical and postmodern perspectives in qualitative inquiry:

> As the 20th century draws to a close, traditional social science has come under increasing scrutiny and attack as those espousing critical and postmodern perspectives challenge objectivist

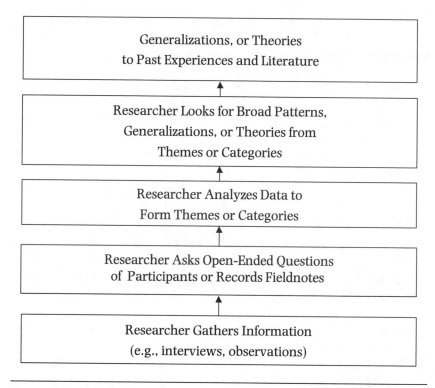

Figure 7.5   The Inductive Logic of Research in a Qualitative Study

assumptions and traditional norms for the conduct of research. Central to this attack are four interrelated notions: (a) Research fundamentally involves issues of power; (b) the research report is not transparent but rather it is authored by a raced, gendered, classed, and politically oriented individual; (c) race, class, and gender are crucial for understanding experience; and (d) historic, traditional research has silenced members of oppressed and marginalized groups. (p. 66)

Distinct from this theoretical orientation are qualitative studies in which theory (or some other broad explanation) becomes the *end point* for a study. It is an inductive process of building from the data to broad themes to a generalized model or theory (see Punch, 1998). The logic of this inductive approach is shown in Figure 7.5. The researcher begins by gathering detailed information from participants and forms this information into categories or themes. These themes or categories are developed into broad patterns, theories, or generalizations that are then compared with personal experiences or with existing literature on the topic.

The development of themes and categories into patterns, theories, or generalizations suggests a varied end point for qualitative studies. For example, in case study research, Stake (1995) refers to an assertion as a propositional generalization—the researcher's summary of interpretations and claims—to which is added the researcher's own personal experiences, called "naturalistic generalizations" (p. 86). As another example, grounded theory provides a different end point. Inquirers hope to discover a theory that is grounded in information from participants (Strauss & Corbin, 1998). Lincoln and Guba (1985) refer to "pattern theories" as an explanation that develops during naturalistic or qualitative research. Rather than the deductive form found in quantitative studies, these "pattern theories" or "generalizations" represent interconnected thoughts or parts linked to a whole. W. L. Neuman (1991) provides additional information about "pattern theories":

> Pattern theory does not emphasize logical deductive reasoning. Like causal theory, it contains an interconnected set of concepts and relationships, but it does not require causal statements. Instead, pattern theory uses metaphor or analogies so that relationship "makes sense." Pattern theories are systems of ideas that inform. The concepts and relations within them form a mutually reinforcing, closed system. They specify a sequence of phases or link parts to a whole. (p. 38)

Finally, some qualitative studies *do not employ any explicit theory*. However, the case can be made that no qualitative study begins from pure observation and that prior conceptual structure composed of theory and method provides the starting point for all observations (Schwandt, 1993). Still, one sees qualitative studies that contain no *explicit* theoretical orientation, such as in phenomenology, in which inquirers attempt to build the essence of experience from participants (e.g., see Riemen, 1986). In these studies, the inquirer constructs a rich, detailed description of a central phenomenon.

My advice on theory-use in a qualitative proposal is this:

● Decide if theory is to be used in the qualitative proposal.

● If it is used, then identify how the theory will be used in the study, such as an up-front explanation, as an end point, or as an advocacy lens.

● Locate the theory in the proposal in a manner consistent with its use.

Locating the Theory or Pattern in Qualitative Research

How theory is used affects its placement in a qualitative study. In those studies with a cultural theme or a theoretical lens, the theory occurs in the opening passages of the study. Consistent with the emerging design of qualitative inquiry, the theory may appear at the beginning and be modified or adjusted based on participant views. Even in the most theory-oriented qualitative design, such as critical ethnography, Lather (1986) qualifies the use of theory:

> Building empirically grounded theory requires a reciprocal relationship between data and theory. Data must be allowed to generate propositions in a dialectical manner that permits use of *a priori* theoretical frameworks, but which keeps a particular framework from becoming the container into which the data must be poured. (p. 267)

Example 7.2   *An Example of Theory-Use Early in a Qualitative Study*

Murguia, Padilla, and Pavel (1991) studied the integration of 24 Hispanic and Native American students into the social system of a college campus. They were curious about how ethnicity influenced social integration, and they began by relating the participants' experiences to a theoretical model, the Tinto model of social integration. They felt that the model had been "incompletely conceptualized and, as a consequence, only imprecisely understood and measured" (p. 433).

Thus, the model was not being tested in the study as one would find in a quantitative project, but modified in the study. At the end of the study, the authors refined Tinto's model and advanced their modification that described the rootedness and functions of ethnicity. In contrast to this approach, in qualitative studies with an end point of a theory (e.g., a grounded theory), a pattern, or a generalization, the theory emerges at the end of the study. This theory might be presented as a logic diagram, a visual representation of relationships among concepts.

Example 7.3   *A Theory at the End*
of a Qualitative Study

Using a national database of 33 interviews with academic department chairpersons, we (Creswell & Brown, 1992) developed a grounded theory interrelating variables (or categories) of chair influence on scholarly performance of faculty. The theory section came into the article as the last section, where the authors presented a visual model of the theory developed inductively from categories of information supplied by interviewees. In addition, the authors also advanced directional hypotheses that logically followed from the model. Moreover, in the section on the model and the hypotheses, the authors compared their results with findings from other studies and theoretical speculations in the literature. For example, the authors stated:

> This proposition and its sub-propositions represent unusual, even contrary evidence, to our expectations. Contrary to proposition 2.1, we expected that the career stages would be similar not in type of issue but in the range of issues. Instead we found that the issues for post-tenure faculty covered almost all the possible problems on the list. Why would this group's needs be more extensive? The research productivity literature suggests that one's research performance does not decline with the award of tenure (Holley 1977). Perhaps diffuse career goals of post-tenure faculty expand the possibilities for "types" of issues. In any case, this sub-proposition focuses attention on the understudied career group that Furniss (1981) reminds us needs to be examined in more detail. (p. 58)

As this example shows, we developed a visual model that interrelated variables, derived this model inductively from informant comments, and placed the model at the end of the study, where the central propositions in it could be contrasted with the existing theories and literature.

MIXED METHODS THEORY-USE

Mixed methods studies may include theory deductively in theory testing and verification, or inductively as in an emerging theory or pattern. In either situation, the use of theory may be directed by the emphasis on either quantitative or qualitative approaches in the mixed methods research. Another way to think about theory in mixed methods research is the use of a *theoretical lens or perspective* to guide the study. Here we have limited information about the procedures involved in using a theoretical lens to study gender, race/ethnicity/disability, sexual orientation, and other bases of diversity (Mertens, 2003). Several authors, however, have begun the discussion.

The first were Greene and Caracelli (1997), who mentioned the use of a "transformative design" as a distinct form of mixed methods research. This design gave primacy to value-based, action-oriented research such as in participatory action research and empowerment approaches. In this design, they suggest mixing the value commitments of different traditions in research (e.g., bias-free from quantitative and bias-laden from qualitative), the use of diverse methods, and a focus on action solutions in research. Unfortunately, they do not specify the procedures involved in incorporating this theoretical perspective into the practice of research.

More information on procedures has appeared in a chapter written by Creswell, Plano Clark, Gutmann, and Hanson (2003). They identify the use of theoretical perspectives such as gendered, feminist perspectives; cultural/racial/ethnic perspectives, lifestyle perspectives, critical perspectives, and class and social status perspectives. In Creswell et al.'s view, these perspectives represent one of the major decisions to be made in the selection of mixed methods strategies. They further develop visual models of these strategies for both sequential and concurrent mixed methods approaches, and they indicate some of the strengths and weaknesses (e.g., it is appealing to those interested in change despite limited discussions about procedures (also see Chapter 11 of this book).

Mertens (2003) continues the discussion. As outlined in Box 7.1, she advocates for the importance of a theory-lens in mixed methods

Box 7.1   Transformative-Emancipatory Questions for Mixed Methods Researchers Throughout the Research Process

Defining the Problem and Searching the Literature

- Did you deliberately search the literature for concerns of diverse groups and issues of discrimination and oppression?

- Did the problem definition arise from the community of concern?

- Did your mixed methods approach arise from spending quality time with these communities? (i.e., building trust? using an appropriate theoretical framework other than a deficit model? developing balanced—positive and negative—questions? developing questions that lead to transformative answers, such as questions focused on authority and relations of power in institutions and communities?)

Identifying the Research Design

- Does your research design deny treatment to any groups and respect ethical considerations of participants?

Identifying Data Sources and Selecting Participants

- Are the participants of groups associated with discrimination and oppression?

- Are the participants appropriately labeled?

- Is there a recognition of diversity within the target population?

- What can be done to improve the inclusiveness of the sample to increase the probability that traditionally marginalized groups are adequately and accurately represented?

Identifying or Constructing Data Collection Instruments and Methods

- Will the data collection process and outcomes benefit the community being studied?

- Will the research findings be credible to that community?

- Will communication with that community be effective?
- Will the data collection open up avenues for participation in the social change process?

Analyzing, Interpreting, and Reporting and Using Results

- Will the results raise new hypotheses?
- Will the research examine subgroups (i.e., multilevel analyses) to analyze the differential impact on diverse groups?
- Will the results help understand and elucidate power relationships?
- Will the results facilitate social change?

SOURCE: Adapted from D. M. Mertens (2003), "Mixed Methods and the Politics of Human Research: The Transformative-Emancipatory Perspective," in A. Tashakkori & C. Teddlie (Eds.), *Handbook of Mixed Methods in the Social and Behavioral Sciences.* Adapted with permission.

research. In detailing a "transformative/emancipatory paradigm" and specific procedures, she emphasizes the role that values play in studying feminist, ethnic/racial, and disability issues. Her "transformative theory" is an umbrella term for research that is emancipatory, anti-discriminatory, participative, Freirian, feminist, racial/ethnic, for individuals with disabilities, and for all marginalized groups.

Mertens identifies the implication of these transformative theories for mixed methods research. These involve integration of the transformative-emancipatory methodology into all phases of the research process. Reading through the questions in Box 7.1, one gains a sense of the importance of studying issues of discrimination and oppression and of recognizing diversity among study participants. These questions also address treating individuals respectfully through gathering and communicating data collection and through reporting results that lead to changes in social processes and relationships.

In using theory in a mixed methods proposal

- Determine if theory is to be used.

- Identify its use in accord with quantitative or qualitative approaches.

● If theory is used as in a transformational strategy of inquiry, define this strategy and discuss the points in the proposed study in which the emancipatory ideas will be used.

Example 7.4   *A Transformative-Emancipatory*
Mixed Methods Study

Hopson, Lucas, and Peterson (2000) studied issues in a urban, predominantly African American HIV/AIDS community. Consistent with a transformative-emancipatory framework, they examined the language of participants with HIV/AIDS within the participants' social context. They first conducted 75 open-ended ethnographic interviews to identify "language themes" (p. 31), such as blame, ownership, and acceptance or non-acceptance. They also collected 40 semistructured interviews that addressed demographics, daily routine, drug use, knowledge of HIV/AIDS risks, and drug and sexual sociobehavioral characteristics. From this qualitative data, the authors used concepts and questions to refine follow-up questions, including the design of a quantitative postintervention instrument. The authors suggested that empowerment approaches in evaluation can be useful, with researchers listening to the voices of real people and acting on what program participants say.

The design in this study gave "primacy to the value-based and action-oriented dimensions of different inquiry traditions" (Greene & Caracelli, 1997, p. 24) in a mixed methods study. The authors used a theoretical lens for reconfiguring the language and dialogue of participants, and they advanced the importance of empowerment in research.

SUMMARY

Researchers use theory in a quantitative study to provide an explanation or prediction about the relationship among variables in the study. A theory explains how and why the variables are related, acting as a bridge between or among the variables. Theory may be broad or narrow in scope, and researchers state their theories in several ways, such as a series of hypotheses, "if . . . then" logic statements, or visual models. Using theories deductively, investigators advance the theories at the beginning of the study in the literature review. They also include them with the hypotheses or research questions or place them in a separate section. A script can help design the theory section for a research proposal.

In qualitative research, inquirers employ theory as a broad explanation much like in quantitative research, such as in ethnographies. It may also be a theoretical lens or perspective that raises questions related to gender, class, or race, or some combination. Theory also appears as an end point of a qualitative study, a generated theory, a pattern, or a generalization that emerges inductively from data collection and analysis. Grounded theorists, for example, generate a theory "grounded" in the views of participants and place it as the conclusion of their studies. Some qualitative studies do not include an explicit theory and present descriptive research of the central phenomenon.

Mixed methods researchers use theory either deductively (as in quantitative research) or inductively (as in qualitative research). Writers also are beginning to identify the use of theoretical lenses or perspectives (e.g., related to gender, lifestyle, race/ethnicity, and class) in their mixed methods studies. A transformational-emancipatory design incorporates this perspective, and recent developments have identified procedures for incorporating this perspective into all phases of the research process.

Writing Exercises

1. Write a "theoretical perspective" section for your research plan following the script for a quantitative theory discussion presented in this chapter.

2. For a quantitative proposal you are planning, draw a visual model of the variables in the theory using the procedures for causal model design advanced in this chapter.

3. Locate qualitative journal articles that (a) use an a priori theory that is modified during the process of research, (b) generate or develop a theory at the end of the study, and (c) represent descriptive research without the use of an explicit theoretical model.

4. Locate a mixed methods study that uses a theoretical lens, such as a feminist, ethnic/racial, or class perspective. Identify specifically in the article how the lens shapes the steps taken in the research process using Box 7.1 as a guide.

ADDITIONAL READINGS

Flinders, D. J., & Mills, G. E. (Eds.). (1993). *Theory and concepts in qualitative research: Perspectives from the field.* **New York: Teachers College Press, Teachers College, Columbia University.**

> David Flinders and Geoffrey Mills have edited a book about perspectives from the field—"theory at work"—as described by different qualitative researchers. The chapters illustrate little consensus about defining theory and whether it is a vice or virtue. Further, theory operates at many levels in research, such as formal theories, epistemological theories, methodological theories, and metatheories. Given this diversity, it is best to see actual theory at work in qualitative studies, and this volume illustrates practice from critical, personal, formal, and educational criticism.

Mertens, D. M. (1998). *Research methods in education and psychology: Integrating diversity with quantitative and qualitative approaches.* **Thousand Oaks, CA: Sage.**

> Throughout this research methods text, Donna Mertens provides an integration of the "emancipatory paradigm" of research. Her brief overview of this paradigm or theoretical perspective is excellent. The paradigm, according to Mertens, places central importance on the lives of individuals who have been marginalized. It analyzes the inequities based on gender, race, ethnicity, or disability, and it is linked to social action. It uses an "emancipatory theory"—a set of beliefs about the ways a program works or why a problem occurs. It also relates theory to the questions asked and the recommenations for action.

Thomas, G. (1997). What's the use of theory? *Harvard Educational Review, 67*(1), 75-104.

> Gary Thomas presents a reasoned critique of the use of theory in educational inquiry. He notes the various definitions of theory and maps out four broad uses of theory: as thinking and reflection, as tighter or looser hypotheses, as explanations for adding to knowledge in different fields, and as formally expressed statements in science. Having noted these uses, he then embraces the thesis that theory unnecessarily structures and constrains thought. Instead, ideas should be in a constant flux, and should be "ad hocery" as characterized by Toffler.

⌘ CHAPTER EIGHT

Definitions, Limitations, and Significance

The use of a theory in effect delimits the scope of the study if researchers use it at the beginning, and it draws parameters around the interpretation if it is used at the end. A researcher needs to delimit the proposal so that readers understand its parameters. Four topics convey these parameters in a proposal: the definitions, the delimitations, the limitations, and the significance of the study. With these boundaries, the investigator clarifies terms used, narrows the scope of a study, suggests potential weaknesses, and identifies the importance of a project for different audiences. In many dissertation and thesis proposals, students include these elements in a distinct section of the proposal. In journal articles, definitions are often contained in introductions to a research study. Researchers writing journal articles may include the delimitations and limitations in method sections and a significance discussion in an introduction. Though these components may not be necessary in all studies, may vary in structural placement, and may not be presented within separate sections, it is important to consider essential decisions for designing them into a study.

THE DEFINITION OF TERMS

Researchers define terms so that readers can understand their precise meaning. In Chapter 5, the "scripts" for a purpose statement included a brief definition of the major variables or the central phenomena. Now, the definitions can be elaborated in a separate section of the research proposal.

Terms to Define

Define terms that individuals outside the field of study may not understand and that go beyond common language (Locke et al., 2000). Clearly, whether a term should be defined is a matter of judgment. A rule of thumb is to define a term if there is likelihood that readers will not know its meaning. Also, define terms when they first appear, so that a reader does not read ahead in the proposal operating with one set of definitions only to find out later that the author is using a different set. As Wilkinson (1991) commented, "scientists have sharply defined terms with which to think clearly about their research and to communicate their findings and ideas accurately" (p. 22). Defining terms also adds precision to a scientific study, as Firestone (1987) stated:

> The words of every day language are rich in multiple meanings. Like other symbols, their power comes from the combination of meaning in a specific setting. . . . Scientific language ostensibly strips this multiplicity of meaning from words in the interest of precision. This is the reason common terms are given "technical meanings" for scientific purposes. (p. 17)

In consideration of this need for precision, one finds terms stated early in the introduction to articles. In dissertations and thesis proposals, terms typically are defined in a special section of the study. The rationale is that in formal research, students must be precise in how they use language and terms. The need to ground thoughts in authoritative definitions constitutes good science.

Define terms as they are introduced in all sections of the research plan. Define terms not understood by readers as found in these sections:

- The title of the study

- The purpose statement

- The research questions, hypotheses, or objectives

- The literature review

- The theory-base of the study

- The methods section

Special terms that need to be defined appear in qualitative, quantitative, and mixed methods studies.

In *qualitative* studies, because of the inductive, evolving methodological design, inquirers may define few terms in the proposal. Instead, in the final study they define terms that arose during data collection. In a qualitative research plan, a writer may advance "tentative" definitions. For example, in a qualitative case study, themes (or perspectives or dimensions) emerge through the data analysis. In the procedure section, authors define these terms as they emerge in the studies. This approach, then, is to delay the definition of terms until they appear in the study. This makes a priori definitions in qualitative studies difficult to include in research proposals. For this reason, qualitative proposals often do not include separate sections on a "definition of terms," but the writers pose tentative qualitative definitions that they use before their entry into the field setting to gather information.

On the other hand, *quantitative* studies—operating more within the deductive model methodology of fixed and set research objectives—includes extensive definitions early in the research proposal. Investigators place them in separate sections in research proposals and precisely define them. The researchers try to comprehensively define all relevant terms at the beginning of studies and to use accepted definitions found in the literature.

In *mixed methods studies*, the approach to definitions might be to include a separate section if the study begins with quantitative data collection. If it begins with qualitative data collection, then the terms will emerge during the research and will be defined in the findings or results section of the final research study. If both quantitative and qualitative data collection occur at the same time, then the priority given to an approach will govern whether the researcher uses a qualitative or quantitative approach for definitions. All mixed methods studies contain terms that may be unfamiliar to readers. For example, include the definition of a mixed methods study in a procedural discussion (see Chapter 11). Also, clarify terms related to the type of mixed methods research strategy used in the study, such as concurrent or sequential, and the specific name for the strategy (e.g., concurrent triangulation model, as discussed in Chapter 11).

No one approach governs how one defines the terms in a study, but several suggestions follow building on recommendations found in Locke et al. (2000):

● Define a term when it first appears in the proposal. In the introduction, for example, a term may require definition to help the reader understand the research problem and the questions or hypotheses in the study.

● Write definitions at a specific operational or applied level. Operational definitions are written in specific language rather than being abstract and conceptual. Because the definition section in a dissertation provides an opportunity for the author to be specific about the terms used in the study, a preference exists for operational definitions, especially in dissertation proposals.

● Do not define the terms in everyday language; instead, use accepted language available in the research literature. In this way, the terms are grounded in the literature and not invented (Locke et al., 2000). It is possible that a precise definition of a term is not available in the literature and definitions created from everyday language will need to be used. In this case, provide a definition and use it consistently throughout the plan and the study (Wilkinson, 1991).

● Researchers might define terms with different intents. A definition may describe a common language word (e.g., "organization"). It may also be paired with a limitation, such as "The *curriculum* will be limited to those after school activities that the current *School District Manual* lists as approved for secondary school students" (Locke et al., 2000, p. 124). It may establish a criterion that will be used in the study, such as "High grade point average means a cumulative GPA of 3.7 or above on a 4.0 scale." It could also define a term operationally with respect to its use in the study, such as "*Reinforcement* will refer to the procedure of listing all club members in the school newspaper, providing special hall passes for members, and listing club memberships on school transcripts" (Locke et al., 2000, p. 124).

● Although no one format exists for defining terms, one approach is to develop a separate section (called the "Definition of Terms") and clearly set the terms and their definitions off by highlighting each term. In this way, the word is assigned an invariant meaning (Locke et al., 2000). Typically, this separate section is not more than two or three pages in length.

Two examples below illustrate varied structures for defining terms in a research study.

Example 8.1   *Terms Defined in a Mixed Methods Dissertation*

This first example illustrates a lengthy definition of terms presented in a mixed methods study. It was placed in a separate section of Chapter 1, which introduced the study. VanHorn-Grassmeyer (1998) studied how 119 new professionals in student affairs in colleges and universities engaged in reflection, either individually or collaboratively. She both surveyed the new professionals and conducted in-depth interviews with them. Because she studied individual and collaborative reflection among student affairs professionals, she provided detailed definitions of these terms in the beginning of the study. I illustrate two of her terms below. Notice how she referenced her definitions in meanings formed by other authors in the literature.

Individual Reflection

Schon (1983) devoted an entire book to concepts he named reflective thinking, reflection-in-action, and reflective practice; this after an entire book was written a decade earlier with Argyris (Argyris & Schon, 1978) to introduce the concepts. Therefore, a concise definition of this researcher's understanding of individual reflection that did justice to something that most aptly had been identified as an intuitive act, was difficult to reach. However, the most salient characteristics of individual reflection for the purposes of this study were these three: a) an "artistry of practice (Schon, 1983)," b) how one practices overtly what one knows intuitively, and c) how a professional enhances practice through thoughtful discourse within the mind.

Student Affairs Professional

A professional has been described in many ways. One description identified an individual who exhibited "a high degree of independent judgement, based on a collective, learned body of ideas, perspectives, information, norms, and habits (and who engage(d) in) professional knowing (Baskett & Marsick, 1992, p. 3)." A student affairs professional has exhibited such traits in service to students in a higher education environment, in any one of a number of functions which support academic and co-curriculuar success. (VanHorn-Grassmeyer, 1998, pp. 11-12)

Example 8.2 *Terms Defined in an Independent Variables Section in a Quantitative Dissertation*

This second example illustrates an abbreviated form of writing definitions for a study. Moreover, the first definition illustrates a specific operational definition of a key term in the study, and the second the procedural definition of a key term. Vernon (1992) studied how divorce in the middle generation impacts grandparents' relationships with their grandchildren (Vernon, 1992). These definitions were included in a section on independent variables.

Kinship Relationship to the Grandchild

Kinship relationship to the grandchild refers to whether the grandparents are maternal grandparents or paternal grandparents. Previous research (e.g., Cherlin & Furstenberg, 1986) suggests that maternal grandparents tend to be closer to their grandchildren.

Sex of Grandparent

Whether a grandparent is a grand*mother* or grand*father* has been found to be a factor in the grandparent/grandchild relationship (i.e., grandmothers tend to be more involved than grandfathers which is thought to be related to the kinkeeping role of women within the family (e.g., Hagestad, 1988). (Vernon, 1992, pp. 35-36)

DELIMITATIONS AND LIMITATIONS

Two more parameters for a research study establish the boundaries, exceptions, reservations, and qualifications inherent in every study: delimitations and limitations (Castetter & Heisler, 1977). They are found in proposals for qualitative, quantitative, and mixed methods studies.

- Use delimitations to narrow the scope of a study. For example, the scope may focus on specific variables or a central phenomenon, delimited to specific participants or sites, or narrowed to one type of research design (e.g., ethnography or experimental research)

- Provide limitations to identify potential weaknesses of the study. At the proposal stage, it is often difficult to identify weaknesses in the study before it has begun. However, advisers like students to anticipate the potential weaknesses in their studies, and students can identify limitations related to the research methods of data collection and analysis. For example, all statistical procedures have limitations; so also do research strategies, such as surveys or grounded theory studies. In introductory discussions about these strategies, authors typically mention both their strengths and their weaknesses (e.g., see Creswell, 2002)

In journal articles, researchers incorporate delimitations into the method or procedure sections, and they write limitations into the final section of their studies. In proposals, authors may include them in a separate section; they also may separate them into two subsections, one on delimitations and the other on limitations. Doctoral and master's committees vary in the extent to which they require these sections to be included in proposals.

Example 8.3   *A Delimitation and a Limitation
in a Doctoral Dissertation Proposal*

The following is an example taken from a dissertation proposal in nursing (Kunes, 1991), and it illustrates passages stating the delimitations and limitations. In the first passage—the delimitations—Kunes suggests how she plans to narrow the scope of her study. In the second passage— a limitation—she indicates a potential weakness in the design of the study. Both points were included in the "Introduction" section of the proposal.

A delimitation:

Initially, this study will confine itself to interviewing and observing the psychiatric staff nurse in a Midwest private psychiatric hospital.

A limitation:

The purposive sampling procedure decreases the generalizability of findings. This study will not be generalizable to all areas of nursing.

A limitation:

In this qualitative study, the findings could be subject to other interpretations. (Kunes, 1991, pp. 21-22).

SIGNIFICANCE OF THE PROPOSED STUDY

In dissertations, writers often include a specific section describing the significance of the study for select audiences. By including this section, the writer creates a rationale for conducting the study and a statement why the results will be important. It expands on introductory audience comments in the "audience" passage made in the introduction (i.e., statement of the problem), in which the writer briefly mentions the importance of the problem for audiences. In contrast, a significance section elaborates on the importance and implications of a study for researchers, practitioners, and policy makers. In designing this section, one might include

● Three or four ways in which the study adds to the scholarly research and literature in the field

● Three or four ways in which the study helps improve practice

● Three or four reasons why the study will improve policy.

In the example to follow, the author stated the significance of the study in the opening paragraphs of the journal article. This study, by Mascarenhas (1989), examined ownership of industrial firms. The author explicitly identified decision makers, organizational members, and researchers as the audience for the study.

Example 8.4   *Significance of the Study Stated in an Introduction to a Quantitative Study*

A study of an organization's ownership and its domain, defined here as markets served, product scope, customer orientation, and technology employed (Abell and Hammond, 1979; Abell, 1980; Perry and Rainey, 1988) is important for several reasons. First, understanding relationships among ownership and domain dimensions can help to reveal the underlying logic of organizations' activities and can help organization members evaluate strategies. . . . Second, a fundamental decision confronting all societies concerns the type of institutions to encourage or adopt for the conduct of activity. . . . Knowledge of the domain consequences of different ownership types can serve as input to that decision. . . . Third, researchers have often studied organizations reflecting one or two ownership types, but their findings may have been implicitly overgeneralized to all organizations. (Mascarenhas, 1989, p. 582)

SUMMARY

Researchers use definitions, delimitations and limitations, and statements about significance to place boundaries on their study plans. Researchers need to define terms to give precise and clear meaning to words used in the proposal. These definitions need to appear when the words are first introduced; should be created using accepted definitions in the literature; should be presented in a detailed, operational way; and should be clearly specified, such as by setting them off in a separate section in the proposal. In qualitative research, the inquirer provides tentative definitions in order to permit definitions to emerge from participants in the study. Also, these terms are few and typically are defined throughout the proposed study. In quantitative research, investigators define many terms in their studies so that the researcher and the readers share a common and consistent definition. In mixed methods research, terms may be specified in an approach consistent with either qualitative or quantitative research; however, mixed methods inquiry presents its own terms about strategies, and these need to be identified for readers not familiar with this form of research.

Turning to delimitations and limitations, delimitations address how the study will be narrowed in scope, whereas limitations identify potential weaknesses of a study. Their placement varies from separate sections (as in a proposal) to their incorporation into the methods and discussion sections (as in a journal article).

Finally, the significance of the study should describe the importance of the study for select audiences. Consider writing statements about the importance of the study for researchers, practitioners, and policy makers.

Writing Exercises

1. Write a definition section for your research plan. As much as possible, use definitions provided by authors in the literature.

2. Identify how your study will be limited in scope. Write three or four of these reasons, including how you will delimit the scope to focus on a specific problem, to certain variables or central phenomena, and to a particular set of study participants.

3. Identify potential limitations for your study. Focus these limitations on methodological weaknesses inherent in all study designs.

4. Write about the significance of your study. Identify how various audiences will profit from the study. Include comments about the significance for other researchers, for practitioners, and for policy makers.

ADDITIONAL READINGS

Locke, L. F., Spirduso, W. W., & Silverman, S. J. (2000). *Proposals that work: A guide for planning dissertations and grant proposals* (4th ed.). Thousand Oaks, CA: Sage.

Lawrence Locke, Waneen Spirduso, and Stephen Silverman discuss the importance in a dissertation proposal of using clear and precise words that have invariant definitions and meanings. They comment about how words in research typically invoke a system language of the discipline or field rather than a common language of everyday vocabulary. Whether researchers use common or system language words, the words need to have a single meaning for the researcher and the reader. Words should have only one referent and need to be used consistently in a proposal. A problem for novice researchers arises when they extend language into the new territory of their project. Locke, Spirduso, and Silverman recommend that a proposal contain a section devoted to the precise definitions used in a proposed study.

Punch, K. F. (2000). *Developing effective research proposals.* **London: Sage.**

Keith Punch discusses the limitations, delimitations, and significance of the study as part of the written research proposal. He describes the limitations as limiting conditions or restrictive weaknesses, which are unavoidably present in a study's design. He notes that researchers should note them in a proposal without slighting the importance of the work. He describes the significance of a study as its justification, importance, or contribution. The arguments made for significance should address its contribution to knowledge, to policy considerations, and to practitioners.

Rossman, G. B., & Rallis, S. F. (1998). *Learning in the field: An introduction to qualitative research.* **Thousand Oaks, CA: Sage.**

Gretchen Rossman and Sharon Rallis discuss the importance of identifying the significance of a study when planning research. They note that formal proposals typically include a section in which the qualitative researcher indicates the potential significance of the study. They recommend that several domains should be included in this section: scholarly research and literature, recurring social policy issues, concerns of practice, and the interests of participants. Further, if the proposal goes to a funding agency, the writer should include statements about the project's match with the needs and priorities of that agency.

Wilkinson, A. M. (1991). *The scientist's handbook for writing papers and dissertations.* **Englewood Cliffs, NJ: Prentice Hall.**

Antoinette Wilkinson devotes an entire chapter to the use of scientific terminology. Social scientists, she suggests, must take a less-than-adequate word from general vocabulary and craft a definition that delimits the exact meaning intended by the researcher. She recommends that social scientists use standard language rather than substitute synonyms for terms. When gathering information through interview schedules, questionnaires, and analyses of texts, language becomes a direct instrument of measurement and terms must be applied uniformly and consistently.

CHAPTER NINE

Quantitative Methods

For many proposal writers, the method section, of all sections discussed thus far, is the most concrete, specific part of a proposal. This chapter presents essential steps in designing a quantitative method for a research proposal or study, with specific focus on survey and experimental modes of inquiry. These modes reflect alternative knowledge claims, as discussed in Chapter 1. For example, determinism suggests that examining the relationships between and among variables is central to answering questions and hypotheses through surveys and experiments. The reduction to a parsimonious set of variables, tightly controlled through design or statistical analysis, provides measures or observations for testing a theory. Objective data result from empirical observations and measures. Validity and reliability of scores on instruments, additional standards for making knowledge claims, lead to meaningful interpretations of data.

In relating these assumptions and the procedures that implement them, this discussion does not exhaustively treat quantitative research methods. Excellent, detailed texts provide information about survey research (e.g., see Babbie, 1990, 2001; Fink, 1995; Salant & Dillman, 1994). For experimental procedures, some traditional books (e.g., D. T. Campbell & Stanley, 1963; Cook & Campbell, 1979), as well as some newer texts, extend ideas presented here (e.g., Bausell, 1994; Boruch, 1998; Keppel, 1991; Lipsey, 1990; Reichardt & Mark, 1998). In this chapter, the focus will be on the essential components of a method section in a proposal for a survey and an experiment.

DEFINING SURVEYS AND EXPERIMENTS

A *survey* design provides a quantitative or numeric description of trends, attitudes, or opinions of a population by studying a sample of that population. From sample results, the researcher generalizes or makes claims about the population. In an *experiment*, investigators may also identify a sample and generalize to a population; however, the basic intent of an *experiment* is to test the impact of a treatment (or an intervention) on an outcome, controlling for all other factors that might influence that outcome. As one form of control, researchers randomly assign individuals to groups. When one group receives a treatment and the other group does not, the experimenter can isolate whether it is the treatment and not the characteristics of individuals in a group (or other factors) that influence the outcome.

COMPONENTS OF A SURVEY METHOD PLAN

The design of a survey method section follows a standard format. Numerous examples of this format appear in scholarly journals, and these examples provide useful models of this strategy of inquiry. The following sections of this chapter detail typical components. In preparing to design these components into a proposal, consider the questions on the checklist shown in Table 9.1 as a general guide.

The Survey Design

In a proposal or plan, one of the first parts of the method section can introduce readers to the basic purpose and rationale for survey research. Begin the discussion by reviewing the purpose of a survey and the rationale for its selection as a design in the proposed study. This discussion can

● Identify the purpose of survey research. This purpose is to generalize from a sample to a population so that inferences can be made about some characteristic, attitude, or behavior of this population (Babbie, 1990). Provide a reference to this purpose from one of the survey method texts identified in this chapter.

● Indicate why a survey is the preferred type of data collection procedure for the study. In this rationale, consider the advantages of survey designs, such as the economy of the design and the rapid turnaround in data collection. Discuss the advantage of identifying attributes of a large population from a small group of individuals (Babbie, 1990; Fowler, 1988).

TABLE 9.1	A Checklist of Questions for Designing a Survey Method
_____	Is the purpose of a survey design stated?
_____	Are the reasons for choosing the design mentioned?
_____	Is the nature of the survey (cross-sectional vs. longitudinal) identified?
_____	Are the population and size of the population mentioned?
_____	Will the population be stratified? If so, how?
_____	How many people will be in the sample? On what basis was this size chosen?
_____	What will be the procedure for sampling these individuals (e.g., random, nonrandom)?
_____	What instrument will be used in the survey? Who developed the instrument?
_____	What are the content areas addressed in the survey? The scales?
_____	What procedure will be used to pilot or field test the survey?
_____	What is the time line for administering the survey?
_____	What are the variables in the study?
_____	How do these variables cross-reference with the research questions and items on the survey?
	What specific steps will be taken in data analysis to
(a)_____	analyze returns?
(b)_____	check for response bias?
(c)_____	conduct a descriptive analysis?
(d)_____	collapse items into scales?
(e)_____	check for reliability of scales?
(f)_____	run inferential statistics to answer the research questions?

● Indicate whether the survey will be cross-sectional, with the data collected at one point in time, or whether it will be longitudinal, with data collected over time.

● Specify the form of data collection. Fink (1995) identifies four types: self-administered questionnaires; interviews; structured record reviews to collect financial, medical, or school information; and structured observations. The data collection may also involve creating a

Web-based or Internet survey and administering it online (Nesbary, 2000). Regardless of the form of data collection, provide a rationale for the data collection procedure using arguments based on its strengths and weaknesses, costs, data availability, and convenience.

The Population and Sample

Specify the characteristics of the population and the sampling procedure. Methodologists have written excellent discussions about the underlying logic of sampling theory (e.g., Babbie, 1990, 2001). This discussion will focus on essential aspects of the population and sample to describe in a research plan.

● Identify the population in the study. Also state the size of this population, if size can be determined, and the means of identifying individuals in the population. Questions of access arise here, and the researcher might refer to availability of sampling frames—mail or published lists—of potential respondents in the population.

● Identify whether the sampling design for this population is single- or multistage (called clustering). Cluster sampling is ideal when it is impossible or impractical to compile a list of the elements composing the population (Babbie, 2001). A single-stage sampling procedure is one in which the researcher has access to names in the population and can sample the people (or other elements) directly. In a multistage, clustering procedure, the researcher first samples groups or organizations (or clusters), obtains names of individuals within groups or clusters, and then samples within the clusters.

● Identify the selection process for individuals. I recommend selecting a *random* sample in which each individual in the population has an equal probability of being selected (a systematic or probabilistic sample). Less desirable is a nonprobability sample (or convenience sample), in which respondents are chosen based on their convenience and availability (Babbie, 1990). With randomization, a representative sample from a population provides the ability to generalize to a population.

● Identify whether the study will involve stratification of the population before selecting the sample. Stratification means that specific characteristics of individuals (e.g., both females and males) are represented in the sample and the sample reflects the true proportion of individuals with certain characteristics of the population (Fowler, 1988). When randomly selecting people from a population, these characteristics may or may not be present in the sample in the same proportions as in the population; stratification ensures their representation. Also identify the characteristics used in stratifying the population (e.g., gender, income levels, education). Within each stratum, identify whether the sample contains individuals with the characteristic in the same proportion as the characteristic appears in the entire population (Babbie, 1990; Miller, 1991).

● Discuss the procedures for selecting the sample from available lists. The most rigorous method for selecting the sample is to choose individuals using a random numbers table, a table available in many introductory statistics texts (e.g., Gravetter & Wallnau, 2000).

● Indicate the number of people in the sample and the procedures used to compute this number. In survey research, I recommend that one use a sample size formula available in many survey texts (e.g., see Babbie, 1990; Fowler, 1988).

Instrumentation

As part of rigorous data collection, the proposal developer also provides detailed information about the actual survey instrument to be used in the proposed study. Consider the following:

● Name the survey instrument used to collect data in the research study. Discuss whether it is an instrument designed for this research, a modified instrument, or an intact instrument developed by someone else. If it is a modified instrument, indicate whether the developer has provided appropriate permission to use it. In some survey projects, the researcher assembles an instrument from components of several instruments. Again, permission to use any part of other instruments needs to be obtained.

● To use an existing instrument, describe the established validity and reliability of scores obtained from past use of the instrument. This means reporting efforts by authors to establish *validity*—whether one can draw meaningful and useful inferences from scores on the instruments. The three traditional forms of validity to look for are content validity (i.e., Do the items measure the content they were intended to measure?), predictive or concurrent validity (i.e., Do scores predict a criterion measure? Do results correlate with other results?), and construct validity (i.e., Do items measure hypothetical constructs or concepts?). In more recent studies, construct validity has also included whether the scores serve a useful purpose and have positive consequences when used (Humbley & Zumbo, 1996). Also discuss whether scores resulting from past use of the instrument demonstrate *reliability*. Look for whether authors report measures of internal consistency (i.e., Are the items' responses consistent across constructs?) and test-retest correlations (i.e., Are scores stable over time when the instrument is administered a second time?). Also determine whether there was consistency in test administration and scoring (i.e., Were errors caused by carelessness in administration or scoring?) (Borg, Gall, & Gall, 1993). When one modifies an instrument or combines instruments in a study, the original validity and reliability may not hold for the new instrument, and it becomes important to re-establish validity and reliability during data analysis in a survey study.

- Include sample items from the instrument so that readers can see the actual items used. In an appendix to the proposal, attach sample items from the instrument or the entire instrument.

- Indicate the major content sections in the instrument, such as the cover letter (Dillman, 1978, provides a useful list of items to include in cover letters), the items (e.g., demographics, attitudinal items, behavioral items, factual items), and the closing instructions. Also mention the type of scales used to measure the items on the instrument, such as continuous scales (e.g., *strongly agree* to *strongly disagree*) and categorical scales (e.g., yes/no, rank from highest to lowest importance).

- Discuss plans for pilot testing or field testing the survey and provide a rationale for these plans. This testing is important to establish the content validity of an instrument and to improve questions, format, and the scales. Indicate the number of people who will test the instrument and the plans to incorporate their comments into final instrument revisions.

- For a mailed survey, identify steps for administering the survey and for following up to ensure a high response rate. Salant and Dillman (1994) suggest a four-phase administration process. The first mail-out is a short advance-notice letter to all members of the sample, and the second mail-out is the actual mail survey, distributed about 1 week after the advance-notice letter. The third mail-out consists of a postcard follow-up sent to all members of the sample 4 to 8 days after the initial questionnaire. The fourth mail-out consists of a personalized cover letter with a handwritten signature, questionnaire, and preaddressed return envelope with postage. This mailing is sent to all nonrespondents. Researchers send this fourth

TABLE 9.2	Variables, Research Questions, and Items on a Survey	
Variable Name	Research Question	Item on Survey
Independent variable #1: Prior publications	Descriptive research question #1: How many publications did the faculty member produce prior to receipt of the doctorate?	See Questions 11, 12, 13, 14, and 15: publication counts before doctorate for journal articles, books, conference papers, book chapters
Dependent variable #1: Grants funded	Descriptive research question #3: How many grants has the faculty member received in the last 3 years?	See Questions 16, 17, and 18: grants from foundations, federal grants, state grants
Control variable #1: Tenure status	Descriptive research question #5: Is the faculty member tenured?	See Question 19: tenured (yes/no)

mail-out 3 weeks after the second mail-out. Thus, in total, the survey researcher concludes the administration period 4 weeks after its start (providing the returns meet project objectives).

Variables in the Study

Although readers of a proposal learn about the variables in earlier sections of the proposal, it is useful in the method section to relate the variables to the specific questions on the instrument. At this stage in a research plan, one technique is to relate the variables, the research questions, and items on the survey instrument so that a reader can easily determine how the researcher will use the questionnaire items. Plan to include a table and a discussion that cross-reference the variables, the questions or hypotheses, and specific survey items. This procedure is especially helpful in dissertations in which investigators test large-scale models. Table 9.2 illustrates such a table using hypothetical data.

Data Analysis

In the proposal, present information about the steps involved in analyzing the data. I recommend presenting them as a series of steps. They are:

Step 1   Report information about the number of members of the sample who did and did not return the survey. A table with numbers and percentages describing respondents and nonrespondents is a useful tool to present this information.

Step 2   Discuss the method by which response bias will be determined. Response bias is the effect of nonresponses on survey estimates (Fowler, 1988). Bias means that if nonrespondents had responded, their responses would have substantially changed the overall results of the survey. Mention the procedures used to check for response bias, such as wave analysis or a respondent/nonrespondent analysis. In wave analysis, the researcher examines returns on select items week by week to determine if average responses change (Leslie, 1972). Based on the assumption that those who return surveys in the final weeks of the response period are nearly nonrespondents, if the responses begin to change, a potential exists for response bias. An alternative check for response bias is to contact by phone a few nonrespondents and determine if their responses differ substantially from respondents. This constitutes a respondent-nonrespondent check for response bias.

Step 3   Discuss a plan to provide a descriptive analysis of data for all independent and dependent variables in the study. This analysis should indicate the means, standard deviations, and range of scores for these variables.

Step 4   If the proposal contains an instrument with scales or a plan to develop scales (combining items into scales), identify the statistical procedure (i.e., factor analysis) for accomplishing this. Also mention reliability checks for the internal consistency of the scales (i.e., the Cronbach alpha statistic).

Step 5   Identify the statistics and the statistical computer
program for testing the major questions or hypo-
theses in the proposed study. Provide a rationale for
the choice of statistical test and mention the assumptions associated with the statistic. Base this choice on
the nature of the research question (e.g., relating
variables or comparing groups as the most popular),
the number of independent and dependent variables,
and the number of covariates (e.g., see Rudestam &
Newton, 1992). Also note that the measurement of
the variables (as continuous or categorical) and the
type of distribution of scores (normal, nonnormal)
affect the choice of statistical test (Creswell, 2002).

Example 9.1   *A Survey Method Section*

Below is an example of a survey method section that illustrates many of
the steps mentioned above. This excerpt (used with permission) comes
from a journal article reporting a study of factors affecting student
attrition in one small liberal arts college (Bean & Creswell, 1980,
pp. 321-322).

Methodology

The site of this study was a small (enrollment 1,000), religious, coedu-
cational, liberal arts college in a Midwestern city with a population
of 175,000 people. **(Authors identified the research site and
population.)**

The dropout rate the previous year was 25%. Dropout rates tend
to be highest among freshmen and sophomores, so an attempt
was made to reach as many freshmen and sophomores as possible by distribution of the questionnaire through classes. Research
on attrition indicates that males and females drop out of college
for different reasons (Bean, 1978, in press; Spady, 1971). Therefore,
only women were analyzed in this study.

During April 1979, 169 women returned questionnaires. A
homogeneous sample of 135 women who were 25 years old or
younger, unmarried, full-time U.S. citizens, and Caucasian was

selected for this analysis to exclude some possible confounding variables (Kerlinger, 1973).

Of these women, 71 were freshmen, 55 were sophomores, and 9 were juniors. Of the students, 95% were between the ages of 18 and 21. This sample is biased toward higher-ability students as indicated by scores on the ACT test. **(Authors presented descriptive information about the sample.)**

Data were collected by means of a questionnaire containing 116 items. The majority of these were Likert-like items based on a scale from "a very small extent" to "a very great extent." Other questions asked for factual information, such as ACT scores, high school grades, and parents' educational level. All information used in this analysis was derived from questionnaire data. This questionnaire had been developed and tested at three other institutions before its use at this college. **(Authors discussed the instrument.)**

Concurrent and convergent validity (D. T. Campbell & Fiske, 1959) of these measures was established through factor analysis, and was found to be at an adequate level. Reliability of the factors was established through the coefficient alpha. The constructs were represented by 25 measures—multiple items combined on the basis of factor analysis to make indices—and 27 measures were single item indicators. **(Validity and reliability were addressed.)**

Multiple regression and path analysis (Heise, 1969; Kerlinger & Pedhazur, 1973) were used to analyze the data.

In the causal model . . . , intent to leave was regressed on all variables which preceded it in the causal sequence. Intervening variables significantly related to intent to leave were then regressed on organizational variables, personal variables, environmental variables, and background variables. **(Data analysis steps were presented.)**

COMPONENTS OF AN EXPERIMENTAL METHOD PLAN

An experimental method discussion follows a standard form: participants, materials, procedures, and measures. These four topics generally

TABLE 9.3	A Checklist of Questions for Designing an Experimental Procedure

	Who are the participants in the study? To what populations do these participants belong?
	How were the participants selected? Was a random selection method used?
	How will the participants be randomly assigned? Will they be matched? How?
	How many participants will be in the experimental and control group(s)?
	What is the dependent variable(s) in the study? How will it be measured? How many times will it be measured?
	What is the treatment condition(s)? How was it operationalized?
	Will variables be covaried in the experiment? How will they be measured?
	What experimental research design will be used? What would a visual model of this design look like?
	What instrument(s) will be used to measure the outcome in the study? Why was it chosen? Who developed it? Does it have established validity and reliability? Has permission been sought to use it?
	What are the steps in the procedure (e.g., random assignment of participants to groups, collection of demographic information, administration of pretest, administration of treatment(s), administration of posttest)?
	What are potential threats to internal and external validity for the experimental design and procedure? How will they be addressed?
	Will a pilot test of the experiment be conducted?
	What statistics will be used to analyze the data (e.g., descriptive and inferential)?

are sufficient. In this section of the chapter, I review these components as well as information about the experimental design and statistical analysis. As with the section on surveys, the intent here is to highlight key topics to be addressed in an experimental method proposal. An overall guide to these topics is found by answering the questions on the checklist shown in Table 9.3.

Participants (Formerly Called Subjects)

Readers need to know about the selection, assignment, and number of participants who will participate in the experiment. Consider the following suggestions when writing the method section for an experiment:

● Describe the selection process for participants as either random or nonrandom (e.g., conveniently selected). The participants might be selected by *random selection* or *random sampling*. With random selection or random sampling, each individual has an equal probability of being selected from the population, ensuring that the sample will be representative of the population (Keppel, 1991). In many experiments, however, only a *convenience* sample is possible because the investigator must use naturally formed groups (e.g., a classroom, an organization, a family unit) or volunteers as participants in the study.

● A convenience sample also makes it difficult to randomly assign individuals to groups, a hallmark of a *true experiment*. If random assignment is made, discuss how the project will involve *randomly assigning* individuals to the treatment groups. This means that of the pool of participants, individual #1 goes to group 1, individual #2 to group 2, and so forth so that there is no systematic bias in assigning the individuals. This procedure eliminates the possibility of systematic differences among participants and the environment of the experiment that could affect the outcomes, so that any differences in outcomes can be attributed to the experimental treatment (Keppel, 1991).

● Identify other controls in the experimental design that will systematically control the variables that might influence the outcome. One approach is to *match* participants in terms of a certain trait or characteristic and then assign one individual from each matched set to each group. For example, scores on a pretest might be obtained. Individuals might then be assigned to groups, with each group having the same numbers as all the other groups of high, medium, and low scorers on the pretest. Alternatively, the criteria for matching might be ability levels or demographic variables. A researcher may decide not to match, however, because it is expensive, takes time (Salkind, 1990), and leads to incomparable groups if participants leave the experiment (Rosenthal & Rosnow, 1991). Other procedures to place control into experiments involve using covariates (e.g., pretest scores) and controlling statistically, selecting homogeneous samples, or blocking the participants into subgroups or categories and analyzing the impact of each subgroup on the outcome (Creswell, 2002).

- Tell the reader about the number of participants in each group and the systematic procedures for determining the size of each group. For experimental research, investigators use a power analysis (Lipsey, 1990) to identify the appropriate sample size for groups. This calculation involves

  - A consideration of the level of statistical significance for the experiment, or alpha

  - The amount of power desired in a study—typically presented as high, medium, or low—for the statistical test of the null hypothesis with sample data when the null hypothesis is, in fact, false

  - The effect size, the expected differences in the means between the control and experimental groups expressed in standard deviation units

Researchers set values for these three factors (e.g., alpha =.05, power = .80, and effect size = .50) and can look up in a table the size needed for each group (see Cohen, 1977; Lipsey, 1990). In this way, the experiment is planned so that the size of each treatment group provides the greatest sensitivity that the effect on the outcome actually is due to the experimental manipulation in the study.

Variables

- Clearly identify the *independent variables* in the experiment (recall the discussion of variables in Chapter 5). One independent variable must be the *treatment variable*. One or more groups receive the experimental manipulation, or treatment, from the researcher. Other independent variables may simply be measured variables in which no manipulation occurs (e.g., attitudes or personal characteristics of participants). Still other independent variables can be statistically controlled in the experiment, such as demographics (e.g., gender or age). The method section must list and clearly identify all the independent variables in an experiment.

- Identify the *dependent variable or variables* in the experiment. The dependent variable is the response or the criterion variable that is presumed to be caused by or influenced by the independent treatment conditions (and any other independent variables). Rosenthal and Rosnow (1991) advanced three prototypic outcomes measures in experiments: the direction of observed change, the amount of this change, and the ease with which the participant changes (e.g., the subject reacquires the correct response as in a single-subject design).

Instrumentation and Materials

During an experiment, one makes observations or obtains measures using instruments at a pre- or posttest (or both) stage of the procedures. As with the selection of all instruments, a sound research plan calls for a thorough discussion about the instrument or instruments—their development, their items, their scales, and reports of reliability and validity of scores on past uses. The researcher also should report on the materials used for the experimental treatment in the study (e.g., the special program or specific activities given to the experimental group).

● Describe the instrument or instruments participants complete in the experiment, typically completed before the experiment begins and at its end. Indicate the established validity and reliability of the scores on instruments, the individuals who developed them, and any permissions needed to use them.

● Thoroughly discuss the materials used for the experimental treatment. One group, for example, may participate in a special computer-assisted learning plan used by a teacher in a classroom. This plan might involve handouts, lessons, and special written instructions to help students in this experimental group learn how to study a subject using computers. A pilot test of these materials may also be discussed, as well as any training required of individuals to administer the materials in a standard way. The intent of this pilot test is to ensure that materials can be administered without variability to the treatment group.

Experimental Procedures

The specific experimental design procedures also need to be identified. This discussion involves indicating the overall experiment type, citing reasons for the design, and advancing a visual model to help the reader understand the procedures.

● Identify the type of experimental design to be used in the proposed study. The types available in experiments are pre-experimental designs, true experiments, quasi-experiments, and single-subject designs. With *pre-experimental* designs, the researcher studies a single group and provides an intervention during the experiment. This design does not have a control group to compare with the experimental group. In *quasi-experiments*, the investigator uses control and experimental groups but does not randomly assign participants to groups (e.g., they may be intact groups available to the researcher). In a *true experiment*, the investigator randomly assigns the participants to treatment groups. A *single-subject* design or N of 1 design involves observing the behavior of a single individual (or a small number of individuals) over time.

● Identify what is being compared in the experiment. In many experiments, those of a type called *between-subject* designs, the investigator compares two or more groups (Keppel, 1991; Rosenthal & Rosnow, 1991). For example, a *factorial design* experiment, a variation on the between-group design, involves using two or more treatment variables to examine the independent and simultaneous effects of these treatment variables on an outcome (Vogt, 1999). This widely used behavioral research design explores not only the effects of each treatment separately but also the effects of variables used in combination, thereby providing a rich and revealing multi-dimensional view (Keppel, 1991). In other experiments, the researcher studies only one group in what is called a *within-group* design. For example, in a *repeated measures* design, participants are assigned to different treatments at different times during the experiment. Another example of a within-group design would be a study of the behavior of a single individual over time in which the experimenter both provides and withholds a treatment, at different times in the experiment, to determine its impact.

● Provide a diagram or a figure to illustrate the specific research design to be used. A standard notation system needs to be used in this figure. I recommend using a classic notation system, the notations provided by Campbell and Stanley (1963, p. 6). This notation is as follows:

  – X represents an exposure of a group to an experimental variable or event, the effects of which are to be measured.

  – O represents an observation or measurement recorded on an instrument.

- X's and O's in a given row are applied to the same specific persons. X's and O's in the same column, or placed vertically relative to each other, are simultaneous.

- The left-to-right dimension indicates the temporal order of procedures in the experiment (sometimes indicated with an arrow).

- The symbol R indicates random assignment.

- Separation of parallel rows by a dashed horizontal line indicates that comparison groups are not equal (or equated) by random assignment. No dashed horizontal line between the groups displays random assignment of individuals to treatment groups.

In the examples below, this notation is used to illustrate pre-experimental, quasi-experimental, true experimental, and single-subject designs.

Example 9.2   *Pre-Experimental Designs*

One-Shot Case Study

This design involves an exposure of a group to a treatment followed by a measure.

Group A   X ——— O

One-Group Pretest-Posttest Design

This design includes a pretest measure followed by a treatment and a posttest for a single group.

Group A O_1 ——— X ——— O_2

Static Group Comparison or Posttest-Only With Nonequivalent Groups

Experimenters use this design after implementing a treatment. After the treatment, the researcher selects a comparison group and provides a posttest to both the experimental group(s) and the comparison group(s).

Group A   X ——— O

Group B   ——— O

Alternative Treatment Posttest-Only With Nonequivalent Groups Design

This design uses the same procedure as the Static Group Comparison, with the exception that the nonequivalent comparison group received a different treatment.

Group A X_1 ————— O
                 - - - - - - - - - - -
Group B X_2 ——— O

Example 9.3   *Quasi-Experimental Designs*

Nonequivalent (Pretest and Posttest) Control-Group Design

In this design, a popular approach to quasi-experiments, the experimental group A and the control group B are selected without random assignment. Both groups take a pretest and posttest. Only the experimental group receives the treatment.

Group A   O ——— X ——— O
                 - - - - - - - - - - - - - - - - - - -
Group B   O ——————————— O

Single-Group Interrupted Time-Series Design

In this design, the researcher records measures for a single group both before and after a treatment.

Group A   O — O — O — O — X — O — O — O — O

Control-Group Interrupted Time-Series Design

A modification of the Single-Group Interrupted Time-Series design in which two groups of participants, not randomly assigned, are observed over time. A treatment is administered to only one of the groups (i.e., Group A).

Group A   O — O — O — O — X — O — O — O — O
                 -
Group B   O — O — O — O — O — O — O — O — O

Example 9.4   *True Experimental Designs*

Pretest-Posttest Control-Group Design

A traditional, classical design, this procedure involves random assignment of participants to two groups. Both groups are administered both a pretest and a posttest to both groups, but the treatment is provided only to experimental Group A.

Group A	R ——— O ——— X ——— O	
Group B	R ——— O ————————— O	

Posttest-Only Control-Group Design

This design controls for any confounding effects of a pretest and is a popular experimental design. The participants are randomly assigned to groups, a treatment is given only to the experimental group, and both groups are measured on the posttest.

Group A	R ——— X ——— O
Group B	R ————————— O

Solomon Four-Group Design

A special case of a 2×2 factorial design, this procedure involves the random assignment of participants to four groups. Pretests and treatments are varied for the four groups. All groups receive a posttest.

Group A	R ——— O ——— X ——— O
Group B	R ——— O ————————— O
Group C	R ————————— X ——— O
Group D	R ————————————— O

Example 9.5   *Single-Subject Designs*

A-B-A Single-Subject Design

This design involves multiple observations of a single individual. The target behavior of a single individual is established over time and is referred to as the baseline behavior. Once this baseline is established, the researcher administers a treatment. Observations continue over time after the treatment has been removed.

Baseline A   Treatment B   Baseline A

X — X — X — X — X — X

O — O — O — O — O — O — O — O — O — O — O — O — O — O — O — O

THREATS TO VALIDITY

There are several threats to validity that will raise potential issues about an experimenter's ability to conclude that the intervention affects an outcome. Experimental researchers need to identify threats to the internal validity of the experiment and relate these threats to the type of design proposed for the study. *Internal validity threats* are experimental procedures, treatments, or experiences of the participants that threaten the researcher's ability to draw correct inferences from the data in an experiment. The threats involve using inadequate procedures (e.g., changing the instrument during the experiment) or aspects or problems in applying treatments (e.g., a diffusion effect when members of the experimental and control groups talk to each other). The threats also can arise from characteristics of the participants (e.g., participants mature during an experiment and change their views or become wiser or more experienced).

Potential threats to external validity also must be identified. *External validity threats* arise when experimenters draw incorrect inferences from the sample data to other persons, other settings, and past or future situations. For example, a threat to external validity arises when the researcher generalizes beyond the groups in the experiment to other racial or social groups not under study.

Other threats that might be mentioned in the method section are the threats to *statistical conclusion validity* that arise when experimenters draw inaccurate inferences from the data because of inadequate statistical power or the violation of statistical assumptions. Threats to *construct validity* occur when investigators use inadequate definitions and measures of variables.

To write these threats into a proposal, as well as threats to internal and external validity, requires first identifying them by consulting methods texts such as Cook and Campbell (1979) or discussions such as found in Reichardt and Mark (1998). Many research methods texts identify and discuss these threats (e.g., Creswell, 2002; Tuckman, 1999).

The Procedure

One needs to describe in detail the procedure for conducting the experiment. A reader should be able to see the design being used, the observations, the treatment, and the timeline of activities.

● Discuss a step-by-step approach for the procedure in the experiment. For example, Borg and Gall (1989, p. 679) outlined six steps typically used in the procedure for a pretest-posttest control-group design with matching:

  1. Administer measures of the dependent variable or a variable closely correlated with the dependent variable to the research participants.

  2. Assign participants to matched pairs on the basis of their scores on the measures described in Step 1.

  3. Randomly assign one member of each pair to the experimental group and the other member to the control group.

  4. Expose the experimental group to the experimental treatment and administer no treatment or an alternative treatment to the control group.

  5. Administer measures of the dependent variables to the experimental and control groups.

  6. Compare the performance of the experimental and control groups on the posttest(s) using tests of statistical significance.

Statistical Analysis

Tell the reader about the types of statistical analysis that will be used during the experiment.

● Report the descriptive statistics calculated for observations and measures at the pretest or posttest stage of experimental designs. These statistics are means, standard deviations, and ranges.

● Indicate the inferential statistical tests used to examine the hypotheses in the study. For experimental designs with categorical information (groups) on the independent variable and continuous information on the dependent variable, researchers use t tests or univariate analysis of variance (ANOVA), analysis of covariance (ANCOVA), or multivariate analysis of variance (MANOVA—multiple dependent measures). In factorial designs, both interaction and main effects of ANOVA are used. When data on a pretest or postest show marked deviation from a normal distribution, use nonparametric statistical tests.

● For single-subject research designs, use line graphs for baseline and treatment observations for abscissa (horizontal axis) units of time and the ordinate (vertical axis) target behavior. Each data point is plotted separately on the graph, and the data points are connected by lines (e.g., see S. B. Neuman & McCormick, 1995). Occasionally, tests of statistical significance, such as t tests, are used to compare the pooled mean of the baseline and the treatment phases, although such procedures may violate the assumption of independent measures (Borg & Gall, 1989).

Example 9.6   *An Experimental Method Section*

The following is a selected passage (used with permission) from an quasi-experimental study by Enns and Hackett (1990) that demonstrates many of the components in an experimental design. Their study addressed the general issue of matching client and counselor interests along the dimensions of attitudes toward feminism. They hypothesized that feminist participants would be more receptive to a radical feminist counselor than would nonfeminist participants and that nonfeminist participants would be more receptive to a nonsexist and liberal feminist counselor. Except for a limited discussion about data analysis, their approach in the method section contains the elements of a good method section for an experimental study.

Method

Participants

The participants were 150 undergraduate women enrolled in both lower- and upper-division courses in sociology, psychology, and communications at a midsized university and a community college, both on the west coast. . . . **(The authors described the participants in this study.)**

Design and Experimental Manipulation

This study used a 3 × 2 × 2 factorial design: Orientation of counselor (nonsexist-humanistic, liberal feminist, or radical feminist) × Statement of Values (implicit or explicit) × Participants' Identification with Feminism (feminist or nonfeminist). Occasional missing data on particular items were handled by a pairwise deletion procedure. **(Authors identified the overall design.)**

The three counseling conditions, nonsexist-humanistic, liberal, and radical feminist, were depicted by 10 min videotape vignettes of a second counseling session between a female counselor and a female client. . . . The implicit statement of values condition used the sample interview only; the counselor's values were therefore implicit in her responses. The explicit statement of values condition was created by adding to each of the three counseling conditions a 2-min leader that portrayed the counselor describing to the client her counseling approach and associated values including for the two feminist conditions a description of her feminist philosophical orientation, liberal or radical. . . . Three counseling scripts were initially developed on the basis of distinctions between nonsexist-humanistic, liberal, and radical feminist philosophies and attendant counseling implications. Client statements and the outcome of each interview were held constant, whereas counselor responses differed by approach. . . . **(Authors described the three treatment conditions variables manipulated in the study.)**

Instruments

Manipulation checks. As a check on participants' perception of the experimental manipulation and as an assessment of participants' perceived similarity to the three counselors, two subscales of Berryman-Fink and Verderber's (1985) Attributions of the Term Feminist Scale were revised and used in this study as the Counselor Description Questionnaire (CDQ) and the Personal Description Questionnaire (PDQ). . . . Berryman-Fink and Verderber (1985) reported internal consistency reliabilities of .86 and .89 for the original versions of these two subscales. . . . **(Authors discussed the instruments and the reliability of the scales for the dependent variable in the study.)**

Procedure

All experimental sessions were conducted individually. The experimenter, an advanced doctoral student in counseling psychology, greeted each subject, explained the purpose of the study as assessing students' reactions to counseling, and administered the ATF. The ATF was then collected and scored while each subject completed a demographic data form and reviewed a set of instructions for viewing the videotape. The first half of the sample was randomly assigned to one of the twelve videotapes (3 Approaches × 2 Statements × 2 Counselors), and a median was obtained on the ATF. The median for the first half of the sample was then used to categorize the second half of the group as feminist or nonfeminist, and the remainder of the participants were randomly assigned to conditions separately from each feminist orientation group to ensure nearly equal cell sizes. The median on the final sample was checked and a few participants recategorized by the final median split, which resulted in 12 or 13 participants per cell.

After viewing the videotape that corresponded to their experimental assignment, participants completed the dependent measures and were debriefed. (pp. 35-36) **(Authors described the procedure used in the experiment.)**

SOURCE: Enns and Hackett (1990). © 1990 by the American Psychological Association. Reprinted with permission.

▓ SUMMARY

This chapter identified essential components in designing a method procedure for a survey or experimental study. The outline of steps for a survey study began with a discussion about the purpose of a survey, the identification of the population and sample for the study, the survey instruments to be used, the relationship between the variables, the research questions, specific items on the survey, and steps to be taken in the analysis of data from the survey. In the design of an experiment, the researcher identifies participants in the study, the variables—the treatment conditions and the outcome variables, and the instruments used for pre- and posttests and the materials to be used in the treatments. The design also includes the specific type of experiment, such as a pre-experimental, quasi-experimental, true experiment, or single-subject design. Then a figure can illustrate the design using appropriate notation. This is followed by comments about potential threats to internal and external validity (and possibly statistical and construct validity) that relate to the experiment and to the statistical analysis used to test the hypotheses or research questions.

Writing Exercises

1. Design a plan for the procedures to be used in a survey study. Review the checklist in Table 9.1 after you write the section to determine if all components have been addressed.

2. Design a plan for procedures for an experimental study. Refer to Table 9.3 after you complete your plan to determine if all questions have been addressed adequately.

ADDITIONAL READINGS

Babbie, E. (2001). *Survey research methods* (9th ed.). Belmont, CA: Wadsworth.

Earl Babbie provides a thorough, detailed text about all aspects of survey design. He reviews the types of study designs, the logic of sampling, and examples of designs. He also discusses the conceptualization of a survey instrument and its scales. He then provides useful ideas about administering a questionnaire and processing the results. Also included is a discussion about data analysis with attention to constructing and understanding tables and writing a survey report. This book is detailed, informative, and technically oriented toward students at the intermediate or advanced level of survey research.

Campbell, D. T., & Stanley, J. C. (1963). Experimental and quasi-experimental designs for research. In N. L. Gage (Ed.), *Handbook of research on teaching* (pp. 1-76). Chicago: Rand-McNally.

This chapter in the Gage *Handbook* is the classical statement about experimental designs. Campbell and Stanley designed a notation system for experiments that is used today; they also advanced the types of experimental designs, beginning with factors that jeopardize internal and external validity, the pre-experimental design types, true experiments, quasi-experimental designs, and correlational and ex post facto designs. The chapter presents an excellent summary of types of designs, their threats to validity, and statistical procedures to test the designs. This is an essential chapter for students beginning their study of experimental studies.

Fink, A. (1995). *The survey handbook* (Vol. 1). Thousand Oaks, CA: Sage.

This is the first volume of a nine-volume set called "The Survey Kit," edited by Arlene Fink. As an introduction to the nine volumes, Fink discusses all aspects of survey research, including how to ask questions, how to conduct surveys, how to engage in telephone interviews, how to sample, and how to measure validity and reliability. Much of the discussion is oriented toward the beginning survey researcher, and the numerous examples and excellent illustrations make it a useful kit to learn the basics of survey research.

Fowler, F. J. (2002). *Survey research methods*. (3rd ed.). Thousand Oaks, CA: Sage.

Floyd Fowler provides a useful text about the decisions that go into the design of a survey research project. He addresses use of alternative sampling procedures, ways of reducing nonresponse rates, data collection, design of good questions, employing sound interviewing techniques, preparation of surveys for analysis, and ethical issues in survey designs.

Keppel, G. (1991). *Design and analysis: A researcher's handbook* (3rd ed.). Englewood Cliffs, NJ: Prentice-Hall.

Geoffrey Keppel provides a detailed, thorough treatment of the design of experiments from the principles of design to the statistical analysis of experimental data. Overall, this book is for the mid-level to advanced statistics student who seeks to understand the design and statistical analysis of experiments. The introductory chapter presents an informative overview of the components of experimental designs.

Lipsey, M. W. (1990). *Design sensitivity: Statistical power for experimental research*. Newbury Park, CA: Sage.

Mark Lipsey has authored a major book on the topics of experimental designs and statistical power of those designs. Its basic premise is that an experiment needs to have sufficient sensitivity to detect those effects it purports to investigate. The book explores statistical power and includes a table to help researchers identify the appropriate size of groups in an experiment.

Neuman, S. B., & McCormick, S. (Eds.). (1995). *Single-subject experimental research: Applications for literacy.* Newark, DE: International Reading Association.

Susan Neuman and Sandra McCormick have edited a useful, practical guide to the design of single-subject research. They present many examples of different types of designs, such as reversal designs and multiple-baseline designs, and they enumerate the statistical procedures that might be involved in analyzing the single-subject data. One chapter, for example, illustrates the conventions for displaying data on line graphs. Although this book cites many applications in literacy, it has broad application in the social and human sciences.

CHAPTER TEN

Qualitative Procedures

Qualitative procedures stand in stark contrast to the methods of quantitative research. Qualitative inquiry employs different knowledge claims, strategies of inquiry, and methods of data collection and analysis. Although the processes are similar, qualitative procedures rely on text and image data, have unique steps in data analysis, and draw on diverse strategies of inquiry.

In fact, the strategies of inquiry chosen in a qualitative project will have a dramatic influence on the procedures. These procedures, even within strategies, are anything but uniform. Looking over the landscape of qualitative procedures shows perspectives ranging from postmodern thinking (Denzin & Lincoln, 2000), to ideological perspectives (Lather, 1991), to philosophical stances (Schwandt, 2000), to systematic procedural guidelines (Creswell, 1998; Strauss & Corbin, 1998). All perspectives vie for center stage in this unfolding model of inquiry called "qualitative" research.

This chapter will attempt to strike a middle ground, provide general procedures, and use examples liberally to illustrate strategy variations. This discussion draws on thoughts provided by several authors writing about qualitative proposal design (e.g., see Berg, 2001; Marshall & Rossman, 1999; Maxwell, 1996; Rossman & Rallis, 1998). The topics in a proposal section on procedures are characteristics of qualitative research, the research strategy, the role of the researcher, steps in data collection and analysis, strategies for validity, the accuracy of findings, and narrative structure. Table 10.1 shows a checklist of questions for designing qualitative procedures.

THE CHARACTERISTICS OF QUALITATIVE RESEARCH

For many years, a proposal writer had to discuss the characteristics of qualitative research and convince faculty and audiences as to their

TABLE 10.1	A Checklist of Questions for Designing a Qualitative Procedure

_____	Are the basic characteristics of qualitative studies mentioned?
_____	Is the specific type of qualitative strategy of inquiry to be used in the study mentioned? Is the history of, a definition of, and applications for the strategy mentioned?
_____	Does the reader gain an understanding of the researcher's role in the study (past experiences, personal connections to sites and people, steps in gaining entry, and sensitive ethical issues)?
_____	Is the purposeful sampling strategy for sites and individuals identified?
_____	Are the specific forms of data collection mentioned and a rationale given for their use?
_____	Are the procedures for recording information (such as protocols) during the data collection procedure mentioned?
_____	Are the data analysis steps identified?
_____	Is there evidence that the researcher has organized the data for analysis?
_____	Has the researcher reviewed the data generally to obtain a sense of the information?
_____	Has coding been used with the data?
_____	Have the codes been developed to form a description or to identify themes?
_____	Are the themes interrelated to show a higher level of analysis and abstraction?
_____	Are the ways that the data will be represented—such as in tables, graphs, and figures—mentioned?
_____	Have the bases for interpreting the analysis (personal experiences, the literature, questions, action agenda) been specified?
_____	Has the researcher mentioned the outcome of the study? (develop a theory? provide a complex picture of themes?)
_____	Have multiple strategies been cited for validating the findings?

legitimacy. Now, there seems to be some consensus as to what constitutes qualitative inquiry and such a discussion is not needed (Flinders & Mills [1993], would dissent on this point). Thus, my suggestions about this section of a proposal are

● Review the needs of potential audiences for the proposal. Decide whether audience members are knowledgeable enough about the characteristics of qualitative research that this section is not necessary.

● If there is some question about their knowledge, present the basic characteristics of qualitative research in the proposal and possibly discuss a recent qualitative research journal article (or study) to use as an example to illustrate the characteristics.

● Several lists of characteristics might be used (e.g., Bogdan & Biklen, 1992; Eisner, 1991; Marshall & Rossman, 1999), but I like the characteristics advanced by Rossman and Rallis (1998) because they capture both traditional perspectives and the newer advocacy, participatory, and self-reflective perspectives of qualitative inquiry. Building on the thoughts of Rossman and Rallis (1998) are the characteristics I would recommend:

  – Qualitative research takes place in the natural setting. The qualitative researcher often goes to the site (home, office) of the participant to conduct the research. This enables the researcher to develop a level of detail about the individual or place and to be highly involved in actual experiences of the participants.

  – Qualitative research uses multiple methods that are interactive and humanistic. The methods of data collection are growing, and they increasingly involve active participation by participants and sensitivity to the participants in the study. Qualitative researchers look for involvement of their participants in data collection and seek to build rapport and credibility with the individuals in the study. They do not disturb the site any more than is necessary. In addition, the actual methods of data collection, traditionally based on open-ended observations, interviews, and documents, now include a vast array of materials, such as sounds, e-mails, scrapbooks, and other emerging forms (see the section on data collection later in this chapter). The data collected involve text (or word) data and images (or picture) data.

  – Qualitative research is emergent rather than tightly prefigured. Several aspects emerge during a qualitative study. The research questions may change and be refined as the inquirer learns what to ask and to whom it should be asked. The data collection process might change as doors open and close for data collection, and the inquirer learns the best sites at which to learn about the central phenomenon of interest. The theory or general pattern of understanding will emerge as it begins with initial codes, develops into broad themes, and coalesces into a grounded theory or broad interpretation. These aspects of an unfolding research model make it difficult to prefigure qualitative research tightly at the proposal or early research stage.

– Qualitative research is fundamentally interpretive. This means that the researcher makes an interpretation of the data. This includes developing a description of an individual or setting, analyzing data for themes or categories, and finally making an interpretation or drawing conclusions about its meaning personally and theoretically, stating the lessons learned, and offering further questions to be asked (Wolcott, 1994). It also means that the researcher filters the data through a personal lens that is situated in a specific sociopolitical and historical moment. One cannot escape the personal interpretation brought to qualitative data analysis.

– The qualitative researcher views social phenomena holistically. This explains why qualitative research studies appear as broad, panoramic views rather than micro-analyses. The more complex, interactive, and encompassing the narrative, the better the qualitative study. Visual models of many facets of a process or a central phenomenon aid in establishing this holistic picture (see, for example, Creswell & Brown, 1992).

– The qualitative researcher systematically reflects on who he or she is in the inquiry and is sensitive to his or her personal biography and how it shapes the study. This introspection and acknowledgment of biases, values, and interests (or *reflexivity*) typifies qualitative research today. The personal-self becomes inseparable from the researcher-self. It also represents honesty and openness to research, acknowledging that all inquiry is laden with values (Mertens, 2003). Procedurally, statements of personal reflection emerge in the "role of the researcher" section (see the discussion of this topic later in the chapter) or an epilogue (see Asmussen & Creswell, 1995), or are embedded throughout a proposal or a study.

– The qualitative researcher uses complex reasoning that is multi-faceted, iterative, and simultaneous. Although the reasoning is largely inductive, both inductive and deductive processes are at work. The thinking process is also iterative, with a cycling back and forth from data collection and analysis to problem reformulation and back. Added to this are the simultaneous activities of collecting, analyzing, and writing up data.

- The qualitative researcher adopts and uses one or more strategies of inquiry as a guide for the procedures in the qualitative study. For beginning researchers, it is enough to use only one strategy and to look in recent procedural books for guidance as to how to design a proposal and conduct the procedures of the strategy.

STRATEGIES OF INQUIRY

Beyond these general characteristics are more specific strategies of inquiry. These strategies focus on data collection, analysis, and writing, but they originate out of disciplines and flow throughout the process of research (e.g., types of problems, ethical issues of importance) (Creswell, 1998). Many strategies exist, such as the 28 approaches identified by Tesch (1990), the 19 types in Wolcott's tree (2001), and the 5 "traditions" of inquiry by Creswell (1998). As discussed in Chapter 1, I recommend now that qualitative researchers choose from among five possibilities, including narrative, phenomenology, ethnography, case study, and grounded theory. I have no authoritative basis for these five, but I do see them used frequently today, and they represent an encompassing focus from narrow to broad. For example, researchers might study individuals (narrative, phenomenology); explore processes, activities, and events (case study, grounded theory); or learn about broad culture-sharing behavior of individuals or groups (ethnography).

In writing a procedure for a qualitative proposal, the tasks listed below are recommended.

- Identify the specific strategy of inquiry that will be used
- Provide some background information about the strategy, such as its discipline origin, the applications of it, and a brief definition of it (see Chapter 1 for the five strategies of inquiry I illustrate)
- Discuss why it is an appropriate strategy to use in the proposed study
- Identify how the use of the strategy will shape the types of questions asked (see Morse, 1994, for questions that relate to strategies), the form of data collection, the steps of data analysis, and the final narrative.

THE RESEARCHER'S ROLE

As mentioned in the list of characteristics, qualitative research is interpretative research, with the inquirer typically involved in a sustained and intensive experience with participants. This introduces a range of strategic, ethical, and personal issues into the qualitative research process (Locke et al., 2000). With these concerns in mind, inquirers explicitly identify their biases, values, and personal interests about their research topic and process. Gaining entry to a research site and the ethical issues that might arise are also elements of the researcher's role.

● Include statements about past experiences that provide background data through which the audience can better understand the topic, the setting, or the participants.

● Comment on connections between the researcher and the participants and on the research sites. "Backyard" research (Glesne & Peshkin, 1992) involves studying the researcher's own organization, or friends, or immediate work setting. This often leads to compromises in the researcher's ability to disclose information and raises difficult power issues. Although data collection may be convenient and easy, the problems of reporting data that are biased, incomplete, or compromised are legend. If studying the "backyard" is necessary, employ multiple strategies of validity (as discussed later) to create reader confidence in the accuracy of the findings.

● Indicate steps taken to obtain permission from the Institutional Review Board (see Chapter 1) to protect the rights of human participants. Attach, as an appendix, the approval letter from the IRB and discuss the process involved in securing permission.

● Discuss steps taken to gain entry to the setting and to secure permission to study the informants or situation (Marshall & Rossman, 1999). It is important to gain access to research or archival sites by seeking the approval of "gatekeepers." A brief proposal might need to be developed and submitted for review by "gatekeepers." Bogdan and Biklen (1992) advance topics that could be addressed in such a proposal:

– Why was the site chosen for study?

– What activities will occur at the site during the research study?

– Will the study be disruptive?

- – How will the results be reported?

- – What will the "gatekeeper" gain from the study?

- Comment about sensitive ethical issues that may arise (see Chapter 1 of this volume and Berg, 2001). For each issue raised, discuss how the research study will address it. For example, when studying a sensitive topic, it is necessary to mask names of people, places, and activities. In this situation, the process for masking information requires discussion in the proposal.

DATA COLLECTION PROCEDURES

Comments about the role of the researcher set the stage for discussion of issues involved in collecting data. The data collection steps include setting the boundaries for the study, collecting information through unstructured (or semi-structured) observations and interviews, documents, and visual materials, as well as establishing the protocol for recording information.

- Identify the *purposefully selected* sites or individuals for the proposed study. The idea behind qualitative research is to *purposefully* select participants or sites (or documents or visual material) that will best help the researcher understand the problem and the research question. This does not necessarily suggest random sampling or selection of a large number of participants and sites, as typically found in *quantitative* research. A discussion about participants and site might include four aspects identified by Miles and Huberman (1994): the *setting* (where the research will take place), the *actors* (who will be observed or interviewed), the *events* (what the actors will be observed or interviewed doing), and the *process* (the evolving nature of events undertaken by the actors within the setting).

- Further, indicate the type or types of data to be collected. In many qualitative studies, inquirers collect multiple forms of data and spend a considerable time in the natural setting gathering information. The collection procedures in qualitative research involve four basic types, as shown in Table 10.2.

    1. *Observations*, in which the researcher takes fieldnotes on the behavior and activities of individuals at the research site. In these fieldnotes, the researcher records, in an unstructured or

TABLE 10.2 Qualitative Data Collection Types, Options, Advantages, and Limitations

Data Collection Types	Options Within Types	Advantages of the Type	Limitations of the Type
Observations	<ul><li>Complete participant: researcher conceals role</li><li>Observer as participant: role of researcher is known</li><li>Participant as observer: observation role secondary to participant role</li><li>Complete observer: researcher observes without participating</li></ul>	<ul><li>Researcher has a firsthand experience with participants</li><li>Researcher can record information as it is revealed</li><li>Unusual aspects can be noticed during observation</li><li>Useful in exploring topics that may be uncomfortable for participants to discuss</li></ul>	<ul><li>Researcher may be seen as intrusive</li><li>"Private" information may be observed that the researcher cannot report</li><li>Researcher may not have good attending and observing skills</li><li>Certain participants (e.g., children) may present special problems in gaining rapport</li></ul>
Interviews	<ul><li>Face-to-face: one on one, in-person interview</li><li>Telephone: researcher interviews by phone</li><li>Group: researcher interviews participants in a group</li></ul>	<ul><li>Useful when participants cannot be observed directly</li><li>Participants can provide historical information</li><li>Allows researcher "control" over the line of questioning</li></ul>	<ul><li>Provides "indirect" information filtered through the views of interviewees</li><li>Provides information in a designated "place" rather than the natural field setting</li><li>Researcher's presence may bias responses</li><li>People are not equally articulate and perceptive</li></ul>

	Examples	Advantages	Limitations
Documents	• Public documents such as minutes of meetings, and newspapers • Private documents such as journals, diaries, and letters • E-mail discussions	• Enables a researcher to obtain the language and words of participants • Can be accessed at a time convenient to the researcher—an unobtrusive source of information • Represents data that are thoughtful, in that participants have given attention to compiling • As written evidence, it saves a researcher the time and expense of transcribing	• May be protected information unavailable to public or private access • Requires the researcher to search out the information in hard-to-find places • Requires transcribing or optically scanning for computer entry • Materials may be incomplete • The documents may not be authentic or accurate
Audiovisual materials	• Photographs • Videotapes • Art objects • Computer software • Film	• May be an unobtrusive method of collecting data • Provides an opportunity for participants to directly share their "reality" • Creative in that it captures attention visually	• May be difficult to interpret • May not be accessible publicly or privately • The presence of an observer (e.g., photographer) may be disruptive and affect responses

NOTE: This table includes material taken from Merriam (1998), Bogdan and Biklen (1992), and Creswell (2002).

semistructured (using some prior questions that the inquirer wants to know) way, activities at the research site. The qualitative observer may also engage in roles varying from a nonparticipant to a complete participant.

2. In *interviews*, the researcher conducts face-to-face interviews with participants, interviews participants by telephone, or engages in focus group interviews with six to eight interviewees in each group. These interviews involve unstructured and generally open-ended questions that are few in number and intended to elicit views and opinions from the participants.

3. During the process of research, the qualitative investigator may collect *documents*. These may be public documents (e.g., newspapers, minutes of meetings, official reports) or private documents (e.g., personal journals and diaries, letters, e-mails).

4. A final category of qualitative data consists of *audio and visual material*. This data may take the form of photographs, art objects, videotapes, or any forms of sound.

● In a discussion about data collection forms, be specific about the types and include arguments concerning the strengths and weaknesses of each type, as discussed in Table 10.2.

● Include data collection types that go beyond typical observations and interviews. These unusual forms create reader interest in a proposal and can capture useful information that observations and interviews may miss. For example, examine the compendium of types of data in Table 10.3 that can be used to stretch the imagination about possibilities, such as gathering sounds or tastes, or using cherished items to elicit comments during an interview.

DATA RECORDING PROCEDURES

Before entering the field, qualitative researchers plan their approach to data recording. The proposal should identify what data the researcher will record and the procedures for recording data.

● Use an *observational protocol* for recording observational data. Researchers often engage in multiple observations during the course of a qualitative study and use a *protocol* or form for recording

TABLE 10.3 A List of Qualitative Data Collection Approaches

- Gather observational notes by conducting an observation as a participant
- Gather observational notes by conducting an observation as an observer
- Conduct an unstructured, open-ended interview and take interview notes
- Conduct an unstructured, open-ended interview, audiotape the interview, and transcribe the interview
- Keep a journal during the research study
- Have a participant keep a journal during the research study
- Optically scan newspaper accounts
- Collect personal letters from participants
- Analyze public documents (e.g., official memos, minutes, records, archival material)
- Examine autobiographies and biographies
- Have a participant write her or his autobiography
- Write your own (the researcher's) autobiography
- Have participants take photographs or videotapes (i.e., photo elicitation)
- Examine physical trace evidence (e.g., footprints in the snow)
- Videotape a social situation or an individual/group
- Examine photographs or videotapes
- Collect sounds (e.g., musical sounds, a child's laughter, car horns honking)
- Collect e-mail or electronic messages
- Examine possessions or ritual objects to elicit views during an interview
- Collect smells, tastes, or sensations through touch

NOTE: Adapted from Creswell (1998) and Creswell (2002).

information. This observational protocol may be a single page with a dividing line down the middle to separate *descriptive notes* (portraits of the participants, a reconstruction of dialogue, a description of the physical setting, accounts of particular events, or activities) from *reflective notes* (the researcher's personal thoughts, such as "speculation, feelings, problems, ideas, hunches, impressions, and prejudices") (Bogdan & Biklen, 1992, p. 121). Also written on this form might be *demographic information* about the time, place, and date of the field setting where the observation takes place.

- Use an *interview protocol* for recording information during a qualitative interview. This protocol includes the following components: a heading, instructions to the interviewer (opening statements), the key research questions, probes to follow key questions, transition messages for the interviewer, space for recording the interviewer's comments, and space in which the researcher records reflective notes.

- Researchers record information from interviews using handwritten notes, audiotaping, or videotaping. During the interview, the researcher should take notes in the event that recording equipment fails. Planning in advance whether a transcriptionist will be used is important.

- The recording of *documents and visual materials* can be based on the researcher's structure for taking notes. Typically, notes reflect information about the document or other material as well as key ideas in the documents. For documents, it is helpful to note whether the information represents primary material (i.e., information directly from the people or situation under study) or secondary material (i.e., secondhand accounts of the people or situation written by others).

DATA ANALYSIS AND INTERPRETATION

Discussion of the plan for analyzing the data might have several components. The process of data analysis involves making sense out of text and image data. It involves preparing the data for analysis, conducting different analyses, moving deeper and deeper into understanding the data, representing the data, and making an interpretation of the larger meaning of the data. Several generic processes might be stated in the proposal that convey a sense of the overall activities of qualitative data analysis, such as the following drawn from my own thoughts and those of Rossman and Rallis (1998):

- It is an ongoing process involving continual reflection about the data, asking analytic questions, and writing memos throughout the study. It is not sharply divided from the other activities in the process, such as collecting data or formulating research questions.

- It involves using open-ended data, for the most part. This requires asking general questions and developing an analysis from the information supplied by participants.

• Researchers need to tailor the data analysis beyond the more generic approaches to specific types of qualitative research strategies (see also Creswell, 1998). *Grounded theory*, for example, has systematic steps (Strauss & Corbin, 1990, 1998). These involve generating categories of information (open coding), selecting one of the categories and positioning it within a theoretical model (axial coding), and then explicating a story from the interconnection of these categories (selective coding). *Case study* and *ethographic research* involve a detailed description of the setting or individuals, followed by analysis of the data for themes or issues (see Stake, 1995; Wolcott, 1994). *Phenomenological research* uses the analysis of significant statements, the generation of meaning units, and the development of an "essence" description (Moustakas, 1994). *Narrative research* employs restorying the participants' stories using structural devices such as plot, setting, activities, climax, and denouement (Clandinin & Connelly, 2000). As these examples illustrate, the processes as well as the terms differ from one analytic strategy to another.

Despite these analytic differences depending on the type of design used, qualitative inquirers often convey a generic process of data analysis into a proposal. An ideal situation is to blend the generic steps with the specific research design steps. The generic steps involve the following steps:

Step 1   *Organize and prepare* the data for analysis. This involves transcribing interviews, optically scanning material, typing up fieldnotes, or sorting and arranging the data into different types depending on the sources of information.

Step 2   Read through all the data. A first general step is to obtain a *general sense* of the information and to reflect on its overall meaning. What general ideas are participants saying? What is the tone of the ideas? What is the general impression of the overall depth, credibility, and use of the information? Sometimes qualitative researchers write notes in margins or start recording general thoughts about the data at this stage.

> **Step 3**   Begin detailed analysis with a coding process. *Coding* is the process of organizing the material into "chunks" before bringing meaning to those "chunks" (Rossman & Rallis, 1998, p. 171). It involves taking text data or pictures, segmenting sentences (or paragraphs) or images into categories, and labeling those categories with a term, often a term based in the actual language of the participant (called an *in vivo* term).

Before proceeding to Step 4, consider some remarks that will provide detailed guidance for the coding process. Tesch (1990, pp. 142-145) provides a useful analysis of the process in eight steps:

1.   Get a sense of the whole. Read all the transcriptions carefully. Perhaps jot down some ideas as they come to mind.

2.   Pick one document (i.e., one interview)—the most interesting one, the shortest, the one on the top of the pile. Go through it, asking yourself "what is this about?" Do not think about the "substance" of the information but its underlying meaning. Write thoughts in the margin.

3.   When you have completed this task for several informants, make a list of all topics. Cluster together similar topics. Form these topics into columns that might be arrayed as major topics, unique topics, and leftovers.

4.   Now take this list and go back to your data. Abbreviate the topics as codes and write the codes next to the appropriate segments of the text. Try this preliminary organizing scheme to see if new categories and codes emerge.

5.   Find the most descriptive wording for your topics and turn them into categories. Look for ways of reducing your total list of categories by grouping topics that relate to each other. Perhaps draw lines between your categories to show interrelationships.

6.   Make a final decision on the abbreviation for each category and alphabetize these codes.

7.   Assemble the data material belonging to each category in one place and perform a preliminary analysis.

8.   If necessary, recode your existing data.

These eight steps engage a researcher in a systematic process of analyzing textual data. Variations exist in this process. For example, some researchers have found it useful to color code different categories on transcripts or cut text segments and place them on notecards.

I encourage qualitative researchers to analyze their data for material that can yield codes that address topics that readers would expect to find, codes that are surprising, and codes that address a larger theoretical perspective in the research. Bogdan and Biklen (1992, pp. 166-172) have their own list of possible types of codes:

● Setting and context codes

● Perspectives held by subjects

● Subjects' ways of thinking about people and objects

● Process codes

● Activity codes

● Strategy codes

● Relationship and social structure codes

● Preassigned coding schemes

One further note about coding: the process can be enhanced by the use of computer qualitative software programs. These programs are now widely available (see www.sagepub.com for software products), and they are useful when the qualitative database is large (e.g., more than 500 pages of transcription) and when the researcher wants to quickly locate useful quotations and multiple perspectives on a category or theme. As with any software program, qualitative software programs require time and skill to learn and employ effectively, although books for learning the programs are widely available (e.g., Weitzman & Miles, 1995).

Step 4   Use the coding process to generate a description of the setting or people as well as categories or themes for analysis. *Description* involves a detailed rendering of information about people, places, or events in a setting. Researchers can generate codes for this description. This analysis is useful in designing detailed descriptions for case studies, ethnographies, and narrative research projects. Then, use the coding to generate a small number of *themes* or categories, perhaps five to seven categories for a research study. These themes are the ones that appear as major findings in qualitative studies and are stated under separate headings in the findings sections of studies. They should display multiple perspectives from individuals and be supported by diverse quotations and specific evidence.

Beyond identifying the themes during the coding process, qualitative researchers can do much with them to build additional layers of complex analysis. For example, researchers interconnect themes into a storyline (as in narratives) or develop them into a theoretical model (as in grounded theory). Themes are analyzed for each individual case and across different cases (as in case studies), or shaped into a general description (as in phenomenology). Sophisticated qualitative studies go beyond description and theme identification and into complex theme connections.

Step 5   Advance how the description and themes will be *represented* in the qualitative narrative. The most popular approach is to use a narrative passage to convey the findings of the analysis. This might be a discussion that mentions a chronology of events, the detailed discussion of several themes (complete with sub-themes, specific illustrations, multiple perspectives from individuals, and quotations), or a discussion with interconnecting themes. Many qualitative researchers also use visuals, figures, or tables as adjuncts to the discussions. They present a process model (as in grounded theory), they advance a drawing of the specific research site (as in ethnography), or they convey descriptive information about each participant in a table (as in case studies and ethnographies).

Step 6   A final step in data analysis involves making an *interpretation* or meaning of the data. "What were the lessons learned" captures the essence of this idea (Lincoln & Guba, 1985). These lessons could be the researcher's personal interpretation, couched in the individual understanding that the inquirer brings to the study from her or his own culture, history, and experiences. It could also be a meaning derived from a comparison of the findings with information gleaned from the literature or extant theories. In this way, authors suggest that the findings confirm past information or diverge from it. It can also suggest new questions that need to be asked—questions raised by the data and analysis that the inquirer had not foreseen earlier in the study. One way ethnographers can end a study, says Wolcott (1994), is to ask further questions. The questioning approach is also used in advocacy and participatory approaches to qualitative research. Moreover, when qualitative researchers use a theoretical lens, they can form interpretations that call for action agendas for reform and change. Thus, interpretation in qualitative research can take many forms, be adapted for different types of designs, and be flexible to convey personal, research-based, and action meanings.

VALIDATING THE ACCURACY OF FINDINGS

Although validation of findings occurs throughout the steps in the process of research, this discussion singles it out in order to emphasize its importance. Proposal developers need to convey the steps they will take in their studies to check for the accuracy and credibility of their findings.

Validity does not carry the same connotations as it does in quantitative research, nor is it a companion of reliability (examining stability or consistency of responses, as discussed in Chapter 9) or generalizability (the external validity of applying results to new settings, people, or samples, also as discussed in Chapter 9). In a limited way, qualitative researchers can use reliability to check for consistent patterns of theme development among several investigators on a team. They can also generalize some facets of multiple case analysis (Yin, 1989) to other cases. Overall, however, reliability and generalizability play a minor role in qualitative inquiry.

Validity, on the other hand, is seen as a strength of qualitative research, but it is used to suggest determining whether the findings are accurate from the standpoint of the researcher, the participant, or the readers of an account (Creswell & Miller, 2000). Terms abound in the qualitative literature that speak to this idea, terms such as "trustworthiness," "authenticity," and "credibility" (Creswell & Miller, 2000), and it is a highly debated topic (Lincoln & Guba, 2000).

A procedural perspective that I recommend for research proposals is to identify and discuss one or more strategies available to check the accuracy of the findings. There are eight primary strategies, organized from those most frequently used and easy to implement to those occasionally used and difficult to implement:

- *Triangulate* different data sources of information by examining evidence from the sources and using it to build a coherent justification for themes.

- Use *member-checking* to determine the accuracy of the qualitative findings through taking the final report or specific descriptions or themes back to participants and determining whether these participants feel that they are accurate.

- Use *rich, thick description* to convey the findings. This may transport readers to the setting and give the discussion an element of shared experiences.

- Clarify the *bias* the researcher brings to the study. This self-reflection creates an open and honest narrative that will resonate well with readers.

- Also present *negative* or *discrepant information* that runs counter to the themes. Because real life is composed of different perspectives that do not always coalesce, discussing contrary information adds to the credibility of an account for a reader.

- Spend *prolonged time* in the field. In this way, the researcher develops an in-depth understanding of the phenomenon under study and can convey detail about the site and the people that lends credibility to the narrative account.

- Use *peer debriefing* to enhance the accuracy of the account. This process involves locating a person (a peer debriefer) who reviews and asks questions about the qualitative study so that the account will resonate with people other than the researcher.

- Use an *external auditor* to review the entire project. As distinct from a peer debriefer, this auditor is new to the researcher and the project and can provide an assessment of the project throughout the process of research or at the conclusion of the study. The role is similar to that of a fiscal auditor, and specific questions exist that auditors might ask (Lincoln & Guba, 1985).

THE QUALITATIVE NARRATIVE

A plan for a qualitative procedure should end with some comments about the narrative that emerges from the data analysis. Numerous varieties of narratives exist, and examples from scholarly journals will illustrate models. In a plan for a study, consider advancing several points about the narrative.

First, indicate the forms to be used in the narrative. These might be an objective account, fieldwork experiences (Van Maanen, 1988), a chronology, a process model, an extended story, an analysis by cases or across cases, or a detailed descriptive portrait (Creswell, 1998).

At the specific level, the conventions might be

- Varying the use of long, short, and text-embedded quotations

- Scripting conversation and stating the conversation in different languages to reflect cultural sensitivity

- Presenting text information in tabular form (e.g., matrices)

- Using the wording from participants

- Intertwining quotations with (the author's) interpretations

- Using indents or other special formatting of the manuscript to call attention to quotations from participants

- Using the first person "I" or collective "we" in the narrative form

- Using metaphors (see, for example, Richardson, 1990, who discusses some of these forms)

- Use the narrative approach typically used within a qualitative strategy of inquiry (e.g., description in case studies and ethnographies, a detailed story in narrative research). Also, describe how the narrative outcome will be compared with theories and the general literature on the topic. In many qualitative articles, researchers discuss the literature at the end of the study (see the discussion in Chapter 2)

Example 10.1   *Qualitative Procedures*

The following is an example of a qualitative procedure written as part of a doctoral proposal (D. Miller, 1992). Miller's project was an ethnographic study of first-year experiences of the president of a 4-year college. As I present this discussion, I will refer back to the sections addressed in this chapter and highlight them in boldfaced type. Also, I have maintained Miller's use of the term *informant*, although today, the more appropriate term, *participant*, should be used.

The Qualitative Research Paradigm

The qualitative research paradigm has its roots in cultural anthropology and American sociology (Kirk & Miller, 1986). It has only recently been adopted by educational researchers (Borg & Gall, 1989). The intent of qualitative research is to understand a particular social situation, event, role, group, or interaction (Locke, Spirduso, & Silverman, 1987). It is largely an investigative process where the researcher gradually makes sense of a social phenomenon by contrasting, comparing, replicating, cataloguing and classifying the object of study (Miles & Huberman, 1984). Marshall and Rossman (1989) suggest that this entails immersion in the everyday life of the setting chosen for the study; the researcher enters the informants' world and through ongoing interaction, seeks the informants' perspectives and meanings. **(Qualitative assumptions are mentioned.)**

Scholars contend that qualitative research can be distinguished from quantitative methodology by numerous unique characteristics that are inherent in the design. The following is a synthesis of commonly articulated assumptions regarding characteristics presented by various researchers.

1. Qualitative research occurs in natural settings, where human behavior and events occur.
2. Qualitative research is based on assumptions that are very different from quantitative designs. Theory or hypotheses are not established *a priori*.
3. The researcher is the primary instrument in data collection rather than some inanimate mechanism (Eisner, 1991; Frankel & Wallen, 1990; Lincoln & Guba, 1985; Merriam, 1988).

4. The data that emerge from a qualitative study are descriptive. That is, data are reported in words (primarily the participant's words) or pictures, rather than in numbers (Fraenkel & Wallen, 1990; Locke et al., 1987; Marshall & Rossman, 1989; Merriam, 1988).

5. The focus of qualitative research is on participants' perceptions and experiences, and the way they make sense of their lives (Fraenkel & Wallen, 1990; Locke et al., 1987; Merriam, 1988). The attempt is therefore to understand not one, but multiple realities (Lincoln & Guba, 1985).

6. Qualitative research focuses on the process that is occurring as well as the product or outcome. Researchers are particularly interested in understanding how things occur (Fraenkel & Wallen, 1990; Merriam, 1988).

7. Idiographic interpretation is utilized. In other words, attention is paid to particulars; and data is interpreted in regard to the particulars of a case rather than generalizations.

8. Qualitative research is an emergent design in its negotiated outcomes. Meanings and interpretations are negotiated with human data sources because it is the subjects' realities that the researcher attempts to reconstruct (Lincoln & Guba, 1985; Merriam, 1988).

9. This research tradition relies on the utilization of tacit knowledge (intuitive and felt knowledge) because often the nuances of the multiple realities can be appreciated most in this way (Lincoln & Guba, 1985). Therefore, data are not quantifiable in the traditional sense of the word.

10. Objectivity and truthfulness are critical to both research traditions. However, the criteria for judging a qualitative study differs from quantitative research. First and foremost, the researcher seeks believability, based on coherence, insight and instrumental utility (Eisner, 1991) and trustworthiness (Lincoln & Guba, 1985) through a process of verification rather than through traditional validity and reliability measures. **(Qualitative characteristics are mentioned.)**

The Ethnographic Research Design

This study will utilize the ethnographic research tradition. This design emerged from the field of anthropology, primarily from the contributions of Bronislaw Malinowski, Robert Park and Franz Boas (Jacob, 1987; Kirk & Miller, 1986). The intent of ethnographic research is to obtain a holistic picture of the subject of study with emphasis on portraying the everyday experiences of individuals by observing and interviewing them and relevant others (Fraenkel & Wallen, 1990). The ethnographic study includes in-depth interviewing and continual and ongoing participant observation of a situation (Jacob, 1987) and in attempting to capture the whole picture reveals how people describe and structure their world (Fraenkel & Wallen, 1990). **(The author used the ethnographic approach.)**

The Researcher's Role

Particularly in qualitative research, the role of the researcher as the primary data collection instrument necessitates the identification of personal values, assumptions and biases at the outset of the study. The investigator's contribution to the research setting can be useful and positive rather than detrimental (Locke et al., 1987). My perceptions of higher education and the college presidency have been shaped by my personal experiences. From August 1980 to May 1990 I served as a college administrator on private campuses of 600 to 5,000. Most recently (1987-1990) I was Dean for Student Life at a small college in the Midwest. As a member of the President's cabinet, I was involved with all top level administrative cabinet activities and decisions and worked closely with the faculty, cabinet officers, president and board of trustees. In addition to reporting to the president, I worked with him through his first year in office. I believe this understanding of the context and role enhances my awareness, knowledge and sensitivity to many of the challenges, decisions and issues encountered as a first year president and will assist me in working with the informant in this study. I bring knowledge of both the structure of higher education and of the role the college presidency. Particular attention will be paid to the role of the new president in initiating change, relationship building, decision making, and providing leadership and vision.

Due to previous experiences working closely with a new college president, I bring certain biases to this study. Although every effort will be made to ensure objectivity, these biases may shape the way I view and understand the data I collect and the way I interpret my experiences. I commence this study with the perspective that the college presidency is a diverse and often difficult position. Though expectations are immense, I question how much power the president has to initiate change and provide leadership and vision. I view the first year as critical; filled with adjustments, frustrations, unanticipated surprises and challenges. **(Author reflected on her role in the study.)**

Bounding the Study

Setting

This study will be conducted on the campus of a state college in the Midwest. The college is situated in a rural Midwestern community. The institution's 1,700 students nearly triple the town's population of 1,000 when classes are in session. The institution awards associate, bachelor and master's degrees in 51 majors.

Actors

The informant in this study is the new President of a state college in the Midwest. The primary informant in this study is the President. However, I will be observing him in the context of administrative cabinet meetings. The president's cabinet includes three Vice Presidents (Academic Affairs, Administration, Student Affairs) and two Deans (Graduate Studies and Continuing Education).

Events

Using ethnographic research methodology, the focus of this study will be the everyday experiences and events of the new college president, and the perceptions and meaning attached to those experiences as expressed by the informant. This includes the assimilation of surprising events or information, and making sense of critical events and issues that arise.

Processes

Particular attention will be paid to the role of the new president in initiating change, relationship building, decision making, and providing leadership and vision. **(Author mentioned data collection boundaries.)**

Ethical Considerations

Most authors who discuss qualitative research design address the importance of ethical considerations (Locke et al., 1982; Marshall & Rossman, 1989; Merriam, 1988; Spradley, 1980). First and foremost, the researcher has an obligation to respect the rights, needs, values, and desires of the informant(s). To an extent, ethnographic research is always obtrusive. Participant observation invades the life of the informant (Spradley, 1980) and sensitive information is frequently revealed. This is of particular concern in this study where the informant's position and institution are highly visible. The following safeguards will be employed to protect the informant's rights: 1) the research objectives will be articulated verbally and in writing so that they are clearly understood by the informant (including a description of how data will be used), 2) written per-mission to proceed with the study as articulated will be received from the informant, 3) a research exemption form will be filed with the Institutional Review Board (Appendixes B1 and B2), 4) the infor-mant will be informed of all data collection devices and activities, 5) verbatim transcriptions and written interpretations and reports will be made available to the informant, 6) the informant's rights, interests and wishes will be considered first when choices are made regarding reporting the data, and 7) the final decision regarding informant anonymity will rest with the informant. **(Author addressed ethical issues and IRB review.)**

Data Collection Strategies

Data will be collected from February through May, 1992. This will include a minimum of bi-monthly, 45 minute recorded interviews with the informant (initial interview questions, Appendix C), bi-monthly two hour observations of administrative cabinet meetings, bi-monthly two hour observations of daily activities and bi-monthly analysis of the president's calendar and documents (meeting minutes, memos, publications). In addition, the informant has agreed to record impressions of his experiences, thoughts and feel-ings in a taped diary (guidelines for recorded reflection, Appendix D). Two follow-up interviews will be scheduled for the end of May 1992 (See Appendix E for proposed timeline and activity schedule). **(The author proposed to use face-to-face interviews, participate as observer, and obtain private documents.)**

To assist in the data collection phase I will utilize a field log, pro-viding a detailed account of ways I plan to spend my time when I am on-site, and in the transcription and analysis phase (also com-paring this record to how time is actually spent). I intend to record details related to my observations in a field notebook and keep a field diary to chronicle my own thinking, feeling, experiences and perceptions throughout the research process. **(The author recorded descriptive and reflective information.)**

Data Analysis Procedures

Merriam (1988) and Marshall and Rossman (1989) contend that data collection and data analysis must be a simultaneous process in qualitative research. Schatzman and Strauss (1973) claim that qualitative data analysis primarily entails classifying things, persons, and events and the properties which characterize them. Typically throughout the data analysis process ethnographers index or code their data using as many categories as possible (Jacob, 1987). They seek to identify and describe patterns and themes from the perspective of the participant(s), then attempt to understand and explain these patterns and themes (Agar, 1980). During data analysis the data will be organized categorically and chronologically, reviewed repeatedly, and continually coded. A list of major ideas that surface will be chronicled (as suggested by Merriam, 1988). Taped interviews and the participant's taped diary will be transcribed verbatim. Field notes and diary entries will be regularly reviewed. **(Author described steps in data analysis.)**

In addition, the data analysis process will be aided by the use of a qualitative data analysis computer program called HyperQual. Raymond Padilla (Arizona State University) designed HyperQual in 1987 for use with the Macintosh computer. HyperQual utilizes HyperCard software and facilitates the recording and analysis of textual and graphic data. Special stacks are designated to hold and organize data. Using HyperQual the researcher can directly "enter field data, including interview data, observations, researcher's memos, and illustrations . . . (and) tag (or code) all or part of the source data so that chunks of data can be pulled out and then be reassembled in a new and illuminating configuration" (Padilla, 1989, pp. 69-70). Meaningful data chunks can be identified, retrieved, isolated, grouped and regrouped for analysis. Categories or code names can be entered initially or at a later date. Codes can be added, changed or deleted with HyperQual editor and text can be searched for key categories, themes, words or phrases. **(Author mentions the proposed use of computer software for data analysis.)**

Verification

In ensuring internal validity, the following strategies will be employed:

1. Triangulation of data—Data will be collected through multiple sources to include interviews, observations and document analysis;

2. Member checking—The informant will serve as a check throughout the analysis process. An ongoing dialogue regarding my interpretations of the informant's reality and meanings will ensure the truth value of the data;

3. Long terms and repeated observations at the research site—Regular and repeated observations of similar phenomena and settings will occur on-site over a four month period of time;

4. Peer examination—a doctoral student and graduate assistant in the Educational Psychology Department will serve as a peer examiner;

5. Participatory modes of research—The informant will be involved in most phases of this study, from the design of the project to checking interpretations and conclusions; and

6. Clarification of researcher bias—At the outset of this study researcher bias will be articulated in writing in the dissertation proposal under the heading, "The Researcher's Role."

The primary strategy utilized in this project to ensure external validity will be the provision of rich, thick, detailed descriptions so that anyone interested in transferability will have a solid framework for comparison (Merriam, 1988). Three techniques to ensure reliability will be employed in this study. First, the researcher will provide a detailed account of the focus of the study, the researcher's role, the informant's position and basis for selection, and the context from which data will be gathered (LeCompte & Goetz, 1984). Second, triangulation or multiple methods of data collection and analysis will be used, which strengthens reliability as well as internal validity (Merriam, 1988). Finally, data collection and analysis strategies will be reported in detail in order to provide a clear and accurate picture of the methods used in this study. All phases of this project will be subject to scrutiny by an external auditor who is experienced in qualitative research methods. **(Author identified strategies of validity to be used in the study.)**

Reporting the Findings

Lofland (1974) suggests that although data collection and analysis strategies are similar across qualitative methods, the way the findings are reported is diverse. Miles and Huberman (1984) address the importance of creating a data display and suggest that narrative text has been the most frequent form of display for qualitative data. This is a naturalistic study. Therefore, the results will be presented in descriptive, narrative form rather than as a scientific report. Thick description will be the vehicle for communicating a holistic picture of the experiences of a new college president. The final project will be a construction of the informant's experiences and the meanings he attaches to them. This will allow readers to vicariously experience the challenges he encounters and provide a lens through which readers can view the subject's world. **(Outcomes of the study were mentioned.)**

⊞ SUMMARY

This chapter explored the steps that go into developing and writing a qualitative procedure. Recognizing the variation that exists in qualitative studies, the chapter advances a general guideline for procedures. This guideline includes a discussion about the general characteristics of qualitative research if audiences are not familiar with this approach to research. These characteristics are that the research takes place in the natural setting, employs multiple methods of data collection, is emergent rather than prefigured, is based on the interpretations of the researcher, is viewed holistically, is reflective, uses both inductive and deductive reasoning processes, and employs a strategy of inquiry. The guideline recommends mentioning a strategy of inquiry, such as the study of individuals (narrative, phenomenology), the exploration of processes, activities and events (case study, grounded theory), or the examination of broad culture-sharing behavior of individuals or groups (ethnography). The choice of strategy needs to be presented and defended. Further, the proposal needs to address the role of the researcher: past experiences, personal connections to the site, steps to gain entry, and sensitive ethical issues. Discussion of data collection should include the purposeful sampling approach and the forms of data to be collected (i.e., observations, interviews, documents, audiovisual materials). It is useful to also indicate the types of data recording protocols that will be used. Data analysis is an ongoing process during research. It involves analyzing participant information, and researchers typically employ the analysis steps found within a specific strategy of inquiry. More generic steps include organizing and preparing the data, an initial reading through the information, coding the data, developing from the codes a description and thematic analysis, and representing the findings in tables, graphs, and figures. It also involves interpreting the data in the light of personal lessons learned, comparing the findings with past literature and theory, raising questions, and/or advancing an agenda for reform. The proposal should also contain a section on the expected outcomes for the study. Finally, an additional important step in planning a proposal is to mention the strategies that will be used to validate the accuracy of the findings.

WRITING EXERCISES

Writing Exercises

1. Write a plan for the procedure to be used in your qualitative study. After writing the plan, use Table 10.1 as a checklist to determine the comprehensiveness of your plan.

2. Develop a table that lists, in a column on the left, the steps you plan to take to analyze your data. In a column on the right, indicate the steps as they apply directly to your project, the research strategy you plan to use, and data that you have collected.

ADDITIONAL READINGS

Bogdan, R. C., & Biklen, S. K. (1992). *Qualitative research for education: An introduction to theory and methods*. Boston: Allyn and Bacon.

Robert Bogdan and Sari Biklen provide chapters on collecting qualitative data, analyzing it, and writing up the results. The chapter on collecting data details the procedures involved in compiling fieldnotes: their types, contents, and format. They suggest useful compositional techniques in writing research in another chapter. Examples of these techniques are the use of quotations, mixing analysis and examples, interpretations, and the use of multiple methods of presentations.

Marshall, C., & Rossman, G. B. (1999*). Designing qualitative research* **(3rd ed.). Thousand Oaks, CA: Sage.**

Catherine Marshall and Gretchen Rossman introduce the procedures for a qualitative proposal. In addition to addressing issues concerning sample selection, they enumerate the researcher's role, involving entry, reciprocity, personal biography, and ethics. Several additional chapters review both primary and secondary methods of data collection, as well as advancing the generic procedures in analyzing qualitative data. This book is an excellent introduction to qualitative research as well as to preparing a proposal.

Tesch, R. (1990). *Qualitative research: Analysis types and software tools***. New York: Falmer.**

Reneta Tesch has compiled a text on qualitative data analysis that spans broad topics such as the types of qualitative designs, the mechanics of coding textual data, and computer software programs available for textual analysis. Her chapter on "Types of Qualitative Research," complete with a graphic overview of 20 types of qualitative designs, presents four categories of qualitative designs—the characteristics of language, the discovery of regularities, the comprehension of meaning of text/action, and reflection. This is a highly detailed and comprehensible taxonomy of types. Her chapter on "Organizing Systems and How to Develop Them" provides a method for coding transcriptions. She also provides a useful discussion of qualitative software programs for textual data analysis.

CHAPTER ELEVEN

Mixed Methods Procedures

With the development and perceived legitimacy of both qualitative and quantitative research in the social and human sciences, mixed methods research, employing the data collection associated with both forms of data, is expanding. A new *Handbook of Mixed Methods in the Social and Behavior Sciences* (Tashakkori & Teddlie, 2003) and journals reporting and promoting mixed methods research (e.g., *Field Methods*) exist as outlets for discussions about mixed methods research. With increasing frequency, published articles are appearing in social and human science journals in such diverse fields as occupational therapy (Lysack & Krefting, 1994), interpersonal communication (Boneva, Kraut, & Frohlich, 2001), AIDS prevention (Janz et al.,1996), dementia caregiving (Weitzman & Levkoff, 2000), and middle school science (Houtz, 1995). Entire books now exist about procedures for conducting mixed methods studies—similar books were not available a decade ago (Greene & Caracelli, 1997; Newman & Benz, 1998; Reichardt & Rallis, 1994; Tashakkori & Teddlie, 1998).

These procedures developed in response to a need to clarify the intent of mixing quantitative and qualitative data in a single study (or a program of study). With the inclusion of multiple methods of data and multiple forms of analysis, the complexity of these designs calls for more explicit procedures. These procedures also developed in part to meet the need to help researchers create understandable designs out of complex data and analyses.

This chapter extends the prior discussion about the pragmatic knowledge claims, the strategies of inquiry, and the use of multiple methods introduced in Chapter 1. It also extends the discussion about a research problem that incorporates the need both to explore and to explain (Chapter 4). It follows a purpose statement and research questions focused on understanding a problem using both qualitative and quantitative methods and the rationale for using multiple forms of data collection and analysis (Chapters 5 and 6).

TABLE 11.1	A Checklist of Questions for Designing a Mixed Methods Procedure
_____	Is a basic definition of mixed methods research provided?
_____	Does the reader have a sense for the potential use of a mixed methods strategy?
_____	Are the criteria identified for choosing a mixed methods strategy?
_____	Is the strategy identified, and are its criteria for selection given?
_____	Is a visual model presented that illustrates the research strategy?
_____	Is the proper notation used in presenting the visual model?
_____	Are procedures of data collection and analysis mentioned as they relate to the model?
_____	Are the sampling strategies for both quantitative and qualitative data collection mentioned? Do they relate to the strategy?
_____	Are specific data analysis procedures indicated? Do they relate to the strategy?
_____	Are the procedures for validating both the quantitative and qualitative data discussed?
_____	Is the narrative structure mentioned, and does it relate to the type of mixed methods strategy being used?

COMPONENTS OF MIXED METHODS PROCEDURES

A checklist of questions for researchers to ask themselves when they design a mixed methods study appears in Table 11.1. These components call for advancing the nature of mixed methods research and the type of strategy being proposed for the study. They also include the need for a visual model of this approach, the specific procedures of data collection and analysis, the researcher's role, and the structure for presenting the final report. Following the discussion of each of these components, an example of a procedures section from a mixed methods study will be presented to apply the ideas.

THE NATURE OF MIXED METHODS RESEARCH

Because mixed methods research is relatively new in the social and human sciences as a distinct research approach, it is useful to convey, in a proposal, a basic definition and description of the approach. This might include the following:

- Trace a brief history of its evolution. Several sources identify its evolution in psychology and in the multitrait-multimethod matrix of Campbell and Fiske (1959) to interest in converging or triangulating different quantitative and qualitative data sources (Jick, 1979) and on to the expanded reasons and procedures for mixing methods (see Creswell, 2002; Tashakkori & Teddlie, 1998).

- Define mixed methods research by incorporating the definition in Chapter 1 that focuses on collecting and analyzing both quantitative and qualitative data in a single study. Highlight the reasons why researchers employ a mixed methods design (e.g., to expand an understanding from one method to another, to converge or confirm findings from different data sources). Also note that "mixing" might be within one study or among several studies in a program of inquiry. Recognize that many different terms are used for this approach, such as integrating, synthesis, quantitative and qualitative methods, multimethod, and multimethodology, but that recent writings use the term "mixed methods" (Tashakkori & Teddlie, 2003).

- Briefly discuss the growth of interest in mixed methods research as expressed in books, journal articles, diverse disciplines, and funded projects.

- Note the challenges this form of research poses for the inquirer. These include the need for extensive data collection, the time-intensive nature of analyzing both text and numeric data, and the requirement for the researcher to be familiar with both quantitative and qualitative forms of research.

TYPES OF MIXED METHODS STRATEGIES

Criteria for Choosing a Strategy

Proposal developers need to convey the specific strategy for data collection they plan to use. They also need to identify the criteria they employ for choosing this strategy. Recent authors have elaborated on the criteria that go into choosing a mixed methods aproach from the many available to use. Several criteria were identified by Morgan

Implementation	*Priority*	*Integration*	*Theoretical Perspective*
No Sequence Concurrent	Equal	At Data Collection	Explicit
Sequential—Qualitative first	Qualitative	At Data Analysis	
Sequential—Qualitative first	Quantitative	At Data Interpretation	Implicit
		With Some Combination	

Figure 11.1   Decision Choices for Determining a Mixed Methods Strategy of Inquiry

SOURCE: Creswell et al. (2003). Reprinted with permission from Sage Publications.

(1998), but others have added important standards that need to be considered (Greene & Caracelli, 1997; Tashakkori & Teddlie, 1998). A matrix, as shown in Figure 11.1, illustrates that four decisions go into selecting a mixed methods strategy of inquiry (see Creswell et al., 2003):

1. What is the implementation sequence of the quantitative and qualitative data collection in the proposed study?

2. What priority will be given to the quantitative and qualitative data collection and analysis?

3. At what stage in the research project will the quantitative and qualitative data and findings be integrated?

4. Will an overall theoretical perspective (e.g., gender, race/ ethnicity, lifestyle, class) be used in the study?

Implementation

Implementation means either that the researchers collect both the quantitative and qualitative data in phases (sequentially) or that they gather it at the same time (concurrently). When the data are collected in phases, either the qualitative or the quantitative data can come first.

It depends on the initial intent of the researcher. When qualitative data are collected first, the intent is to explore the topic with participants at sites. Then the researcher, in the second phase, expands the understanding through a second phase in which data are collected from a large number of people (typically representative). When data are collected concurrently, both quantitative and qualitative data are gathered at the same time in the project and the implementation is simultaneous.

Priority

A second factor that goes into the choice of a strategy is whether greater priority or weight is given to the quantitative or the qualitative approach, especially the use of quantitative data and analysis. The priority might be equal, or it might be skewed toward either qualitative or quantitative data. A priority for one type of data or the other depends on the interests of the researcher, the audience for the study (e.g., faculty committee, professional association), and what the investigator seeks to emphasize in the study. In practical terms, priority occurs in a mixed methods study through such strategies as whether quantitative or qualitative information is emphasized first in the study, the extent of treatment of one type of data or the other, and the use of a theory as an inductive or deductive framework for the study. In the first edition of this book, the terms "dominant" and "less-dominant" were used to express priority. Having a major form of data collection and analysis and a minor form is well suited for studies undertaken by graduate students.

Integration

Integration of the two types of data might occur at several stages in the process of research: the data collection, the data analysis, interpretation, or some combination of places. Integration means that the researcher "mixes" the data. For example, in data collection, this "mixing" might involve combining open-ended questions on a survey with closed-ended questions on the survey. Mixing at the stage of data analysis and interpretation might involve transforming qualitative themes or codes into quantitative numbers and comparing that information with quantitative results in an "interpretation" section of a study. The place in the process for integration seems related to whether phases (a sequence) or a single phase (concurrent) of data collection occurs.

Sequential Exploratory Design (11.2a)

Sequential Exploratory Design (11.2b)

Sequential Transformative Design (11.2c)

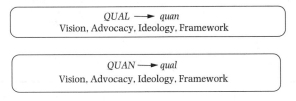

Figure 11.2   Sequential Strategies

A Theoretical Perspective

A final factor to consider is whether a larger, theoretical perspective guides the entire design. This perspective may be one from the social sciences or from an advocacy/participatory lens (e.g., gender, race, class). Although all designs have implicit theories (see Chapter 7), mixed methods researchers can make the theory explicit as a guiding framework for the study. This framework would operate regardless of the implementation, priority, and integrative features of the strategy of inquiry.

ALTERNATIVE STRATEGIES AND VISUAL MODELS

Mixed methods researchers can make decisions about these four factors to select a particular research strategy. Although the following discussion does not exhaust all the possibilities, the six major strategies identified below are choices for inquirers in a research proposal, adapted from the discussion by Creswell et al. (2003). A proposal would contain a description of the strategy and a visual model of it, as well as including

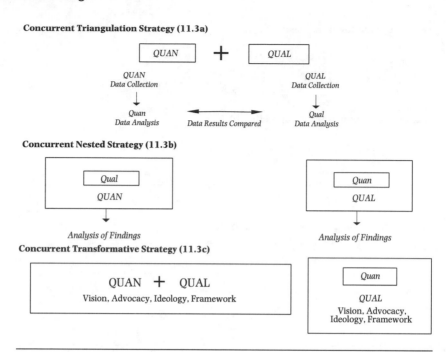

Figure 11.3 Concurrent Strategies

basic procedures that the investigator will use in implementing the strategy. Each strategy will be briefly described and illustrated in Figures 11.2 and 11.3 (see Creswell et al., 2003).

The notation in these figures is adapted from Morse (1991) and Tashakkori and Teddlie (1998), who suggested

● A "+" indicates a simultaneous or concurrent form of data collection.

● A "→" indicates a sequential form of data collection.

● Capitalization indicates an emphasis or priority on the quantitative or qualitative data and analysis in the study.

● "Quan" and "Qual" stand for quantitative and qualitative, respectively, and they use the same number of letters to indicate equality between the forms of data.

● Below each figure are specific data collection, analysis, and interpretation procedures to help the reader understand the more specific procedures used.

● Boxes highlight the quantitative and qualitative data collection.

Sequential Explanatory Strategy

The sequential explanatory strategy is the most straightforward of the six major mixed methods approaches. It is characterized by the collection and analysis of quantitative data followed by the collection and analysis of qualitative data. The priority typically is given to the quantitative data, and the two methods are integrated during the interpretation phase of the study. The steps of this strategy are pictured in Figure 11.2a. This strategy may or may not have a specific theoretical perspective. The purpose of the sequential explanatory design typically is to use qualitative results to assist in explaining and interpreting the findings of a primarily quantitative study. It can be especially useful when unexpected results arise from a quantitative study (Morse, 1991). In this case, the qualitative data collection that follows can be used to examine these surprising results in more detail. The straightforward nature of this design is one of its main strengths. It is easy to implement because the steps fall into clear, separate stages. In addition, this design feature makes it easy to describe and to report. The main weakness of this design is the length of time involved in data collection, with the two separate phases. This is especially a drawback if the two phases are given equal priority.

Sequential Exploratory Strategy

The sequential exploratory strategy has many features similar to the sequential explanatory strategy. It is conducted in two phases, with the priority generally given to the first phase, and it may or may not be implemented within a prescribed theoretical perspective (see Figure 11.2b). In contrast to the sequential explanatory approach, this model is characterized by an initial phase of qualitative data collection and analysis, which is followed by a phase of quantitative data collection and analysis. Therefore, the priority is given to the qualitative aspect of the study. The findings of these two phases are then integrated during the interpretation phase.

At the most basic level, the purpose of this strategy is to use quantitative data and results to assist in the interpretation of qualitative findings. Unlike the sequential explanatory approach, which is better suited to explaining and interpreting relationships, the primary focus of this model is to explore a phenomenon. Morgan (1998) suggested that this design is appropriate to use when testing elements of an emergent theory resulting from the qualitative phase and that it can also be used to generalize qualitative findings to different samples. Similarly, Morse (1991) cited one purpose for selecting this approach: to determine the distribution of a phenomenon within a chosen population. Finally, the sequential exploratory strategy is often discussed as the model used when a researcher develops and tests an instrument (e.g., see Creswell, 1999).

The sequential exploratory strategy has many of the same advantages as the sequential explanatory model. Its two-phase approach makes it easy to implement and straightforward to describe and report. It is useful to a researcher who wants to explore a phenomenon but also wants to expand on the qualitative findings. This model is especially advantageous when a researcher is building a new instrument. In addition, this model could make a largely qualitative study more palatable to a quantitative adviser, committee, or research community that may be unfamiliar with the naturalistic tradition. As with the sequential explanatory approach, the sequential exploratory model requires a substantial length of time to complete both data collection phases, which can be a drawback for some research situations. In addition, the researcher may find it difficult to build from the qualitative analysis to the subsequent quantitative data collection.

Sequential Transformative Strategy

As did the previously described sequential model, the transformative sequential strategy has two distinct data collection phases, one following the other (see Figure 11.2c). However, in this design either method may be used first, and the priority can be given to either the quantitative or the qualitative phase, or even to both if sufficient resources are available. In addition, the results of the two phases are integrated during the interpretation phase. Unlike the sequential exploratory and explanatory approaches, the sequential transformative model has a theoretical perspective to guide the study. The aim of this theoretical perspective, whether it be a conceptual framework, a specific ideology, or advocacy, is more important in guiding the study than the use of methods alone.

The purpose of a sequential transformative strategy is to employ the methods that will best serve the theoretical perspective of the researcher. By using two phases, a sequential transformative researcher may be able to give voice to diverse perspectives, to better advocate for participants, or to better understand a phenomenon or process that is changing as a result of being studied.

The sequential transformative model shares the methodological strengths and weaknesses of the other two sequential mixed methods approaches. Its use of distinct phases facilitates its implementation, description, and sharing of results, although it also requires the time to complete two data collection phases. More important, this design places mixed methods research within a transformative framework. Therefore, this strategy may be more appealing and acceptable to those researchers already using a transformative framework within one distinct methodology, such as qualitative research. Unfortunately, because little has been written to date on this approach, one weakness is that there is little guidance on how to use the transformative vision to guide the methods. Likewise, it may be unclear how to move between the analysis of the first phase into the data collection of the second phase.

Concurrent Triangulation Strategy

The concurrent triangulation approach is probably the most familiar of the six major mixed methods models (see Figure 11.3a). It is selected as the model when a researcher uses two different methods in an attempt to confirm, cross-validate, or corroborate findings within a single study (Greene et al., 1989; Morgan, 1998; Steckler, McLeroy, Goodman, Bird, & McCormick, 1992). This model generally uses separate quantitative and qualitative methods as a means to offset the weaknesses inherent within one method with the strengths of the other method. In this case, the quantitative and qualitative data collection is concurrent, happening in one phase of the research study. Ideally, the priority would be equal between the two methods, but in practical application the priority may be given to either the quantitative or the qualitative approach. This strategy usually integrates the results of the two methods during the interpretation phase. This interpretation can either note the convergence of the findings as a way to strengthen the knowledge claims of the study or explain any lack of convergence that may result.

This traditional mixed methods model is advantageous because it is familiar to most researchers and can result in well-validated and substantiated findings. In addition, the concurrent data collection results in a shorter data collection time period as compared to one of the sequential approaches.

This model also has a number of limitations. It requires great effort and expertise to adequately study a phenomenon with two separate methods. It also can be difficult to compare the results of two analyses using data of different forms. In addition, a researcher may be unclear how to resolve discrepancies that arise in the results.

Concurrent Nested Strategy

Like the concurrent triangulation approach, the concurrent nested model can be identified by its use of one data collection phase, during which both quantitative and qualitative data are collected simultaneously (see Figure 11.3b). Unlike the traditional triangulation model, a nested approach has a predominant method that guides the project. Given less priority, the method (quantitative or qualitative) is embedded, or nested, within the predominant method (qualitative or quantitative). This nesting may mean that the embedded method addresses a different *question* than the dominant method or seeks information from different *levels* (the analogy to hierarchical analysis in quantitative research is helpful in conceptualizing these levels—see Tashakkori and Teddlie, 1998). The data collected from the two methods are mixed during the analysis phase of the project. This strategy may or may not have a guiding theoretical perspective.

The concurrent nested model may be used to serve a variety of purposes. Often, this model is used so that a researcher can gain broader perspectives as a result of using the different methods as opposed to using the predominant method alone. For example, Morse (1991) noted that a primarily qualitative design could embed some quantitative data to enrich the description of the sample participants. Likewise, she described how qualitative data could be used to describe an aspect of a quantitative study that cannot be quantified. In addition, a concurrent nested model may be employed when a researcher chooses to utilize different methods to study different groups or levels. For example, if an organization is being studied, then employees could be studied quantitatively, managers could be interviewed qualitatively, entire divisions could be analyzed with quantitative data, and so forth. Tashakkori and Teddlie (1998) described this approach as a multilevel design. Finally, one method could be used within a framework of the other method, such as if a researcher designed and conducted an experiment but used case study methodology to study each of the treatment conditions.

This mixed methods model has many strengths. A researcher is able to collect the two types of data simultaneously, during a single data collection phase. It provides a study with the advantages of both quantitative and qualitative data. In addition, by using the two different methods in this fashion, a researcher can gain perspectives from the different types of data or from different levels within the study.

There are also limitations to consider when choosing this approach. The data need to be transformed in some way so that they can be integrated within the analysis phase of the research. There is little written at this time to guide a researcher through this process. In addition, there is little advice to be found for how a researcher should resolve discrepancies that occur between the two types of data. Because the two methods are unequal in their priority, this approach also results in unequal evidence within a study, which may be a disadvantage when interpreting the final results.

Concurrent Transformative Strategy

As with the sequential transformative model, the concurrent transformative approach is guided by the researcher's use of a specific theoretical perspective (see Figure 11.3c). This perspective can be based on ideologies such as critical theory, advocacy, participatory research, or a conceptual or theoretical framework. This perspective is reflected in the purpose or research questions of the study. It is the driving force behind all methodological choices, such as defining the problem, identifying the design and data sources, analyzing, interpreting, and reporting results throughout the research process. The choice of a concurrent model (whether it is triangulation or nested design) is made to facilitate this perspective. For example, the design may nested so that diverse participants are given a voice in the change process of an organization that is studied primarily quantitatively. It may involve a triangulation of quantitative and qualitative data to best converge information to provide evidence for an inequality of policies in an organization.

Thus, the concurrent transformative model may take on the design features of either a triangulation or a nested approach. That is, the two types of data are collected at the same time during one data collection phase and may have equal or unequal priority. The integration of these different data would most often occur during the analysis phase, although integration during the interpretation phase is a possible variation. Because the concurrent transformative model shares features with the triangulation and nested approaches, it also shares their specific strengths and weaknesses. However, this model has the added advantage of positioning mixed methods research within a transformative framework, which may make it especially appealing to those qualitative or quantitative researchers already using a transformative framework to guide their inquiry.

DATA COLLECTION PROCEDURES

Although the visual model and the discussion about the specific strategies provide a picture of the procedures, it is helpful in a proposal to discuss the specific types of data to be collected. It is also important to identify the sampling strategies and the approaches used to establish validity of the data.

● Identify and be specific about the type of data—both quantitative and qualitative—that will be collected during the proposed study. Refer to Table 1.3, which shows both quantitative and qualitative data. They differ in terms of open-ended versus closed-ended responses. Some forms of data, such as interviews and observations, can be either quantitative or qualitative. Although reducing information to numbers is the approach used in quantitative research, it is also used in qualitative research.

● Recognize that quantitative data often involve random sampling, so that each individual has an equal probability of being selected and the sample can be generalized to the larger population. In qualitative data collection, purposeful sampling is used so that individuals are selected because they have experienced the central phenomenon.

● Relate the procedures specifically to the visual model. For example, as shown in Figure 11.2a, in a sequential explanatory model, the general procedures below the figure can be detailed even further. For example, a discussion of this approach might include describing the use of survey data collection followed by both descriptive and inferential data analysis in the first phase. Then qualitative observations and coding and thematic analysis within an ethnographic design might be mentioned for the second phase.

DATA ANALYSIS AND VALIDATION PROCEDURES

Data analysis in mixed methods research relates to the type of research strategy chosen for the procedures. Thus, in a proposal, the procedures need to be identified within the design. However, analysis occurs both *within* the quantitative (descriptive and inferential numeric analysis) approach and the qualitative (description and thematic text or image analysis) approach, and often *between* the two approaches. For example, some of the more popular approaches are the following (see Caracelli & Greene, 1993; Tashakkori & Teddlie, 1998):

● *Data transformation:* In the concurrent strategies, a researcher may quantify the qualitative data. This involves creating codes and themes qualitatively, then counting the number of times they occur in the text data (or possibly the extent of talk about a code or theme by counting lines or sentences). This quantification of qualitative data then enables a researcher to compare quantitative results with the qualitative data. Alternatively, an inquirer may qualify quantitative data. For instance, in a factor analysis of data from a scale on an instrument, the researcher may create factors or themes that then can be compared with themes from the qualitative database.

● *Explore outliers:* In a sequential model, an analysis of quantitative data in the first phase can yield extreme or outlier cases. Follow-up qualitative interviews with these outlier cases can provide insight about why they diverged from the quantitative sample.

● *Instrument development:* In a sequential approach, obtain themes and specific statements from participants in an initial qualitative data collection. In the next phase, use these statements as specific items and the themes for scales to create a survey instrument that is grounded in the views of the participants. A third, final phase might be to validate the instrument with a large sample representative of a population.

● *Examine multiple levels:* In a concurrent nested model, conduct a survey at one level (e.g., with families) to gather quantitative results about a sample. At the same time, collect qualitative interviews (e.g., with individuals) to explore the phenomenon with specific individuals in families.

Another aspect of data analysis in mixed methods research to describe in a proposal is the series of steps taken to check the validity of both the quantitative data and the accuracy of the qualitative findings. Writers on mixed methods advocate for the use of validity procedures for both the quantitative and qualitative phases of the study (Tashakkori & Teddlie, 1998). The proposal writer discusses the validity and reliability of the scores from past uses of instruments employed in the study. In addition, potential threats to internal validity (see Chapter 9) for experiments and surveys are noted. For the qualitative data, the strategies that will be used to check the accuracy of the findings need to be mentioned. These may include triangulating data sources, member-checking, detailed description, or other approaches as noted in Chapter 10.

REPORT PRESENTATION STRUCTURE

The structure for the report, like the data analysis, follows the type of strategy chosen for the proposed study. Because mixed methods studies may not be familiar to audiences, it is helpful to provide some guidance as to how the final report will be structured.

- For a sequential study, mixed methods researchers typically organize the report of procedures into quantitative data collection and quantitative data analysis followed by qualitative data and collection and analysis. Then, in the conclusions or interpretation phase of the study, the researcher comments on how the qualitative findings helped to elaborate on or extend the quantitative results. Alternatively, the qualitative data collection and analysis could come first followed by the quantitative data collection and analysis. In either structure, the writer typically will present the project as two distinct phases, with separate headings for each phase.

- In a concurrent study, the quantitative and qualitative data collection may be presented in separate sections, but the analysis and interpretation combines the two forms of data to seek convergence among the results. The structure of this type of mixed methods study does not as clearly make a distinction between the quantitative and qualitative phases.

- In a transformative study, the structure typically involves advancing the advocacy issue in the beginning of the study and then using either the sequential or concurrent structure as a means of organizing the content of the study. In the end of the study, a separate section may advance an agenda for change or reform that has developed as a result of the research.

EXAMPLES OF MIXED METHODS PROCEDURES

The following are illustrations of mixed methods studies that use both the sequential and concurrent strategies and procedures.

Example 11.1   *A Sequential Strategy of Inquiry*

Kushman (1992) studied two types of teacher workplace commitment—organizational commitment and commitment to student learning—in 63 urban elementary and middle schools. He posed a two-phase
mixed methods study, as presented in the purpose statement:

> The central premise of this study was that organizational commit-
> ment and commitment to student learning address distinct but
> equally important teacher attitudes for an organizationally effec-
> tive school, an idea that has some support in the literature but
> requires further empirical validation. . . . Phase 1 was a quantitative
> study that looked at statistical relationships between teacher com-
> mitment and organizational antecedents and outcomes in ele-
> mentary and middle schools. Following this macrolevel analysis,
> Phase 2 looked within specific schools, using qualitative/case
> study methods to better understand the dynamics of teacher
> commitment. (Kushman, 1992, p. 13)

This purpose statement illustrates the combination of a purpose with
the *rationale* for mixing ("to better understand") as well as the specific
types of data collected during the study. The introduction focused on
the need to examine organizational commitment and commitment to
student learning leading to a *priority* for the quantitative approach. This
priority was further illustrated in sections defining organizational commitment and commitment to student learning and the use of extensive
literature to document these two concepts. A conceptual framework
then followed (complete with a visual model), and research questions
were posed to explore relationships. This provided a theoretical lead for
the quantitative phase of the study (Morse, 1991). The *implementation*
was QUAN → qual in this two-phase study. The author presented results
in two phases, with the first—the quantitative results—displaying and
discussing correlations, regressions, and two-way ANOVAs. Then the
case study results were presented in terms of themes and subthemes
supported by quotations. The *integration* of the quantitative results and
qualitative findings occurred in the final discussion, in which the
researcher highlighted the quantitative results and the complexities
that surfaced from the qualitative results. In addition, the author did not
use a *theoretical* perspective as a lens in the study.

Example 11.2   *A Concurrent Strategy of Inquiry*

In 1993, Hossler and Vesper conducted a study examining the factors associated with parental savings for children attending higher education campuses. Using longitudinal data collected from students and parents over a 3-year period, the authors examined factors most strongly associated with parental savings for postsecondary education. Their results found that parental support, educational expectations, and knowledge of college costs were important factors. Most important, for our purposes, the authors collected information from parents and students on 182 surveys and from 56 interviews. Their purpose indicated an interest in triangulating the findings:

> In an effort to shed light on parental saving, this article examines parental saving behaviors. Using student and parent data from a longitudinal study employing multiple surveys over a three-year period, logistic regression was used to identify the factors most strongly associated with parental saving for postsecondary education. In addition, insights gained from the interviews of a small subsample of students and parents who were interviewed five times during the three-year period are used to further examine parental savings. (p. 141)

The actual data collected was from 182 student and parent participants from surveys over a 4-year period of time and from 56 students and their parents in interviews. From the purpose statement, we can see that they collected data concurrently as an *implementation* strategy. Further, they provide extensive discussion of the quantitative analysis of the survey data, including a discussion about the measurement of variables and the details of the logistic regression data analysis. They also mention the limitations of the quantitative analysis and specific *t*-test and regression results. In contrast, they devote one page to the qualitative data analysis and note briefly the themes that occurred in the discussion. The *priority* in this mixed methods study was assigned to quantitative data collection and analysis, and the notation for the study would be: QUAN + qual. The *integration* of the two data sources occurred in a section titled "Discussion of Survey and Interview Results" (p. 155), at the interpretation stage of the research process. In this section, they compared the importance of the factors explaining parental savings for the quantitative results, on one hand, with the findings from the interview data on the other. Similar to Example 11.1, no *theoretical* lens guided the study, although the article began with the literature on econometric studies and research on college choice and ended with an "Augmented Model of Parental Savings." Thus, we might characterize the use of theory in this mixed methods study as inductive (as in qualitative inquiry), drawn from the literature (as in quantitative research), and ultimately as generated during the process of research.

▦ SUMMARY

In designing the procedures for a mixed methods study, begin by conveying the nature of mixed methods research. This includes tracing its history, defining it, and mentioning its applications in many fields of research. Then, state and employ four criteria to select an appropriate mixed methods strategy. Indicate the implementation strategy for data collection (concurrent or sequential). Also state the priority or weight given to the quantitative or qualitative approach in the study, such as equal weight, or a priority to quantitative or qualitative data. Mention the phase of research (e.g., data collection, analysis, interpretation) in which integration of the approaches will occur. Finally, identify whether a theoretical lens or framework will guide the study, such as a theory from the social sciences or a lens from an advocacy perspective (e.g., feminism, racial perspective). These four factors help in choosing the strategy to use.

Six strategies are organized around whether the data are collected sequentially (explanatory and exploratory), concurrently (triangulation and nested), or with a transformative lens (sequential or concurrent). Each model has strengths and weaknesses, although the sequential approach is the easiest to implement. A choice of strategy also can be presented in a figure in the research proposal. Then, specific procedures can be related to the figure to help the reader understand the flow of activities in a project. These procedures will include the types of quantitative and qualitative data to be collected as well as the procedures for data analysis. Typically, data analysis involves data transformation, exploring outliers, and examining multiple levels. Validity procedures also need to be explicitly described. The final written report, because it may be unfamiliar to audiences, can also be described in a proposal. Each of the three types of strategies—sequential, concurrent, and transformative—has a different structural approach to writing a mixed methods study.

Writing Exercises

1. Design a combined qualitative and quantitative study that employs two phases sequentially. Discuss and provide a rationale for why the phases are ordered in the sequence you propose.

2. Design a combined qualitative and quantitative study that gives *priority* to qualitative data collection and less priority to quantitative data collection. Discuss the approach to be taken in writing the introduction, the purpose statement, the research questions, and the specific forms of data collection.

3. Develop a visual figure and specific procedures that illustrate the use of a theoretical lens such as a feminist perspective in the research. Use the procedures of either a sequential or concurrent model for conducting the study. Use appropriate notation in the figure.

ADDITIONAL READINGS

Creswell, J. W. (1999). Mixed-method research: Introduction and application. In G. J. Cizek (Ed.), *Handbook of educational policy* (pp. 455-472). San Diego: Academic Press.

In this chapter, I present an overview of discussions about mixed methods research. This includes reviewing the terms for this type of research, including a brief history of mixed methods research, and advancing nine steps in the design of a study. As an aid to designing a mixed methods proposal, I present an early version of the format for design that was introduced in Chapter 3 of this book. I also include an example of a mixed methods study and illustrate how the authors engaged in the steps of mixed methods research.

Greene, J. C., Caracelli, V. J., & Graham, W. F. (1989). Toward a conceptual framework for mixed-method evaluation designs. *Educational Evaluation and Policy Analysis*, 11(3), 255-274.

Jennifer Greene and associates undertook a study of 57 mixed-methods evaluation studies reported from 1980 to 1988. From this analysis, they developed five different mixed methods purposes and seven design characteristics. They found the purposes of mixed methods studies to be based on seeking convergence (triangulation), on examining different facets of a phenomenon (complementarity), on using the methods sequentially (development), on discovering paradox and fresh perspectives (initiation), and on adding breadth and scope to a project (expansion). They also found that the studies varied in terms of the assumptions, strengths, and limitations of the method; whether they addressed different phenomena or the same phenomena; were implemented within the same or different paradigms; were given equal or different weight in the study; and were implemented independently, concurrently, or sequentially. Using the purposes and the design characteristics, the authors recommended several mixed methods designs.

Morse, J. M. (1991). Approaches to qualitative-quantitative methodological triangulation. *Nursing Research, 40*(l), 120-123.

Janice Morse suggests that using qualitative and quantitative methods to address the same research problem leads to issues of weighing each method and their sequence in a study. Based on these ideas, she then advances two forms of methodological triangulation: simultaneous, using both methods at the same time; and sequential, using the results of one method for planning the next method. Further, these two forms are described using a notation of capital and lowercase letters that signify the relative weight given to a method as well as sequence. The different approaches to triangulation are then discussed in the light of their purpose, limitations, and approaches.

Tashakkori, A., & Teddlie, C. (Eds.). (2003). *Handbook of mixed methods in the social and behavioral sciences*. Thousand Oaks, CA: Sage.

This new *Handbook*, edited by Abbas Tashakkori and Charles Teddlie, represents the most substantial effort to date to bring together the leading writers about mixed methods research. In 27 chapters, the *Handbook* introduces the reader to mixed methods, illustrates methodological and analytic issues in its use, identifies applications in the social and human sciences, and plots future directions. Separate chapters, for example, illustrate the use of mixed methods research in evaluation, management and organization, health sciences, nursing, psychology, sociology, and education.

References

Aikin, M. C. (Ed.). (1992). *Encyclopedia of educational research* (6th ed.). New York: Macmillan.

American Psychological Association. (1927-). *Psychological abstracts.* Washington, DC: Author.

American Psychological Association. (2001). *Publication manual of the American Psychological Association* (5th ed.). Washington, DC: Author.

Annual review of psychology. (1950-). Stanford, CA: Annual Reviews.

Ansorge, C., Creswell, J. W., Swidler, S., & Gutmann, M. (2001). *Use of Ibook laptop computers in teacher education.* Unpublished manuscript, University of Nebraska–Lincoln.

Asmussen, K. J., & Creswell, J. W. (1995). Campus response to a student gunman. *Journal of Higher Education, 66,* 575-591.

Babbie, E. (1990). *Survey research methods* (2nd ed.). Belmont, CA: Wadsworth.

Babbie, E. (2001). *The practice of social research* (9th ed.). Belmont, CA: Wadsworth/Thomson Learning.

Bailey, E. P. (1984). *Writing clearly: A contemporary approach.* Columbus, OH: Charles Merrill.

Bausell, R. B. (1994). *Conducting meaningful experiments.* Thousand Oaks, CA: Sage.

Bean, J., & Creswell, J. W. (1980). Student attrition among women at a liberal arts college. *Journal of College Student Personnel, 3,* 320-327.

Beisel, N. (1990, February). Class, culture, and campaigns against vice in three American cities, 1872-1892. *American Sociological Review, 55,* 44-62.

Bem, D. (1987). Writing the empirical journal article. In M. Zanna & J. Darley (Eds.), *The compleat academic: A practical guide for the beginning social scientist* (pp. 171-201). New York: Random House.

Berg, B. L. (2001). *Qualitative research methods for the social sciences* (4th ed.). Boston: Allyn and Bacon.

Berger, P. L., & Luckmann, T. (1967). *The social construction of reality: A treatise in the sociology of knowledge.* Garden City, NJ: Anchor Books.

Blalock, H. (1969). *Theory construction: From verbal to mathematical formulations.* Englewood Cliffs, NJ: Prentice-Hall.

Blalock, H. (1985). *Causal models in the social sciences.* New York: Aldine.

Blalock, H. (1991). Are there any constructive alternatives to causal modeling? *Sociological Methodology, 21,* 325-335.

Blase, J. J. (1989). The micropolitics of the school: The everyday political orientation of teachers toward open school principals. *Educational Administration Quarterly, 25*(4), 379-409.

Boeker, W. (1992). Power and managerial dismissal: Scapegoating at the top. *Administrative Science Quarterly, 37,* 400-421.

Bogdan, R. C., & Biklen, S. K. (1992). *Qualitative research for education: An introduction to theory and methods.* Boston: Allyn and Bacon.

Boice, R. (1990). *Professors as writers: A self-help guide to productive writing.* Stillwater, OK: New Forums.

Boneva, B., Kraut, R., & Frohlich, D. (2001). Using e-mail for personal relationships. *American Behavioral Scientist, 45*(3), 530-549.

Booth-Kewley, S., Edwards, J. E., & Rosenfeld, P. (1992). Impression management, social desirability, and computer administration of attitude questionnaires: Does the computer make a difference? *Journal of Applied Psychology, 77*(4), 562-566.

Borg, W. R., & Gall, M. D. (1989). *Educational research: An introduction* (5th ed.). New York: Longman.

Borg, W. R., Gall, J. P., & Gall, M. D. (1993). *Applying educational research: A practical guide.* New York: Longman.

Boruch, R. F. (1998). Randomized controlled experiments for evaluation and planning. In L. Bickman & D. J. Rog (Eds.), *Handbook of applied social research methods* (pp. 161-191). Thousand Oaks, CA: Sage.

Bunge, N. (1985). *Finding the words: Conversations with writers who teach.* Athens: Swallow Press, Ohio University Press.

Cahill, S. E. (1989). Fashioning males and females: Appearance management and the social reproduction of gender. *Symbolic Interaction, 12*(2), 281-298.

Campbell, D. T., & Fiske, D. (1959). Convergent and discriminant validation by the multitrait-multimethod matrix. *Psychological Bulletin, 56,* 81-105.

Campbell, D. T., & Stanley, J. C. (1963). Experimental and quasi-experimental designs for research. In N. L. Gage (Ed.), *Handbook of research on teaching* (pp. 1-76). Chicago: Rand-McNally.

Campbell, W. G., & Ballou, S. V. (1977). *Form and style: Theses, reports, term papers* (5th ed.). Boston: Houghton Mifflin.

Caracelli, V. J., & Greene, J. C. (1993). Data analysis strategies for mixed-method evaluation designs. *Educational Evaluation and Policy Analysis, 15*(2), 195-207.

Carroll, D. L. (1990). *A manual of writer's tricks.* New York: Paragon House.

Carstensen, L. W., Jr. (1989). A fractal analysis of cartographic generalization. *The American Cartographer, 16*(3), 181-189.

Castetter, W. B., & Heisler, R. S. (1977). *Developing and defending a dissertation proposal.* Philadelphia: Center for Field Studies, Graduate School of Education, University of Pennsylvania.

Cherryholmes, C. H. (1992, August-September). Notes on pragmatism and scientific realism. *Educational Researcher, 14,* 13-17.

Clandinin, D. J., & Connelly, F. M. (2000). *Narrative inquiry; Experience and story in qualitative research.* San Francisco: Jossey-Bass.

Cohen, J. (1977). *Statistical power analysis for the behavioral sciences.* New York: Academic Press.

Cook, T. D., & Campbell, D. T. (1979). *Quasi-experimentation: Design & analysis issues for field settings.* Chicago: Rand McNally College Publishing.

Cooper, H. (1984). *The integrative research review: A systematic approach.* Newbury Park, CA.: Sage.

Cooper, J. O., Heron, T. E., & Heward, W. L. (1987). *Applied behavior analysis.* Columbus, OH: Merrill.

Creswell, J. W. (1994). *Research design: Qualitative and quantitative approaches.* Thousand Oaks, CA: Sage.

Creswell, J. W. (1998). *Qualitative inquiry and research design: Choosing among five traditions.* Thousand Oaks, CA: Sage.

Creswell, J. W. (1999). Mixed-method research: Introduction and application. In G. J. Cizek (Ed.), *Handbook of educational policy* (pp. 455-472). San Diego: Academic Press.

Creswell, J. W. (2002). *Educational research: Planning, conducting, and evaluating quantitative and qualitative research.* Upper Saddle River, NJ: Merrill/Pearson.

Creswell, J. W., & Brown, M. L. (1992). How chairpersons enhance faculty research: A grounded theory study. *The Review of Higher Education, 16*(1), 41-62.

Creswell, J. W., & Miller, D. L. (2000). Determining validity in qualitative inquiry. *Theory into Practice, 39*(3), 124-130.

Creswell, J. W., Plano Clark, V., Gutmann, M., & Hanson, W. (2003). Advances in mixed method design. In A. Tashakkori & C. Teddlie (Eds.), *Handbook of mixed methods in the social and behavioral sciences.* Thousand Oaks, CA: Sage.

Creswell, J., Seagren, A., & Henry, T. (1979). Professional development training needs of department chairpersons: A test of the Biglan model. *Planning and Changing, 10,* 224-237.

Crotty, M. (1998). *The foundations of social research: Meaning and perspective in the research process.* London: Sage.

Crutchfield, J. P. (1986). *Locus of control, interpersonal trust, and scholarly productivity.* Unpublished doctoral dissertation, University of Nebraska–Lincoln.

DeGraw, D. G. (1984). *Job motivational factors of educators within adult correctional institutions from various states.* Unpublished doctoral dissertation, University of Nebraska.

Denzin, N. K., & Lincoln, Y. S. (Eds.). (2000). *The handbook of qualitative research* (2nd ed.). Thousand Oaks, CA: Sage.

Dillard, A. (1989). *The writing life.* New York: Harper & Row.

Dillman, D. A. (1978). *Mail and telephone surveys: The total design method.* New York: John Wiley & Sons.

Duncan, O. D. (1985). Path analysis: Sociological examples. In H. M. Blalock, Jr. (Ed.), *Causal models in the social sciences* (2nd ed., pp. 55-79). New York: Aldine.

Educational Resources Information Center. (1969-   ). *Current index to journals in education.* New York: Macmillan.

Educational Resources Information Center. (1975-   ). *Resources in education.* Washington, DC: U.S. Department of Health, Education, and Welfare.

Educational Resources Information Center. (1975). *Thesaurus of ERIC descriptors* (12th ed.). Phoenix, AZ: Oryx Press.

Eisner, E. W. (1991). *The enlightened eye: Qualitative inquiry and the enhancement of educational practice.* New York: Macmillan.

Elbow, P. (1973). *Writing without teachers.* London: Oxford University Press.

Enns, C. Z., & Hackett, G. (1990). Comparison of feminist and nonfeminist women's reactions to variants of nonsexist and feminist counseling. *Journal of Counseling Psychology, 37*(1), 33-40.

Fay, B. (1987). *Critical social science.* Ithaca, NY: Cornell University Press.

Finders, M. J. (1996). Queens and teen zines: Early adolescent females reading their way toward adulthood. *Anthropology and Education Quarterly, 27,* 71-89.

Fink, A. (1995). *The survey handbook* (Vol. 1). Thousand Oaks, CA: Sage.

Firestone, W. A. (1987). Meaning in method: The rhetoric of quantitative and qualitative research. *Educational Researcher, 16,* 16-21.

Flinders, D. J., & Mills, G. E. (Eds.). (1993). *Theory and concepts in qualitative research: Perspectives from the field.* New York: Teachers College Press.

Fowler, F. J. (2002). *Survey research methods* (3rd ed). Thousand Oaks, CA: Sage.

Franklin, J. (1986). *Writing for story: Craft secrets of dramatic nonfiction by a two-time Pulitzer prize-winner.* New York: Atheneum.

Gamson, J. (2000). Sexualities, queer theory, and qualitative research. In N. K. Denzin & Y. S. Lincoln (Eds.), *Handbook of qualitative research* (pp. 347-365). Thousand Oaks, CA: Sage.

Glesne, C., & Peshkin, A. (1992). *Becoming qualitative researchers: An introduction.* White Plains, NY: Longman.

Goldberg, N. (1986). *Writing down the bones.* Boston: Shambhala.

Gravetter, F. J., & Wallnau, L. B. (2000). *Statistics for the behavioral sciences* (5th ed.). Belmont, CA: Wadsworth/Thomson Learning.

Greene, J. C., & Caracelli, V. J. (Eds.). (1997). *Advances in mixed-method evaluation: The challenges and benefits of integrating diverse paradigms* (New Directions for Evaluation No. 74). San Francisco: Jossey-Bass.

Greene, J. C., Caracelli, V. J., & and Graham, W. F. (1989). Toward a conceptual framework for mixed-method evaluation designs. *Educational Evaluation and Policy Analysis, 11*(3), 255-274.

Heron, J., & Reason, P. (1997). A participatory inquiry paradigm. *Qualitative Inquiry, 3,* 274-294.

Homans, G. C. (1950). *The human group.* New York: Harcourt, Brace.

Hopkins, T. K. (1964). *The exercise of influence in small groups.* Totowa, NJ: The Bedmister Press.

Hopson, R. K., Lucas, K. J., & Peterson, J. A. (2000). HIV/AIDS talk: Implications for prevention intervention and evaluation. In R. K. Hopson (Ed.), *How and why language matters in evaluation* (New Directions for Evaluation No. 86). San Francisco: Jossey-Bass.

Hossler, D., & Vesper, N. (1993). An exploratory study of the factors associated with parental savings for postsecondary education. *Journal of Higher Education, 64*(2), 140-165.

Houtz, L. E. (1995). Instructional strategy change and the attitude and achievement of seventh- and eighth-grade science students. *Journal of Research in Science Teaching, 32*(6), 629-648.

Huber, J., & Whelan, K. (1999). A marginal story as a place of possibility: Negotiating self on the professional knowledge landscape. *Teaching and Teacher Education, 15,* 381-396.

Humbley, A. M., & Zumbo, B. D. (1996). A dialectic on validity: Where we have been and where we are going. *The Journal of General Psychology, 123,* 207-215.

Institute for Scientific Information. (1969-   ). *Social sciences citation index.* Philadelphia: Institute for Scientific Information.

Isaac, S., & Michael, W. B. (1981). *Handbook in research and evaluation: A collection of principles, methods, and strategies useful in the planning, design, and evaluation of studies in education and the behavioral sciences* (2nd ed.). San Diego: EDITS Publisher.

Janovec, T. (2001). *Procedural justice in organizations: A literature map.* Unpublished manuscript, University of Nebraska–Lincoln.

Janz, N. K., Zimmerman, M. A., Wren, P. A., Israel, B. A., Freudenberg, N., & Carter, R. J. (1996). Evaluation of 37 AIDS prevention projects: Successful approaches and barriers to program effectiveness. *Health Education Quarterly, 23*(1), 80-97.

Jick, T. D. (1979, December). Mixing qualitative and quantitative methods: Triangulation in action. *Administrative Science Quarterly, 24,* 602-611.

Jungnickel, P. W. (1990). *Workplace correlates and scholarly performance of pharmacy clinical faculty members.* Unpublished manuscript, University of Nebraska–Lincoln.

Kalof, L. (2000). Vulnerability to sexual coercion among college women: A longitudinal study. *Gender Issues, 18*(4), 47-58.

Keeves, J. P. (Ed.). (1988). *Educational research, methodology, and measurement: An international handbook.* Oxford, UK: Pergamon.

Kemmis, S., & Wilkinson, M. (1998). Participatory action research and the study of practice. In B. Atweh, S. Kemmis, & P. Weeks (Eds.), *Action research in practice: Partnerships for social justice in education* (pp. 21-36). New York: Routledge.

Keppel, G. (1991). *Design and analysis: A researcher's handbook* (3rd ed.). Englewood Cliffs, NJ: Prentice-Hall.

Kerlinger, F. N. (1979). *Behavioral research: A conceptual approach.* New York: Holt, Rinehart and Winston.

Kline, R. B. (1998). *Principles and practice of structural equation modeling.* New York: Guilford.

Kos, R. (1991). Persistence of reading disabilities: The voices of four middle school students. *American Educational Research Journal, 28*(4), 875-895.

Krol, E. (1993). *The whole Internet: User's guide and catalog.* Sebastopol, CA: O'Reilly & Associates.

Kunes, M. V. (1991). *How the workplace affects the self-esteem of the psychiatric nurse.* Unpublished proposal, University of Nebraska–Lincoln.

Kushman, J. W. (1992, February). The organizational dynamics of teacher workplace commitment: A study of urban elementary and middle schools. *Educational Administration Quarterly, 28*(1), 5-42.

Labovitz, S., & Hagedorn, R. (1971). *Introduction to social research.* New York: McGraw-Hill.

Ladson-Billings, G. (2000). Racialized discourses and ethnic epistemologies. In N. K. Denzin & Y. S. Lincoln (Eds.), *Handbook of qualitative research* (2nd ed., pp. 257-277). Thousand Oaks, CA: Sage.

Lather, P. (1986). Research as praxis. *Harvard Educational Review, 56*, 257-277.

Lather, P. (1991). *Getting smart: Feminist research and pedagogy with/in the postmodern.* New York: Routledge.

Lauterbach, S. S. (1993). In another world: A phenomenological perspective and discovery of meaning in mothers' experience with death of a wished-for baby: Doing phenomenology. In P. L. Munhall & C. O. Boyd (Eds.), *Nursing research: A qualitative perspective* (pp. 133-179). New York: National League for Nursing Press.

LeCompte, M. D., & Schensul, J. J. (1999). *Designing and conducting ethnographic research.* Walnut Creek, CA: AltaMira.

Leslie, L. L. (1972). Are high response rates essential to valid surveys? *Social Science Research, 1*, 323-334.

Lincoln, Y. S., & Guba, E. G. (1985). *Naturalistic inquiry.* Beverly Hills, CA: Sage.

Lincoln, Y. S., & Guba, E. G. (2000). Paradigmatic controversies, contradictions, and emerging confluences. In N. K. Denzin & Y. S. Lincoln (Eds.), *Handbook of qualitative research* (2nd ed., pp. 163-188). Thousand Oaks, CA: Sage.

Lipsey, M. W. (1990). *Design sensitivity: Statistical power for experimental research.* Newbury Park, CA: Sage.

Locke, L. F., Spirduso, W. W., & Silverman, S. J. (2000). *Proposals that work: A guide for planning dissertations and grant proposals* (4th ed.). Thousand Oaks, CA: Sage.

Lysack, C. L., & Krefting, L. (1994). Qualitative methods in field research: An Indonesian experience in community based practice. *The Occupational Therapy Journal of Research, 14*(20), 93-110.

A manual of style. (1982). Chicago: University of Chicago Press.

Marshall, C., & Rossman, G. B. (1999). *Designing qualitative research* (3rd ed.). Thousand Oaks, CA: Sage.

Mascarenhas, B. (1989). Domains of state-owned, privately held, and publicly traded firms in international competition. *Administrative Science Quarterly, 34,* 582-597.

Maxwell, J. A. (1996). *Qualitative research design: An interactive approach.* Thousand Oaks, CA: Sage.

McCracken, G. (1988). *The long interview.* Newbury Park, CA: Sage.

Megel, M. E., Langston, N. F., & Creswell, J. W. (1988). Scholarly productivity: A survey of nursing faculty researchers. *Journal of Professional Nursing, 4,* 45-54.

Merriam, S. B. (1998). *Qualitative research and case study applications in education.* San Francisco: Jossey-Bass.

Mertens, D. M. (1998). *Research methods in education and psychology: Integrating diversity with quantitative and qualitative approaches.* Thousand Oaks, CA: Sage.

Mertens, D. M. (2003). Mixed methods and the politics of human research: The transformative-emancipatory perspective. In A. Tashakkori & C. Teddlie (Eds.), *Handbook of mixed methods in the social and behaviorial sciences.* Thousand Oaks, CA: Sage.

Miles, M. B., & Huberman, A. M. (1994). *Qualitative data analysis: A sourcebook of new methods* (2nd ed.). Newbury Park, CA: Sage.

Miller, D. (1992). *The experiences of a first-year college president: An ethnography.* Unpublished dissertation proposal, University of Nebraska–Lincoln.

Miller, D. C. (1991). *Handbook of research design and social measurement* (5th ed.). Newbury Park, CA: Sage.

Moore, D. (2000). Gender identity, nationalism, and social action among Jewish and Arab women in Israel: Redefining the social order? *Gender Issues, 18*(2), 3-28.

Morgan, D. (1998). Practical strategies for combining qualitative and quantitative methods: Applications to health research. *Qualitative Health Research, 8*(3), 362-376.

Morse, J. M. (1991). Approaches to qualitative-quantitative methodological triangulation. *Nursing Research, 40*(1), 120-123.

Morse, J. M. (1994). Designing funded qualitative research. In N. K. Denzin & Y. S. Lincoln (Eds.), *Handbook of qualitative research* (pp. 220-235). Thousand Oaks, CA: Sage.

Moustakas, C. (1994). *Phenomenological research methods.* Thousand Oaks, CA: Sage.

Murguia, E., Padilla, R. V., & Pavel, M. (1991). Ethnicity and the concept of social integration in Tinto's model of institutional departure. *Journal of College Student Development, 32,* 433-439.

Murphy, J. P. (with Rorty, R.). (1990). *Pragmatism: From Peirce to Davidson.* Boulder, CO: Westview Press.

Nesbary, D. K. (2000). *Survey research and the World Wide Web.* Boston: Allyn and Bacon.

Neuman, S. B., & McCormick, S. (1995). (Eds.). *Single-subject experimental research: Applications for literacy.* Newark, DE: International Reading Association.

Neuman, W. L. (1991). *Social research methods: Qualitative and quantitative approaches.* Boston: Allyn and Bacon.

Neuman, W. L. (2000). *Social research methods: Qualitative and quantitative approaches* (4th ed.). Boston: Allyn and Bacon.

Newman, I., & Benz, C. R. (1998). *Qualitative-quantitative research methodology: Exploring the interactive continuum.* Carbondale: Southern Illinois University Press.

Nieswiadomy, R.M. (1993). *Foundations of nursing research* (2nd ed.). Norwalk, CT: Appleton & Lange.

Olesen, V. L. (2000). Feminism and qualitative research at and into the millennium. In N. K. Denzin & Y. S. Lincoln (Eds.), *Handbook of qualitative research* (2nd ed., pp. 215-255). Thousand Oaks, CA: Sage.

Padula, M. A., & Miller, D. L. (1999). Understanding graduate women's reentry experiences. *Psychology of Women Quarterly, 23,* 327-343.

Patton, M. Q. (1990). *Qualitative evaluation and research methods* (2nd ed.). Newbury Park, CA: Sage.

Phillips, D. C., & Burbules, N. C. (2000). *Postpositivism and educational research.* Lanham, MD: Rowman & Littlefield.

Punch, K. F. (1998). *Introduction to social research: Quantitative and qualitative approaches.* London: Sage.

Reichardt, C. S., & Mark, M. M. (1998). Quasi-experimentation. In L. Bickman & D. J. Rog (Eds.), *Handbook of applied social research methods* (pp. 193-228). Thousand Oaks, CA: Sage.

Reichardt, C. S., & Rallis, S. E. (Eds.). (1994). *The qualitative-quantitative debate: New perspectives* (New Directions for Program Evaluation No. 61). San Francisco: Jossey-Bass.

Rhoads, R. A. (1997). Implications of the growing visibility of gay and bisexual male students on campus. *NASPA Journal, 34*(4), 275-286.

Richardson, L. (1990). *Writing strategies: Reaching diverse audiences.* Newbury Park, CA: Sage.

Richie, B. S., Fassinger, R. E., Linn, S. G., Johnson, J., Prosser, J., & Robinson, S. (1997). Persistence, connection, and passion: A qualitative study of the career development of highly achieving African American-Black and White women. *Journal of Counseling Psychology, 44*(2), 133-148.

Riemen, D. J. (1986). The essential structure of a caring interaction: Doing phenomenology. In P. M. Munhall & C. J. Oiler (Eds.), *Nursing research: A qualitative perspective* (pp. 85-105). Norwalk, CT: Appleton-Century-Crofts.

Rorty, R. (1983). *Consequences of pragmatism.* Minneapolis: University of Minnesota Press.

Rorty, R. (1990). Pragmatism as anti-representationalism. In J. P. Murphy (Ed.), *Pragmatism: From Peirce to Davidson* (pp. 1-6). Boulder, CO: Westview Press.

Rosenthal, R., & Rosnow, R. L. (1991). *Essentials of behavioral research: Methods and data analysis.* New York: McGraw-Hill.

Ross-Larson, B. (1982). *Edit yourself: A manual for everyone who works with words.* New York: W. W. Norton.

Rossman, G. B., & Rallis, S. F. (1998). *Learning in the field: An introduction to qualitative research.* Thousand Oaks, CA: Sage.

Rossman, G. B., & Wilson, B. L. (1985). Numbers and words: Combining quantitative and qualitative methods in a single large-scale evaluation study. *Evaluation Review, 9*(5), 627-643.

Rudestam, K. E., & Newton, R. R. (1992). *Surviving your dissertation.* Newbury Park, CA: Sage.

Salant, P., & Dillman, D. A. (1994). *How to conduct your own survey.* New York: John Wiley & Sons.

Salkind, N. (1990). *Exploring research.* New York: Macmillan.

Schwandt, T. A. (1993). Theory for the moral sciences: Crisis of identity and purpose. In D. J. Flinders & G. E. Mills (Eds.), *Theory and concepts in qualitative research: Perspectives from the field* (pp. 5-23). New York: Teachers College Press.

Schwandt, T. A. (2000). Three epistemological stances for qualitative inquiry. In N. K. Denzin and Y. S. Lincoln (Eds.), *Handbook of qualitative research* (2nd ed., pp. 189-213). Thousand Oaks, CA: Sage.

Schwandt, T. A. (2001). *Dictionary of qualitative inquiry* (2nd ed.). Thousand Oaks, CA: Sage.

Sieber, J. E. (1998). Planning ethically responsible research. In L. Bickman & D. J. Rog (Eds.), *Handbook of applied social research methods* (pp. 127-156). Thousand Oaks, CA: Sage.

Sieber, S. D. (1973). The integration of field work and survey methods. *American Journal of Sociology, 78,* 1335-1359.

Slife, B. D., & Williams, R. N. (1995). *What's behind the research? Discovering hidden assumptions in the behavioral sciences.* Thousand Oaks, CA: Sage.

Smith, J. K. (1983, March). Quantitative versus qualitative research: An attempt to clarify the issue. *Educational Researcher, 12,* 6-13.

Sociological abstracts. (1953-   ). San Diego: Author.

Spradley, J. P. (1980). *Participant observation.* New York: Holt, Rinehart & Winston.

Stake, R. E. (1995). *The art of case study research.* Thousand Oaks, CA: Sage.

Steckler, A., McLeroy, K. R., Goodman, R. M., Bird, S. T., & McCormick, L. (1992). Toward integrating qualitative and quantitative methods: An introduction. *Health Education Quarterly, 19*(1), 1-8.

Steinbeck, J. (1969). *Journal of a novel: The East of Eden letters.* New York: Viking.

Strauss, A., & Corbin, J. (1990). *Basics of qualitative research: Grounded theory procedures and techniques.* Thousand Oaks, CA: Sage.

Strauss, A., & Corbin, J. (1998). *Basics of qualitative research: Grounded theory procedures and techniques* (2nd ed.). Thousand Oaks, CA: Sage.

Sudduth, A. G. (1992). *Rural hospitals' use of strategic adaptation in a changing health care environment.* Unpublished doctoral dissertation, University of Nebraska.

Tarshis, B. (1982). *How to write like a pro: A guide to effective nonfiction writing.* New York: New American Library.

Tashakkori, A., & Teddlie, C. (1998). *Mixed methodology: Combining qualitative and quantitative approaches.* Thousand Oaks, CA: Sage.

Tashakkori, A., & Teddlie, C. (Eds.). (2003). *Handbook of mixed methods in the social and behavioral sciences.* Thousand Oaks, CA: Sage.

Terenzini, P. T., Cabrera, A. F., Colbeck, C. L., Bjorklund, S. A., & Parente, J. M. (2001). Racial and ethnic diversity in the classroom. *The Journal of Higher Education, 72*(5), 509-531.

Tesch, R. (1990). *Qualitative research: Analysis types and software tools.* New York: Falmer.

Thomas, G. (1997). What's the use of theory? *Harvard Educational Review, 67*(1), 75-104.

Thomas, J. (1993). *Doing critical ethnography.* Newbury Park, CA: Sage.

Thorndike, R. M. (1997). *Measurement and evaluation in psychology and education* (6th ed.). New York: Macmillan.

Trujillo, N. (1992). Interpreting (the work and the talk of) baseball: Perspectives on ballpark culture. *Western Journal of Communication, 56,* 350-371.

Tuckman, B. W. (1999). *Conducting educational research* (5th ed.). Fort Worth, TX: Harcourt, Brace College Publishers.

Turabian, K. L. (1973). *A manual for writers of term papers, theses, and dissertations* (4th ed.). Chicago: University of Chicago Press.

University Microfilms. (1938-   ). *Dissertation abstracts international.* Ann Arbor, MI: Author.

VanHorn-Grassmeyer, K. (1998). *Enhancing practice: New professional in student affairs.* Unpublished doctoral dissertation, University of Nebraska–Lincoln.

Van Maanen, J. (1988). *Tales of the field: On writing ethnography.* Chicago: University of Chicago Press.

Vernon, J. E. (1992). *The impact of divorce on the grandparent/grandchild relationship when the parent generation divorces.* Unpublished doctoral dissertation, University of Nebraska–Lincoln.

Vogt, W. P. (1999). *Dictionary of statistics and methodology: A nontechnical guide for the social sciences* (2nd ed.). Thousand Oaks, CA: Sage.

Webb, R. B., & Glesne, C. (1992). Teaching qualitative research. In M. D. LeCompte, W. L. Millroy, & J. Preissle (Eds.), *The handbook of qualitative research in education* (pp. 771-814). San Diego: Academic Press.

Webb, W. H., Beals, A. R., & White, C. M. (1986). *Sources of information in the social sciences: A guide to the literature* (3rd ed.). Chicago: American Library Association.

Weitzman, E. A., & Miles, M. B. (1995). *Computer programs for qualitative data analysis.* Thousand Oaks, CA: Sage.

Weitzman, P. F., & Levkoff, S. E. (2000). Combining qualitative and quantitative methods in health research with minority elders: Lessons from a study of dementia caregiving. *Field Methods, 12*(3), 195-208.

Wilkinson, A. M. (1991). *The scientist's handbook for writing papers and dissertations.* Englewood Cliffs, NJ: Prentice Hall.

Wolcott, H. T. (1994). *Transforming qualitative data: Description, analysis, and interpretation.* Thousand Oaks, CA: Sage.

Wolcott, H. T. (1999). *Ethnography: A way of seeing.* Walnut Creek, CA: AltaMira.

Wolcott, H. T. (2001). *Writing up qualitative research* (2nd ed.). Thousand Oaks, CA: Sage.

Yin, R. K. (1989). *Case study research: Design and methods.* Newbury Park, CA: Sage.

Ziller, R. C. (1990). *Photographing the self: Methods for observing personal orientations.* Newbury Park, CA: Sage.

Zinsser, W. (1983). *Writing with a word processor.* New York: Harper Colophon Books.

Author Index

Subject Index

About the Author

John W. Creswell is Professor of Educational Psychology in the graduate program of Quantitative and Qualitative Methods in Education (QQME) at the University of Nebraska–Lincoln. He specializes in research methods, qualitative inquiry, and mixed methods designs, and methodological applications in education, the social sciences, and family medicine. He has authored seven books and numerous chapters and journal articles. He recently completed an introductory research methods text for Merrill/Pearson Education and is currently writing articles and chapters on mixed methods research and completing a book on applied qualitative research for Sage Publications. He lives in Lincoln, Nebraska, with his wife. Their two grown children are pursuing careers in psychology and neuroscience. He is learning to write poetry, actively participates in water aerobics, and serves as a national consultant and research methodologist for many projects in the social and human sciences.